CAMBRIDGE TEXTBOOKS IN LINGUISTICS

General editors: S. R. ANDERSON, J. BRESNAN, B. COMRIE, W. DRESSLER, C. EWEN, R. HUDDLESTON, R. LASS, D. LIGHTFOOT, J. LYONS, P. H. MATTHEWS, R. POSNER, S. ROMAINE, N. V. SMITH, N. VINCENT

DIALECTOLOGY

REFERENCE

D0321164

In this series

DIALECTOLOGY

J. K. CHAMBERS
AND
PETER TRUDGILL

SECOND EDITION

CAMBRIDGE
UNIVERSITY PRESS

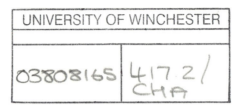
CAMBRIDGE UNIVERSITY PRESS
Cambridge, New York, Melbourne, Madrid, Cape Town, Singapore,
São Paulo, Delhi, Dubai, Tokyo, Mexico City

Cambridge University Press
The Edinburgh Building, Cambridge CB2 8RU, UK

Published in the United States of America by Cambridge University Press, New York

www.cambridge.org
Information on this title: www.cambridge.org/9780521596466

First published 1980
Seventh printing 1994
Second edition 1998
Fifteenth printing 2009

A catalogue record for this publication is available from the British Library

ISBN 978-0-521-59378-6 Hardback
ISBN 978-0-521-59646-6 Paperback

CONTENTS

Contents

Contents

MAPS

FIGURES

TABLES

PREFACE TO THE SECOND EDITION

In revising this textbook, we have taken pains to retain the features that have made it a staple for linguists and students for eighteen years. *Dialectology* presents the fundamentals of studying language variation between and within communities. More than one reviewer of the first edition noted that ours was the first book to survey those fundamentals although dialect studies have been pursued systematically for about a century and a half. For this second edition, one of the topics most in need of updating was dialect geography, which had lost much of its impetus in the decades before our first edition but has since been revitalised. Partly this revitalisation is mechanical, stemming from technological advances in the handling of large databases, but partly it is theoretical, resulting from increased representativeness in sample populations and closer attention to the social dynamics of diffusion and change. Our integration of socio-linguistics with more venerable traditions as a highly influential new branch of urban dialectology surprised a few readers but was generally received as an interesting innovation. Now it would be shocking, and hopelessly muddled, if someone tried to keep them apart.

JKC, PT
Toronto, Lausanne 1997

THE INTERNATIONAL PHONETIC ALPHABET (revised to 1993)

CONSONANTS (PULMONIC)

	Bilabial	Labiodental	Dental	Alveolar	Postalveolar	Retroflex	Palatal	Velar	Uvular	Pharyngeal	Glottal
Plosive	p b			t d		ʈ ɖ	c ɟ	k ɡ	q ɢ		ʔ
Nasal	m	ɱ		n		ɳ	ɲ	ŋ	N		
Trill	ʙ			r					R		
Tap or Flap				ɾ		ɽ					
Fricative	ɸ β	f v	θ ð	s z	ʃ ʒ	ʂ ʐ	ç ʝ	x ɣ	χ ʁ	ħ ʕ	h ɦ
Lateral fricative				ɬ ɮ							
Approximant		ʋ		ɹ		ɻ	j	ɰ			
Lateral approximant				l		ɭ	ʎ	L			

Where symbols appear in pairs, the one to the right represents a voiced consonant. Shaded areas denote articulations judged impossible.

CONSONANTS (NON-PULMONIC)

Clicks	Voiced implosives	Ejectives
ʘ Bilabial	ɓ Bilabial	’ as in:
ǀ Dental	ɗ Dental/alveolar	p’ Bilabial
ǃ (Post)alveolar	ʄ Palatal	t’ Dental/alveolar
ǂ Palatoalveolar	ɠ Velar	k’ Velar
ǁ Alveolar lateral	ʛ Uvular	s’ Alveolar fricative

VOWELS

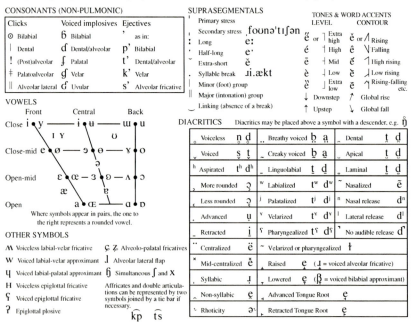

Where symbols appear in pairs, the one to the right represents a rounded vowel.

OTHER SYMBOLS

ʍ Voiceless labial-velar fricative
w Voiced labial-velar approximant
ɥ Voiced labial-palatal approximant
ʜ Voiceless epiglottal fricative
ʢ Voiced epiglottal fricative
ʡ Epiglottal plosive

ɕ ʑ Alveolo-palatal fricatives
ɺ Alveolar lateral flap
ɧ Simultaneous ʃ and x

Affricates and double articulations can be represented by two symbols joined by a tie bar if necessary.

k͡p t͡s

SUPRASEGMENTALS

ˈ	Primary stress
ˌ	Secondary stress

ˌfoʊnəˈtɪʃən

ː	Long	eː
ˑ	Half-long	eˑ
˘	Extra-short	ĕ
.	Syllable break	ɹi.ækt
		Minor (foot) group	
‖	Major (intonation) group	
‿	Linking (absence of a break)	

TONES & WORD ACCENTS

LEVEL			CONTOUR	
e̋ or ˥	Extra high	ě or ˩˥	Rising
é	˦	High	ê	˥˩	Falling
ē	˧	Mid	e᷄	˧˥	High rising
è	˨	Low	e᷅	˩˧	Low rising
ȅ	˩	Extra low	e᷈	˧˩˧	Rising-falling etc.
↓	Downstep		↗	Global rise
↑	Upstep		↘	Global fall

DIACRITICS

Diacritics may be placed above a symbol with a descender, e.g. ŋ̊

̥	Voiceless	n̥ d̥	̤	Breathy voiced	b̤ a̤	̪	Dental	t̪ d̪
̬	Voiced	s̬ t̬	̰	Creaky voiced	b̰ a̰	̺	Apical	t̺ d̺
ʰ	Aspirated	tʰ dʰ	̼	Linguolabial	t̼ d̼	̻	Laminal	t̻ d̻
̹	More rounded	ɔ̹	ʷ	Labialized	tʷ dʷ	̃	Nasalized	ẽ
̜	Less rounded	ɔ̜	ʲ	Palatalized	tʲ dʲ	ⁿ	Nasal release	dⁿ
̟	Advanced	u̟	ˠ	Velarized	tˠ dˠ	ˡ	Lateral release	dˡ
̠	Retracted	i̠	ˤ	Pharyngealized	tˤ dˤ	̚	No audible release	d̚
̈	Centralized	ë	̴	Velarized or pharyngealized	ɫ			
̽	Mid-centralized	e̽	̝	Raised	e̝	(ɹ̝ = voiced alveolar fricative)
̩	Syllabic	ɹ̩	̞	Lowered	e̞	(β̞ = voiced bilabial approximant)
̯	Non-syllabic	e̯	̘	Advanced Tongue Root	e̘			
˞	Rhoticity	ɚ	̙	Retracted Tongue Root	e̙			

xiv

BACKGROUND

1
Dialect and language

Dialectology, obviously, is the study of dialect and dialects. But what exactly is a dialect? In common usage, of course, a dialect is a substandard, low-status, often rustic form of language, generally associated with the peasantry, the working class, or other groups lacking in prestige. DIALECT is also a term which is often applied to forms of language, particularly those spoken in more isolated parts of the world, which have no written form. And dialects are also often regarded as some kind of (often erroneous) deviation from a norm – as aberrations of a correct or standard form of language.

In this book we shall not be adopting any of these points of view. We will, on the contrary, accept the notion that all speakers are speakers of at least one dialect – that standard English, for example, is just as much a dialect as any other form of English – and that it does not make any kind of sense to suppose that any one dialect is in any way linguistically superior to any other.

1.1 Mutual intelligibility

It is very often useful to regard dialects as DIALECTS OF A LANGUAGE. Dialects, that is, can be regarded as subdivisions of a particular language. In this way we may talk of the Parisian dialect of French, the Lancashire dialect of English, the Bavarian dialect of German, and so on.

This distinction, however, presents us with a number of difficulties. In particular, we are faced with the problem of how we can distinguish between a LANGUAGE and a DIALECT, and the related problem of how we can decide what a language is. One way of looking at this has often been to say that 'a language is a collection of mutually intelligible dialects'. This definition has the benefit of characterising dialects as subparts of a language and of providing a criterion for distinguishing between one language and another.

This characterisation of 'language' and 'dialect', however, is not entirely successful, and it is relatively simple to think of two types of apparent counterexample. If we consider, first, the Scandinavian languages, we observe that Norwegian, Swedish and Danish are usually considered to be different languages. Unfortunately for our definition, though, they are mutually intelligible. Speakers of these three languages can readily understand and communicate with one another. Secondly, while we would normally consider German to be a single language, there are some types of German which are not intelligible to speakers of other types. Our definition, therefore, would have it that Danish is less than a language, while German is more than a language.

There are also other difficulties with the criterion of mutual intelligibility. The main problem is that it is a criterion which admits of degrees of more or less. While it is true, for example, that many Swedes can very readily understand many Norwegians, it is also clear that they often do not understand them so well as they do other Swedes. For this reason, inter-Scandinavian mutual intelligibility can be less than perfect, and allowances do have to be made: speakers may speak more slowly, and omit certain words and pronunciations that they suspect may cause difficulties.

Mutual intelligibility may also not be equal in both directions. It is often said, for instance, that Danes understand Norwegians better than Norwegians understand Danes. (If this is true it may be because, as Scandinavians sometimes say, 'Norwegian is pronounced like Danish is spelt', while Danish pronunciation bears a rather more complex relationship to its own orthography. It may be due, alternatively or additionally, to more specifically linguistic factors.) Mutual intelligibility will also depend, it appears, on other factors such as listeners' degree of exposure to the other language, their degree of education and, interestingly enough, their willingness to understand. People, it seems, sometimes do not understand because, at some level of consciousness, they do not want to. A study carried out in Africa, for example, demonstrated that, while one ethnic group A claimed to be able to understand the language of another ethnic group B, ethnic group B claimed *not* to be able to understand language A. It then emerged that group A, a larger and more powerful group, wanted to incorporate group B's territory into their own on the grounds that they were really the same people and spoke the same language. Clearly, group B's failure to comprehend group A's language was part of their resistance to this attempted takeover.

1.2 Language, dialect and accent

It seems, then, that while the criterion of mutual intelligibility may have some relevance, it is not especially useful in helping us to decide what is and is not a language. In fact, our discussion of the Scandinavian languages and German suggests that (unless we want to change radically our everyday assumptions about what a language is) we have to recognise that, paradoxically enough, a 'language' is not a particularly linguistic notion at all. Linguistic features obviously come into it, but it is clear that we consider Norwegian, Swedish, Danish and German to be single languages for reasons that are as much political, geographical, historical, sociological and cultural as linguistic. It is of course relevant that all three Scandinavian languages have distinct, codified, standardised forms, with their own orthographies, grammar books, and literatures; that they correspond to three separate nation states; and that their speakers consider that they speak different languages.

The term 'language', then, if from a linguistic point of view a relatively nontechnical term. If therefore we wish to be more rigorous in our use of descriptive labels we have to employ other terminology. One term we shall be using in this book is VARIETY. We shall use 'variety' as a neutral term to apply to any particular kind of language which we wish, for some purpose, to consider as a single entity. The term will be used in an ad hoc manner in order to be as specific as we wish for a particular purpose. We can, for example, refer to the variety 'Yorkshire English', but we can equally well refer to 'Leeds English' as a variety, or 'middle-class Leeds English' – and so on. More particular terms will be ACCENT and DIALECT. 'Accent' refers to the way in which a speaker pronounces, and therefore refers to a variety which is phonetically and/or phonologically different from other varieties. 'Dialect', on the other hand, refers to varieties which are grammatically (and perhaps lexically) as well as phonologically different from other varieties. If two speakers say, respectively, *I done it last night* and *I did it last night*, we can say that they are speaking different dialects.

The labels 'dialect' and 'accent', too, are used by linguists in an essentially ad hoc manner. This may be rather surprising to many people, since we are used to talking of accents and dialects as if they were well-defined, separate entities: 'a southern accent', 'the Somerset dialect'. Usually, however, this is actually not the case. Dialects and accents frequently merge into one another without any discrete break.

1.3 Geographical dialect continua

There are many parts of the world where, if we examine dialects spoken by people in rural areas, we find the following type of situation. If we travel from village to village, in a particular direction, we notice linguistic differences which distinguish one village from another. Sometimes these differences will be larger, sometimes smaller, but they will be CUMULATIVE. The further we get from our starting point, the larger the differences will become. The effect of this may therefore be, if the distance involved is large enough, that (if we arrange villages along our route in geographical order) while speakers from village A understand people from village B very well and those from village F quite well, they may understand village M speech only with considerable difficulty, and that of village Z not at all. Villagers from M, on the other hand, will probably understand village F speech quite well, and villagers from A and Z only with difficulty. In other words, dialects on the outer edges of the geographical area may not be mutually intelligible, but they will be linked by a chain of mutual intelligibility. At no point is there a complete break such that geographically adjacent dialects are not mutually intelligible, but the cumulative effect of the linguistic differences will be such that the greater the geographical separation, the greater the difficulty of comprehension.

Map 1-1. European dialect continua

This type of situation is known as a GEOGRAPHICAL DIALECT CONTINUUM. There are many such continua. In Europe, for example, the standard varieties of French, Italian, Catalan, Spanish and Portuguese are not really mutually intelligible. The rural dialects of these languages, however, form part of the West Romance dialect continuum which stretches from the coast of Portugal to the centre of Belgium (with speakers immediately on either side of the Portuguese–Spanish border, for instance, having no problems in understanding each other) and from there to the south of Italy, as shown in Map 1-1. Other European dialect continua include the West Germanic continuum, which includes all dialects of what are normally referred to as German, Dutch and Flemish (varieties spoken in Vienna and Ostend are not mutually intelligible, but they are linked by a chain of mutual intelligibility); the Scandinavian dialect continuum, comprising dialects of Norwegian, Swedish and Danish; the North Slavic dialect continuum, including Russian, Ukrainian, Polish, Czech and Slovak; and the South Slavic continuum, which includes Slovenian, Serbian, Croatian, Macedonian and Bulgarian.

The notion of the dialect continuum is perhaps a little difficult to grasp because, as has already been noted, we are used to thinking of linguistic varieties as discrete entities, but the fact that such continua exist stresses the legitimacy of using labels for varieties in an ad hoc manner. Given that we have dialect continua, then the way we divide up and label particular bits of a continuum may often be, from a purely linguistic point of view, arbitrary. Note the following forms from the Scandinavian dialect continuum:

(1)	/hemːɑ	hɑʀ	jɑ intə sɔ meːd	sɔm et gamːɑlt	gɑusabɑin/	
(2)	/hemːɑ	hɑr	jɑ intə sɔ mykːət	sɔm et gamːɑlt	gɔːsbeːn/	
(3)	/jemːə	hɑr	jæ ikːə sɔ myːə	sɔm et gamːɑlt	gɔːsəbeːn/	
(4)	/heimə	hɑr	eg içːə sɔ myçːə	sɔm et gamːɑlt	gɔːsəbein/	
	At home	have	I not so much	as an old	goose-leg	

Some of these forms we label 'Swedish' and some 'Norwegian'. As it happens, (1) and (2) are southern and central Swedish respectively, (3) and (4) eastern and western Norwegian respectively. But there seems to be no particular linguistic reason for making this distinction, or for making it where we do. The motivation is mainly that we have a linguistically arbitrary but politically and culturally relevant dividing line in the form of the national frontier between Sweden and Norway.

In some cases, where national frontiers are less well established, dialect continua can cause political difficulties – precisely because people are used to thinking in terms of discrete categories rather than in ad hoc or continuum-type terms. The South Slavic dialect continuum, as we have seen, incorporates the standard languages, Slovenian, Serbian, Croatian, Macedonian and Bulgarian. This description, however, conceals a number of problems to do with autonomy and heteronomy. Until recently, for example, Serbian and Croatian were thought of in Yugoslavia as a single language. Since the break-up of that country, however, many politicians have wanted to stress their separateness, while the government of Bosnia has argued that Bosnian constitutes a third language distinct from the other two. Similarly, Bulgarian politicians often argue that Macedonian is simply a dialect of Bulgarian – which is really a way of saying, of course, that they feel Macedonia ought to be part of Bulgaria. From a purely linguistic point of view, however, such arguments are not resolvable, since dialect continua admit of more-or-less but not either-or judgements.

1.4 Social dialect continua

Dialect continua can also be social rather than geographical, and continua of this type can also pose problems. A good example of this is provided by Jamaica. The linguistic history of Jamaica, as of many other areas of the Caribbean, is very complex. One (simplified) interpretation of what happened is that at one time the situation was such that those at the top of the social scale, the British, spoke English, while those at the bottom of the social scale, the African slaves, spoke Jamaican Creole. This was a language historically related to English but very different from it, and in its earlier stages probably was not too unlike modern Sranan (another English-based

Upper classes ———————— English

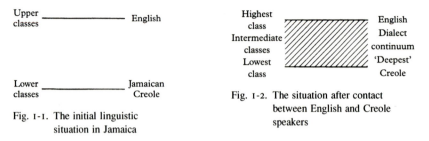

Highest class
Intermediate classes
Lowest class

English
Dialect continuum
'Deepest' Creole

Lower classes ———————— Jamaican Creole

Fig. 1-1. The initial linguistic situation in Jamaica

Fig. 1-2. The situation after contact between English and Creole speakers

Creole spoken in Surinam). The following extract from a poem in Sranan demonstrates that it is a language clearly related to English (most words appear to be derived from English) but nevertheless distinct from it and not mutually intelligible with it:

mi go – m'e kon,	I've gone – I come,
sootwatra bradi,	the sea is wide.
tak wan mofo,	Say the words,
ala mi mati,	you all my friends,
tak wan mofo,	say the words.
m'go,	I've gone,
m'e kon . . .	I come . . .

The initial linguistic situation in Jamaica, therefore, can be diagrammatically represented as in Fig. 1-1. Over the centuries, however, English, the international and prestigious language of the upper social strata, exerted a considerable influence on Jamaican Creole. (Jamaican Creole was recognised as being similar to English, and was therefore often (erroneously) regarded, because of the social situation, as an inferior or debased form of it.) The result is the situation shown in Fig. 1-2. Two things have happened. First, the 'deepest' Creole is now a good deal closer to English than it was (and than Sranan is). Secondly, the gap between English and Jamaican Creole has been filled in. The result is that, while people at the top of the social scale speak something which is clearly English, and those at the bottom speak something which clearly is not, those in between speak something in between. The range of varieties from 'pure' English to 'deepest' Creole forms the social dialect continuum. Most speakers command quite a wide range of the continuum and 'slide' up and down it depending on stylistic context. The following examples from different points on West Indian dialect continua illustrate the nature of the phenomenon:

It's my book	*I didn't get any*	*Do you want to cut it?*
its mai buk	ai didnt get eni	du ju wɔnt tu kᵛt it
iz mai buk	ai didn get non	du ju waːn tu kot it
iz mi buk	a din get non	ju waːn kot it
a mi buk dat	a in get non	iz kot ju waːn kot it
a fi mi buk dat	mi na bin get non	a kot ju waːn fu kot it

8

The problem with the Jamaican social dialect continuum is that, while any division of it into two parts would be linguistically as arbitrary as the division of the northern part of the Scandinavian continuum into Norwegian and Swedish, there is no social equivalent of the political geographical dividing line between Norway and Sweden. There is no well-motivated reason for saying, of some point on the continuum, that 'English stops here' or 'Jamaican Creole starts here'. The result is that, whether in Jamaica or in, say, Britain, Jamaicans are considered to speak English. In fact, some Jamaicans do speak English, some do not, and some speak a variety or varieties about which it is not really possible to adjudicate. Clearly, the varieties spoken by most Jamaicans are not foreign to, say, British English speakers in the same way that French is, but they do constitute in many cases a *semi*-foreign language. Again this is a diffi-cult notion for many people to grasp, since we are used to thinking of languages as being well-defined and clearly separated entities: either it is English or it is not. The facts, however, are often somewhat different. The most obvious difficulty to arise out of the Jamaican situation (and that in many other parts of the West Indies) is edu-cational. West Indian children are considered to be speakers of English, and this is therefore the language which they are taught to read and write in and are examined in. Educationists have only recently come to begin to realise, however, that the relative educational failure of certain West Indian children may be due to a failure by educa-tional authorities to recognise this semi-foreign language problem for what it is.

1.5 Autonomy and heteronomy

A useful concept in looking at the relationship between the notions of a 'language' and 'dialect continuum' is the concept of heteronomy. Heteronomy is simply the opposite of autonomy, and thus refers to dependence rather than inde-pendence. We say, for example, that certain varieties on the West Germanic dialect continuum are dialects of Dutch while others are dialects of German because of the relationship these dialects bear to the respective standard languages. The Dutch dia-lects are heteronomous with respect to standard Dutch, and the German dialects to standard German. This means, simply, that speakers of the Dutch dialects consider that they are speaking Dutch, that they read and write in Dutch, that any standardis-ing changes in their dialects will be towards Dutch, and that they in general look to Dutch as the standard language which naturally corresponds to their vernacular varieties. Fig. 1-3 is an attempt to represent this diagrammatically by showing how the superposed autonomous varieties, standard Dutch and German, have been imposed over the dialect continuum.

Since heteronomy and autonomy are the result of political and cultural rather than purely linguistic factors, they are subject to change. A useful example of this is pro-vided by the history of what is now southern Sweden. Until 1658 this area was part of Denmark (see Map 1-2), and the dialects spoken on that part of the Scandinavian

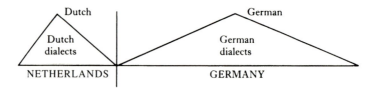

Fig. 1-3. West Germanic dialect continuum

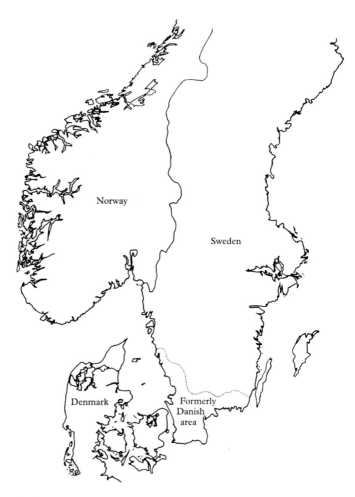

Map 1-2. Sweden and Denmark, showing the southern region of Sweden which was formerly Danish territory

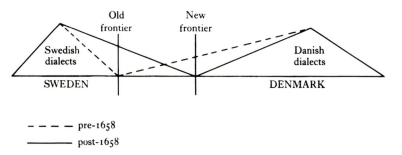

Fig. 1-4. Scandinavian dialect continuum

dialect continuum were considered to be dialects of Danish. As the result of war and conquest, however, the territory became part of Sweden, and it is reported that it was a matter of only forty years or so before those same dialects were, by general consent as it were, dialects of Swedish. The dialects themselves, of course, had not changed at all linguistically. But they had become heteronomous with respect to standard Swedish rather than Danish (see Fig. 1-4).

We can now, therefore, expand a little on our earlier discussion of the term 'language'. Normally, it seems, we employ this term for a variety which is autonomous together with all those varieties which are dependent (heteronomous) upon it. And just as the direction of heteronomy can change (e.g., Danish to Swedish), so formerly heteronomous varieties can achieve autonomy, often as the result of political developments, and 'new' languages can develop. (The linguistic forms will not be new, of course, simply their characterisation as forming an independent language.) Until the beginning of the nineteenth century, for instance, the standard language used in Norway was actually Danish, and it was only with the re-emergence of Norway as an independent nation that a distinct, autonomous standard Norwegian was developed. Similarly, what we now call Afrikaans became regarded as an independent language (and acquired a name, and an orthography and standardised grammar of its own) only in the 1920s. Prior to that it had been regarded as a form of Dutch.

In other cases, political separation may lead not to autonomy but to semi-autonomy (as in the case of Swiss German) or to a kind of double or shared autonomy. North American English, for example, used to look to British English as its norm, but now the autonomous standard English variety comes in a number of different forms, with British, American and Canadian English all being regarded as equally legitimate.

The same cannot be said of Canadian French, which still looks to European French as the norm (with the bizarre result that English-speaking Canadians are often still taught European French rather than Canadian French – rather as if Mexican Americans were taught British rather than American English). And Jamaican Creole is still to a very considerable extent heteronomous with respect to standard English. It has been said that 'a language is a dialect with an army and a navy'. There is considerable truth in this claim, which stresses the political factors that lie behind linguistic autonomy. Nevertheless, the Jamaican situation shows that it is not the whole truth. Perhaps a time will come when Jamaican Creole will achieve complete autonomy, like Norwegian, or shared autonomy, like American English. Certainly there are educational grounds for suggesting that such a development in Jamaica would be desirable.

It is also possible for autonomy to be lost, and for formerly independent varieties to become heteronomous with respect to other varieties. This is what has happened to those varieties of the English dialect continuum spoken in Scotland. Scots was formerly an autonomous variety, but has been regarded for most purposes as a variety of English for the last two hundred years or so. Movements are currently afoot, however, linked to the rise of Scottish nationalism, for the reassertion of Scottish English/Scots as a linguistic variety in its own right, and it is possible that some form of Scots will achieve at least semi-autonomy at some future date.

1.6   Discreteness and continuity

We shall be looking frequently at dialect continua in the rest of this book, and observing that traditional work in dialectology has not always been very success-ful in handling linguistic phenomena such as variability, gradience and fuzziness that result from the fact that such continua exist. We shall, it is true, be using labels for linguistic varieties that may suggest that we regard them as discrete entities. It will be as well, nevertheless, to bear in mind that this will in most cases be simply an ad hoc device and that the use of labels such as 'language', 'dialect' and 'variety' does not imply that continua are not involved.

Further information

A useful discussion of the problem of 'language' and 'dialect' can be found in Hockett 1958: chapter 38. The problem of mutual intelligibility in Scandinavia is interestingly dealt with in Haugen 1966b. The African intelligibility study referred to is Wolff 1959. Further discussion on dialect, accent and speech can be found in Trudgill 1955. For a more theoretical discus-sion of dialectologists' approaches to variability, gradience and fuzziness, see Chambers 1993. Information on Scandinavian dialects is provided by Walshe 1965. Information on creoles, including Jamaican Creole and Sranan, can be found in Todd 1974 and in Hymes 1971, from which the Caribbean examples in this chapter are taken, as well as in Mühlhäusler 1986; Romaine 1988; and Holm 1988. Haugen's writings are also informative on the switch of some dialects from Danish to Swedish and on the rise of Norwegian; see, respectively, Haugen 1968 and 1966a. On the achievement of autonomy by Afrikaans, see Combrink 1978.

2
Dialect geography

Casual observations about the way people speak are common topics of conversation. English people in America, for instance, soon come to expect that they will be told they have just said *idear* for 'idea', and Australians in England quickly grow immune to the remark that they pronounce the second syllable of 'Australia' as if it were *rile*. Among linguists, observations like these are so frequent that they sometimes impede normal conversation. But they are by no means restricted to linguists.

Indeed, it is very likely that dialect differences have been topics of conversation for as long as people have been talking to one another. One of the most venerable dialect observations, and perhaps the most fatal one, is recorded in the Old Testament, when the Gileadites were battling the Ephraimites along the Jordan. Whenever the Gileadites captured a fugitive, they asked him if he was an Ephraimite. If he said no, they would then ask him to name an ear of corn, which the Gileadites called a *shibboleth*. According to the scriptural account (Judges xii, 6), 'He said *sibboleth*, for he could not frame to pronounce it right. Then they took him and slew him.'

The word *shibboleth* has entered English and many other languages with the meaning 'test word' or more generally 'a distinguishing trait'. A more recent (and less fatal) example: United States customs officers are said to identify Canadians crossing the border by their use of *eh* in sentences like, 'Let's hope we have this kind of weather all the way to Florida, eh?'

2.1 The impetus for dialect geography

Observations of dialect differences are so common that it is perhaps surprising to find that the major thrust towards studying dialects systematically begins only in the latter half of the nineteenth century. There is, of course, a long history of astute commentary prior to this time. In France, the primary dialect division between the north and the south was characterised as early as 1284 by the poet Bernart d'Auriac, who coined the terms *langue d'oil* and *langue d'oc* from the words for 'yes' which were used in the north (*oil*, now *oui*) and in the south (*oc*), respectively. D'Auriac's terms are used to this day to characterise the dialect split which still persists. In England, Trevisa made the following statement in 1387 (modernised somewhat in this version):

'Men of the east with men of the west, as it were under the same part of heaven, accordeth more in sownynge of speech [i.e. are more similar sounding] than men of the north with men of the south: therefore it is that Mercia, that is, men of middle England, as it were partners of the ends, understandeth better the end languages, northern and southern, than northern and southern understandeth each other.' Trevisa's description of a dialect continuum in England from north to south has been supported by the systematic studies that began more than five centuries after he wrote about it. (Some documentation of the *langue d'oil/langue d'oc* boundary will be found in 7.3 and 7.5 below; and dialect gradation in England is the central topic in Chapter 8.)

Until the latter half of the nineteenth century, characterisations of dialect areas were intuitive and casual. Only then did it become apparent that such characterisations were inadequate beside the striking advances in philology and other language studies which were leading to the modern discipline of linguistics. The first attempts to systematise observations of dialect difference were a direct response to those advances (see Chapter 3). The Neogrammarians, whose study of classical languages led them to revelatory discoveries about the interrelationship of many modern and classical languages, had begun the search for general principles of language change. One of the foundations of their research was the explanatory power of what is known as VERNER'S LAW, a statement of the phonological conditions which determine the class of Germanic words which can be exceptions to GRIMM'S LAW, an earlier discovery stating the major phonological change from Proto-Indo-European to the Germanic dialects. The theoretical significance of Verner's Law was that it eliminated the largest set of apparent exceptions to Grimm's Law by showing that the so-called exceptions also exhibited lawful or rule-governed properties. This discovery led to the hypothesis that all sound changes are rule-governed. The Neogrammarian principle stated: *Ausnahmslosigkeit der Lautgesetze*, or 'sound changes are exceptionless'. With such a hypothesis, so bold and admirably refutable, dialect evidence would be obviously relevant.

The result was the development of DIALECT GEOGRAPHY, a methodology or (more accurately) a set of methods for gathering evidence of dialect differences systematically. (Dialect geography is sometimes called simply DIALECTOLOGY: however, in this book the latter term is used more generally to mean the study of language variety by any methodology.)

The very first results of the dialectologists seemed to demolish any claim about the exceptionlessness of sound changes, since they revealed a heterogeneity that was unimaginable beforehand (see 3.1). Furthermore, the heterogeneity seemed almost random to the first researchers, with neighbours in some cases giving wildly inconsistent responses to questioned items, and sometimes even being inconsistent in their own responses from day to day. Such variability has only in recent years become the focus of linguistic theorising, with its own principles and rule-governed systematicity (as will be made clearer in Chapter 5).

The first reaction of the dialect geographers seems to have been a profound suspicion of linguistic theorising under almost any guise. This came about partly because general linguistic theories shed very little light on the kind of variability that dialectologists encountered in their field studies. In any case, dialect geography, for much of its history, scarcely involved itself with general linguistic issues. Some of its practitioners became preoccupied with the study of minutiae that could hardly affect our understanding of language as human knowledge. The English dialect collector, Alexander Ellis, remarked in 1875 that 'collecting country words is looked upon as an amusement, not as laying a brick in the temple of science'.

The result was that dialectology and linguistics came to have little contact with one another. Attempts at integrating dialect research with structuralist and generativist linguistics (as discussed in Chapter 3) were thought-provoking but not notably influential.

Recently there has been a rapprochement, with the recognition that the study of variation in language is manageable and, concomitantly, that studying dialect is a central source of variation data. It is interesting to note that in the present rapprochement neither of the positions traditionally assumed by linguists and by dialectologists underwent a kind of radical change that swung it towards the other position. Instead, the rise of sociolinguistics provided dialectologists with natural allies and broadened the constituency studying language variation.

2.2 An outline history of dialect geography

More than a century has elapsed since the first major project in dialect geography was undertaken, and in that time there have been hundreds of projects, great and small, that have made use of the methodology. We consider here only a few of them, and particularly those that have been national in their scope. It should be readily apparent that the national scope is by no means a requisite of dialect geography. Indeed, more local projects, involving, say, a few square kilometres of Gascony (as discussed below in 9.3.1) or an even smaller area of northwestern Ohio (9.3.2 below) or the Golden Horseshoe (10.2.3), can be the focus of study as well. Our predilection for the larger projects in this section merely reflects the accessibility of their documentation and the greater influence which they have exerted in the history of dialectology.

The first dialect survey that can properly be called dialect geography was begun in Germany by Georg Wenker in 1876. Wenker's first attempt at a survey involved sending a list of sentences written in standard German to schoolmasters in the north of Germany and asking them to return the list transcribed into the local dialect. Between 1877 and 1887, he made successive mailings which eventually blanketed the entire nation. The breadth of coverage is staggering: he ultimately sent his list of sentences to nearly 50,000 schoolmasters, and he received completed questionnaires from about 45,000 of them.

Each questionnaire contained forty sentences, and few of the sentences were simple. For example, the first one was this: *Im Winter fliegen die trocknen Blätter durch die Luft herum* 'In winter the dry leaves fly around through the air'. Each sentence clearly offers several points at which the schoolmasters could record regional variants.

The wealth of data, not surprisingly, turned out to be a hindrance rather than an advantage. In order to make any of his findings accessible, Wenker was forced to limit his analysis to the variants of certain words within a closely circumscribed area of north and central Germany. In addition, the problem of displaying the complex variants on a set of maps impeded the accessibility of his work. Wenker ended up making two sets of maps by hand, with each map charting a single feature. The maps were bound under the title *Sprachatlas des Deutschen Reichs*. One copy was deposited in Marburg and the other in Berlin in 1881. These beautiful tomes are the first linguistic atlases (*Sprachatlas*) to be published.

Wenker's work did not end with the publication of his atlas. He carried on gathering questionnaires, and made them available to other scholars. However, it took more than four decades, until 1926, for the project to reach fruition. In that year, the first volume of the *Deutscher Sprachatlas* appeared, under the editorship of Ferdinand Wrede and based largely on Wenker's files. Ironically, the wealth of data gathered by Wenker turned out to be too sparse in one sense. Later dialectologists in Germany were disappointed by the few lexical variants that Wenker's questionnaire had elicited and, in 1939, W. Mitzka supplemented Wenker's files by sending a list of about 200 standard German lexical items to 50,000 schools and asking for regional synonyms for them.

Despite the problems encountered by Wenker and his successors on the German project, dialect geography had made a beginning and it soon spread. In Denmark, a similar but less ambitious project began a few years after Wenker's first questionnaire was sent out, under the direction of Marius Kristensen. Publication of the results began within about fifteen years of the initiation of the project, in 1898, and was completed in 1912.

Since the time of these early surveys, the use of a postal questionnaire has been largely supplanted in favour of sending trained observers into the field to conduct interviews and record the data in a consistent phonetic notation. Apart from local surveys, a few large-scale projects make use of postal questionnaires. One is the Survey of Scottish Dialects, begun in 1952 under the direction of Angus McIntosh, which distributed a postal questionnaire to all the schools in Scotland as the first phase of its research. Two regional projects of the American national survey, both in the upper midwest (described below), supplemented their field research with postal surveys. And the Dialect Topography project in Canada, of which some results are discussed in 8.7 and 10.2.3 below, uses a postal questionnaire. But this is no longer the primary method of data-gathering.

The use of trained fieldworkers had an auspicious beginning with the linguistic survey of France, which began in 1896. The Swiss director, Jules Gilliéron, quite consciously set out to improve upon the methods that Wenker had employed. He began by devising a questionnaire that isolated specific items for which responses could be elicited. Although the questionnaire was continually revised as the survey proceeded, it always included a core of about 1,500 such items. Gilliéron then chose a fieldworker to record the responses to the questionnaire at each interview.

The man he chose, Edmond Edmont, is a legendary figure among dialectologists. A grocer by profession, Edmont was chosen for the astuteness of his ear, and was trained to use phonetic notation. From 1896 to 1900, he cycled through the French countryside selecting informants and conducting interviews. When he finished, he had recorded the results of no fewer than 700 such interviews at 639 different sites. It is never clear whether the informants he chose formed a fairly homogeneous social group by choice or by chance, but of the 700 informants, only sixty were women and only 200 were educated beyond the norms of the rural population of the time. Edmont's results were sent to Gilliéron and his assistants periodically, and were incorporated into their analysis. In this way, publication got underway almost immediately, beginning in 1902; the thirteenth and final volume was published in 1910.

Gilliéron's French survey has been enormously influential, and due to the efficacy of the project from inception to publication, and also to the quality of its results, it remains the touchstone for subsequent surveys. Some idea of its influence is seen in the fact that two of Gilliéron's students, Karl Jaberg and Jakob Jud, went from the French project to direct their own project on the Italian dialects of Italy and southern Switzerland. Then, in 1931, when the first few volumes of their *Sprach- und Sachatlas des Italiens und der Südschweiz* had just been published (the final volume was published in 1940), Jakob Jud and one of the three fieldworkers for the Italian project, Paul Scheurmeier, arrived in the United States to participate in the training of fieldworkers for the Linguistic Atlas of the United States and Canada, which was just getting underway. Similar ties, in the form of personal contact and professional consultation, link Gilliéron directly or indirectly with the national dialect surveys in Spain, Romania and England, as well as with several regional surveys in Europe.

The Linguistic Atlas of the United States and Canada (LAUSC) was funded in 1930, and work got underway the following year with the training of fieldworkers. Because of the enormous geographical spread in North America and the relatively recent settlement history of many regions west of the Atlantic seaboard, it was necessary to divide the survey area into several regions and treat each one as if it were a self-contained project in its own right, with its own directors and fieldworkers, while at the same time coordinating each regional survey from a central office in order to ensure comparability of results. The job of coordinating the project fell to Hans Kurath, who also served as the director for the first region to be surveyed, the New England states.

The New England survey proceeded apace, stimulated no doubt by the newness of the project and also abetted by the fact that the area is compact and long settled – in these respects it is the part of North America most comparable to the survey areas of Europe. The *Linguistic Atlas of New England*, consisting of three massive, folio-size volumes of maps, was published with a *Handbook* discussing and explaining the maps in 1939–43.

The second survey area, consisting of the Atlantic states south of New England, also long-settled but much less compact, was begun immediately after the interviews were completed in New England, and the work there progressed as smoothly as could perhaps be expected, granting the inevitable disruption caused by World War II and by the death of the principal fieldworker, Guy S. Loman, Jr, who had also been the principal fieldworker in New England.

Four volumes based on the field records of this survey have now appeared, and the distended publication schedule documents as well as anything else the accumulation of practical and financial problems for the project. Kurath's *Word Geography of the Eastern United States* appeared in 1949, and soon after, in 1953, came *A Survey of Verb Forms in the Eastern United States* by E. Bagby Atwood. However, it was not until 1961 that the next volume appeared: *The Pronunciation of English in the Atlantic States*, by Kurath and Raven I. McDavid, Jr. After another long hiatus, the *Handbook* appeared in 1994, marking a fresh start under new director William Kretzschmar, who is overseeing computerisation of the vast database and comprehensive electronic publication.

Two other regional projects of LAUSC took more direct routes to their completion. *The Linguistic Atlas of the Upper Midwest* was published in three volumes from 1973 to 1976. In a sense, this publication reveals how much the Linguistic Atlas of the United States and Canada depends upon the enthusiasm with which it was begun in 1930. The publication of the materials on the upper midwest (Minnesota, Iowa, Nebraska, North and South Dakota) came into being from the labours of its regional director, Harold B. Allen, one of the original fieldworkers in an earlier phase of the project, who conducted more than half of the interviews in the upper midwest himself as well as analysing and compiling most of the results and arranging for publication through his own university.

A more recent project, *The Linguistic Atlas of the Gulf States*, appears to be the wave of the future for dialect geography. Beginning in 1968, director Lee Pederson deployed a relatively small fieldworker team in the vast southeastern region of the United States from Georgia to east Texas, and he supervised an even smaller team of transcribers, thus ensuring an enviable consistency in the phonetic records. Pederson also anticipated technological advances or at least accommodated them as they came available, and the resulting publications incorporate numerous innovations both in access and in presentation. In 1981, the entire database was published on over 1,000 microfiche sheets, and five years later a categorised concordance appeared, also on microfiche. Starting in 1986, seven large volumes, about one a year to 1992, completed the project, providing a handbook, indexes and mappings. The volumes are so minutely detailed and so rich in resources that they are almost overwhelming. The data displays and interpretations embody Pederson's revaluation of the atlas tradition, which is so extensive that even experienced atlas users will need a guide to get oriented. Future dialect surveys will inevitably turn to the *Gulf States* project for its many precedents.

Compared to the LAUSC project, the national survey of England has a compact history, commensurate with the compact geography of the land. The Survey of English Dialects (SED) was conceived by Eugen Dieth of Zurich and Harold Orton of Leeds, inaugurated in 1948, researched in the field from 1950 to 1961, and published in several volumes which appeared between 1962 and 1978. The survey was organised by dividing the country into four regions: the north, the east and west midlands and the south. In each region, between seventy and eighty interviews were conducted (making a total of 313 when the fieldwork was finished) using a long questionnaire which elicited about 1,200 items.

When the results were in, Orton decided to publish them by making a compendium of each informant's response to each question at the interview. The result is four volumes of *Basic Material*, each with three parts, which give a comprehensive list of informant responses. This format was determined out of economic necessity, as a less expensive way of publishing the results than the usual set of maps with responses overlaid. However, Orton's decision has proved entirely felicitous for researchers who are interested in the data in order to frame and test hypotheses on linguistic variation, rather than to discover, say, the whereabouts of a particular lexical item. The format renders the English data more readily accessible than any of the other surveys so far.

The SED has also published interpretive volumes with the data arranged on maps: the *Phonological Atlas of the Northern Region* by Edouard Kolb (who took over the work after Dieth's death) appeared in 1964; *A Word Geography of England* by Orton and Nathalia Wright in 1974; *The Linguistic Atlas of England* by Orton, Stewart Sanderson and John Widdowson in 1978; and after a lapse of several years, three more volumes, *Word Maps* (1987) by Clive Upton with Sanderson and Widdowson, the *Dictionary and Grammar* (1994) by Upton, David Parry and Widdowson, and *An Atlas of English Dialects* (1996) by Upton and Widdowson. Harold Orton died in 1975, but his work for the SED seems to have left no loose ends.

In retrospect, the history of dialect geography shows a period of growth and expansion in the first half of this century, followed by a decline in the middle decades, and a significant revitalisation in recent years.

The period of expansion was stimulated by the publication of Gilliéron's French survey and by the belated public awareness of Wenker's pioneering work. The broadly based national surveys came into being for the most part in the wake of these results, flourished in Italy, southern Switzerland, Spain, Romania, the United States,

England and elsewhere in this period, and produced monumental publications which attest to the intellectual enthusiasm with which dialect geography was practised. So too did numerous smaller projects in dialect geography which have been slighted in this outline in favour of the larger ones which provided their impetus.

Around mid-century, there was a decline in activity to such an extent that dialect geography all but disappeared as an international discipline. New projects were shelved, and many old projects stalled at various stages of incompletion. One of the few exceptions was the *Survey of Scottish Dialects*, which got underway in 1952, completed its first phase by means of a postal questionnaire, as noted above, and published two volumes in 1975 and 1977. But, generally, the future of dialect geography looked bleak.

The resurgence began in the 1980s. We have already noted some of its benchmarks: the revival of the Middle and South Atlantic States project under Kretzschmar, the resumption of analysis of the Survey of English Dialects by Upton and his associates, and, of course, Pederson's Gulf States publications. In addition to these, significant regional projects are taking place in Spain directed by Manuel Alvar, in France sponsored by the Centre national de la recherche scientifique, and in many other places, including Mexico, Canary Islands, Vanuatu and Réunion. Dialect atlases are appearing in relative profusion, some of them belated culminations of old fieldwork and others the end-products of more recent research.

One reason for the resurgence is technological. Dialectology, the most data-oriented branch of language studies, finally found itself with tools commensurate to its task. As Kretzschmar, Schneider and Johnson say:

> the development of dialect studies, whether geographical or sociolinguistic, has always been hampered by a superfluity of data . . . Even smaller surveys have had to settle for selective analysis of their data because the wealth of possibilities for analysis overran the editors' time and the human capacity for holding in mind only so much information at once. Computers can help overcome these problems: they are wonderful tools for quickly sorting and matching pieces of information and for performing complex calculations on the results, and these days they are practically unlimited in their ability to store data. (1989: v)

Another reason, surely equal in importance to the new technologies though less concrete, is the development of a conceptual framework for analysing language variation. Sociolinguistics, because of the nature of its enterprise, has had to devise analytic tools and a set of hypotheses for dealing with idiolectal variability in actual speech events. In doing so, it inaugurated a science of *parole*, in Saussurean terms, whereas linguistics had formerly restricted itself to the science of *langue*. Sociolinguistics thus provided a conceptual framework into which dialectology fit quite naturally and to which it could contribute significantly. The term 'sociolinguistic dialectology' is sometimes used for the intersection of the two disciplines. Dialectologists have discovered a broader, more integral context for their work.

2.3   The methods of dialect geography

The rationale for a discipline of dialect geography is disarmingly simple: it seeks to provide an empirical basis for conclusions about the linguistic variety that occurs in a certain locale. In that respect, it is exactly the same as many other branches of linguistics, and, indeed, much of its methodology is shared with other branches.

The recording of data, to take an obvious example, is no different from the recording of data by anthropological linguists and requires the same practical training in phonetics. The analysis of the data once it is gathered is properly subsumed by theoretical linguistics, with the goals shared by the disciplines of phonology, morphology, syntax and semantics (although, in practice, this relationship has not always been straightforward, as the next chapter indicates). If the variability has social correlates, so that the old people in the survey differ from the young or the men differ from the women, then the analysis must be sociolinguistic. In so far as dialect variation is the result of waves of linguistic innovation spreading throughout a region, there is an intrinsic chronological dimension (in terms of 'apparent' time rather than real time, a distinction that is discussed in Chapter 10), a domain shared with comparative-historical linguistics.

However, in addition to these, there are other aspects of dialect geography which are uniquely associated with it or, if they are shared by some other branch of linguistics, grew out of it. No account of dialect geography would be complete without some discussion of them.

2.3.1   *The questionnaire*

From the very beginning, interviews of informants by fieldworkers engaged in a survey have been conducted within the guidelines established by a questionnaire. The interviews can thus be conducted by different fieldworkers and under wildly varying circumstances, and still elicit a common core of linguistic data. The immediate advantage of the questionnaire is thus to ensure that the results of all the interviews conducted in the survey will be comparable.

The actual use of the questionnaire can be either DIRECT or INDIRECT. The classic example of the direct use was Edmond Edmont's application of Gilliéron's questionnaire, which was simply a list of about 1,500 items. For each item, Edmont apparently asked his informant outright questions such as, 'What do you call a "cup"?' or 'How do you say "fifty"?' Wenker's postal questionnaire, though written rather than oral, was also a direct use, since the informants were presented with the standard (or, more accurately, the written standard) form of the words and asked for their regional variants.

One of the innovations of Jaberg and Jud in their survey of Italian-speaking areas was to make use of indirect questions, which they felt would encourage informants to give more natural responses. Their fieldworkers would ask, 'What is this?', holding up a cup, or would ask the informant to count. Since then, most surveys have used indirect questions.

Another distinction in the use of the questionnaire might be termed FORMAL or INFORMAL, although these terms perhaps emphasise the difference rather more than is appropriate. The distinction is nicely illustrated by the use of the questionnaires in the American and the English surveys. In both cases, the fieldworkers were to use indirect questions, but beyond that the American fieldworkers were free to frame their questions as they pleased as long as they elicited the desired response, whereas the English fieldworkers were supplied with the form of the question in advance. The American fieldworkers could thus be informal, at least in theory. In actual practice, it is doubtful that this difference was a real one, or at least a very significant one, since it is likely that, with experience, the American fieldworkers discovered that a certain form was best for eliciting a response to a certain item, and that the English field-workers soon learned to put the questionnaire aside and ask the questions in a more natural way.

One result of the decision to use identical forms in eliciting responses for the SED was that Eugen Dieth and Harold Orton, who devised the questionnaire, had to work out the various possibilities for framing indirect questions. They ended up by classifying five different question types, which we recognise as essentially two different types with subtypes. The basic types are NAMING questions and COMPLETING questions.

NAMING questions simply involve eliciting a response by quizzing the informant. The Dieth–Orton questionnaire contains hundreds of examples of this, including these:

> What do you say to a caller at the door if you want him to enter? (*come in*)
> What's in my pocket? [Show an empty pocket.] (*nothing, nought*)

A subtype of naming is what came to be called a TALKING question, which is simply a quiz which elicits more than one word, as in these questions:

> What can you make from milk? (*butter, cheese*)
> How do you mark your sheep to tell them from somebody else's? (*cut, punch, brand, colour*, etc.)

And so-called REVERSE questions, which attempt to elicit a particular word from the informant by getting him to talk about it at some length, have the following form:

> What's the *barn* for, and where is it?

Whatever the length of the response to a reverse question, the only word of it that is recorded in *The Basic Material* is the pronunciation of 'barn'.

COMPLETING questions differ by supplying a blank for the informant to fill in. There are numerous examples of these as well, including the following:

> You sweeten tea with . . . ? (*sugar*)
> Coal is got out of a mine, but stone out of a . . . ? (*quarry*)

A subtype of completing questions is called CONVERTING questions, which simply require completing a sequence of sentences with blanks, like these:

> A tailor is a man who . . . suits. (*makes*)
> You go to a tailor and ask him to . . . a suit. (*make*)
> I might say: That's a nice suit you're wearing. Tell me, who . . . it? (*made*)

In the questionnaire devised by Dieth and Orton for the SED, basic naming questions dominate, with basic completing questions also very common. Converting questions and talking questions occur infrequently, the former to elicit paradigmatic examples of verbs and the latter to elicit a set of closely associated items. Reverse questions are very rare.

Whether they are presented formally or informally, indirect questions have been favoured in almost all surveys. Their advantages seem quite obvious, but there is also an obvious disadvantage to them. Interviewing by indirect questioning takes a lot longer than does interviewing by direct questioning. We have no way of knowing how long an average interview by Edmond Edmont, using direct questions, might have taken, but the fact that in less than four years he completed 700 interviews in 639 villages, which were probably on average more than a day's bicycle ride apart, suggests that each interview probably took no more than a single day to complete. If that is so, then it is a striking testimony to the efficiency of direct questioning, because Edmont was eliciting and transcribing about 1,500 items, and in some interviews the number of items was much closer to 2,000, depending upon the state of revision of Gilliéron's questionnaire at the time.

By contrast, the surveys which have used indirect questioning have required lengthy interviews. For the Linguistic Atlas of the United States and Canada, with a questionnaire containing 700 items, interviews last ten to twelve hours. If the inform-ant has sufficient leisure, that requires at least two sittings, and several more if the informant has to work the interview time into a busy schedule. Even so, that length of time pales beside the time required for interviews by the Survey of English Dia-lects. With a questionnaire of about 1,200 items, and all questions framed in a formal way, each interview took twenty to twenty-four hours. It is not surprising, then, that most interviews were begun with one informant and completed with another, or that several interviews are incomplete.

The basic organisation of the questionnaire is generally according to semantic fields. Once the lexical items and grammatical categories that are expected to reveal dialectal variants are determined, they are then clustered into semantically similar groups in the hope that the informant will be encouraged to focus on the subject matter rather than on the form of his answers. For both the English and the American surveys, the semantic fields include such areas as farming techniques, flora and fauna, the weather, social activities, kinship and so on.

A persistent criticism of the elicitation techniques for dialect surveys is that they result in only one style of the informant's speech, a relatively formal or careful style. It is well known that more casual styles increase the occurrences of regional accents and homelier vocabulary. To elicit casual speech, however, requires a close rapport being established in the interview, and that in turn requires a freer form being given to the interview, especially by encouraging the informant to speak at length on matters that affect him intimately. It is not particularly difficult to devise questions that might work in this way, perhaps by asking a rural informant about occasions when the weather conditions have seriously damaged the crops, or by asking an older person for his opinions about the younger generation. By contrast, the use of questions designed to elicit particular responses, however indirect, maintains a level of formality. Many of the questions have the flavour of an interchange between a schoolmaster and pupil, and not a particularly happy interchange at that when the response is trivial or obvious, as in:

> What makes you sweat? Not the cold, but . . . ? (*the heat*)
> Who are the two most important members of a family? (*father, mother*)

Of course, the freer form of the American interviews potentially alleviates some of their artificiality, and even in the stricter form of the English interviews, the personality of the interviewer can go a long way towards breaking down the barriers. The success of fieldworkers in this respect remains highly personal, and they can hardly be trained in the matter of developing rapport. Moreover, the trappings of the interview situation do not encourage it.

The deliberate design of interviews to elicit a formal or careful style presumably arose not out of choice but out of necessity. The fieldworker, faced with the task of making a phonetically accurate transcription of a core of items that could later be compared with the same items from other speakers, could hardly be expected to pick such items out of the stream of speech elicited by an open question. To do that would require a permanent record of the discourse by means of tape-recording.

Much of the work done in the field since the tape-recorder became widely available in the middle of this century remained squarely in the tradition established by Gilliéron, making only peripheral or inconsequential use of the new technology. In this respect, the *Linguistic Atlas of the Gulf States* made a notable departure. From the beginning, Pederson had his fieldworkers tape-record their interviews for later transcription. Conversations could thus be freer, and the fieldworkers, no longer burdened with noting phonetic detail instantaneously, as they heard it, could make eye contact, drink tea, move around, and otherwise act like normal visitors with their informants.

2.3.2 *Linguistic maps*

Once the interviews have been completed and the responses for particular items tabulated, the results are prepared for publication. The form that publication takes is a set of maps, one for each of the items indicative of dialectal variation. (The one notable exception to this is the *Basic Material* volumes of the SED, discussed earlier, which publish the responses in tables rather than on maps.) The substantive contributions of linguistic mapping are discussed in Chapters 7 and 8, and need not concern us here. However, it is worth discussing the form which linguistic maps have taken, especially to provide a general orientation to the maps that are found in the published atlases.

Linguistic maps can be either DISPLAY maps or INTERPRETIVE maps. Display maps simply transfer the tabulated responses for a particular item onto a map, putting the tabulation into a geographical perspective. Interpretive maps attempt to make a more general statement, by showing the distribution of predominant variants from region to region. By far the more common are display maps, which are used in Gilliéron's *Atlas linguistique de la France*, Kurath's *Linguistic Atlas of New England*, Kolb's *Phonological Atlas of the Northern Region*, and virtually every other well-known linguistic atlas.

Interpretive maps are more often found in secondary studies which use the data of a dialect geography project as the primary source from which a specific topic is developed. Thus, the study of the linguistic boundary between the north and south of France by George Jochnowitz, based on Gilliéron's survey, uses interpretive maps based on Gilliéron's display maps. The maps in Chapter 8 below are interpretive maps based on the tabular data of the SED. The reason Orton and Wright could use interpretive maps in their *Word Geography of England* is because the tabular data on which they are based had previously been published in the volumes of *Basic Material*.

Evidently, Harold Orton and his fellow researchers on the SED originally intended to publish the *Word Geography* as a series of display maps rather than interpretive maps, because the draft maps which were published in various articles as early as 1960 take this form. We can thus contrast the two kinds of maps by comparing the draft map for a particular item with the interpretive map published in 1974. The map for 'newt' makes an instructive contrast in this regard, because it elicited no fewer than thirty-four responses when the raw data were tabulated, but these were resolved into two main groups when the data were interpreted. The display map (Map 2-1) lists the thirty-four responses in the upper right-hand corner. Each response is keyed to a distinct symbol, which identifies it on the map. By studying the map, it is possible

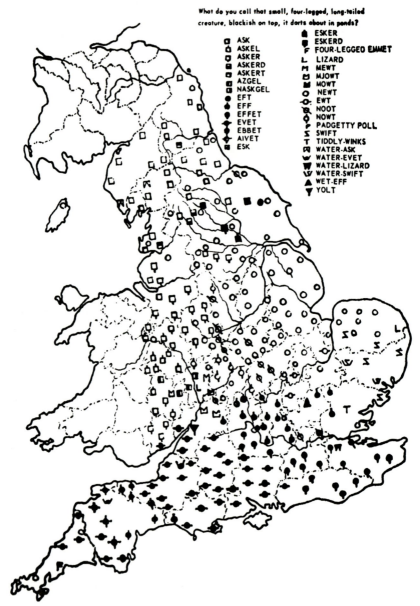

IV. 9. 8. NEWT

What do you call that small, four-legged, long-tailed creature, blackish on top, it darts about in ponds?

ASK		ESKER	
ASKEL		ESKERD	
ASKER		FOUR-LEGGED EMMET	
ASKERD		LIZARD	
ASKERT		MEWT	
AZGEL		MJOWT	
NASKGEL		MOWT	
EFT		NEWT	
EFF		EWT	
EFFET		NOOT	
EVET		NOWT	
EBBET		PADGETTY POLL	
AIVET		SWIFT	
ESK		TIDDLY-WINKS	
		WATER-ASK	
		WATER-EVET	
		WATER-LIZARD	
		WATER-SWIFT	
		WET-EFF	
		YOLT	

Map 2-1. Display map for 'newt' (Orton 1960: 343)

to pick out responses that predominate in various regions. For example, *ask* holds sway in the far north, *evet* in the southwest, and *ebbet* in the southeast. In between, the variety is a little daunting perhaps, but it is possible to discern a trend for *askel* and *asker* in the west midlands and a trend for *newt* in East Anglia and the east midlands. Closer inspection will reveal four isolated occurrences of *swift* in East Anglia and an apparently nonce occurrence of *four-legged emmet* in Cornwall. In this way, the display map collates the 313 responses (more or less) given for this item during the interviews and puts them into geographical perspective.

The interpretive map (Map 2-2) must be based on a display map like Map 2-1, or some comparable representation. What it does, essentially, is to give a representation of the predominant responses and their distribution, based on some criterion. In looking at the display map, we attempted to pick out various trends; those trends could then be represented on a separate map, with the rare items like *swift* and *four-legged emmet* omitted out of deference to the very frequent words like *ask, evet, ebbet, askel* and *asker*. The result would give a plausible interpretation of the display map. However, it is important to note that the interpretation thus given takes some liberties with the data, and other interpretations are obviously possible. An equally valid interpretation might combine the terms *askel* and *asker*, which are obviously closely related both etymologically and geographically, and both are also closely related to *ask*; similarly, *evet* and *ebbet* could be combined for the same reasons. The interpretation can simplify the display map to varying degrees. Orton's interpretation of Map 2-1 resolves the thirty-four separate terms into two categories, based on the etymology of the words, as shown in the upper right-hand corner of Map 2-2. Areas where the words for 'newt' are ultimately derived from Old English *aðexe*, including *ask, askel, asker, azgel, nazgel* and the rest, are to the north of the dark line which meanders across the map, in the area numbered **1**. The largest part of the map, the area numbered **2**, is dominated by words which originated as Old English *efeta*, including *evet, ebbet, eft, ewt, newt* and so on. The meandering dividing line (called an ISOGLOSS, and discussed in detail in Chapter 7) is obviously not as absolute a dividing line as it might appear, as a comparison with the display map will make clear. The 'irregular' occurrences of words from the other side of the line, as it were, are marked on the interpretive map by placing the special symbols shown in the upper corner of the map beside *ask* and *newt* where they occur. Thus, the three-sided cube occurs in four places in the northeast corner of the map where the word *newt* was given instead of the expected *ask*. Also shown on the interpretive map are xs which indicate that a completely unrelated word occurs at these places. The use *of four-legged emmet* which we noticed in Cornwall falls appropriately to the south of the dividing line by virtue of *emmet* being derived from *efeta*, and the co-occurrence of the adjective *four-legged* is noted under the map, in a note attached to the word *evet*. As for the occurrence of *swift*, a word etymologically unrelated to either *ask* or *newt* which actually

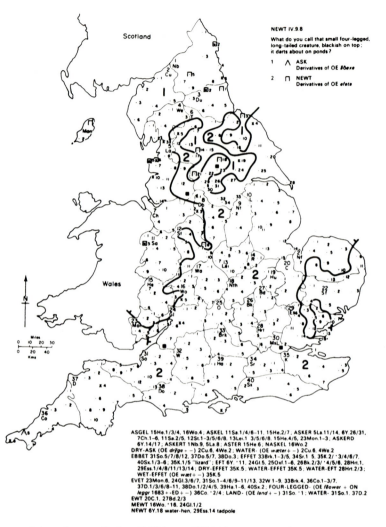

Map 2-2. Interpretive map for 'newt' (Orton and Wright 1974: map 37)

predominates in a small area of East Anglia, that area is separated from the rest of the map by its own dividing line.

It should be clear from this discussion that the interpretive map requires ancillary information to be completely lucid. The display map elucidates it here and the volumes of *Basic Material* elucidate the other 250 maps of *A Word Geography of England* for anyone who wishes to sort out the information in all its detail. On the other hand, the interpretive map in its own right is sufficient to indicate the predominant areas of a particular category of lexical items, something which the display map does not

28

do. For most linguistic purposes, neither map is entirely adequate. The display map represents too much information and the interpretive map too little. Having both maps is certainly useful, though it is prohibitively expensive and no linguistic atlas has yet been published with both types. The publishing of information gleaned from a dialect survey requires a choice between the two.

2.3.3 *The selection of informants*

Perhaps the most typical feature shared by all of the major projects in dialect geography is the type of informant selected. No matter how diverse the culture, how discrepant the socioeconomic climate, and how varied the topography, the majority of informants has in all cases consisted of *nonmobile, older, rural males.* For want of an established term to characterise this population, here and elsewhere throughout this book we refer to them as NORMs, an acronym based on the description given in the preceding sentence.

In the French survey, the selection of informants was left to the discretion of Edmont. In the final tally, as we saw in 2.2, Edmont's 700 informants included only sixty women; about 200 of the informants were educated, and the rest were virtually uneducated; and all of them were from small French villages.

In Wenker's survey, we have no way of knowing whose local speech the schoolmasters used as their model when they were transcribing the set of forty sentences, but we can be very certain that it was not their own; in all likelihood, their responses were made by recollecting localisms they had heard rather than by interviewing a particular member of the community. However, the postal questionnaire used in the Survey of Scottish Dialects is absolutely clear on this point. Although the questionnaires were sent to schools throughout Scotland, the instructions called for them to be answered by a person with at least one parent born in the same district; the youngest informants were middle-aged.

Research for the *Linguistic Atlas of New England* took as one of its aims the broadening of the database by interviewing people of different backgrounds. Kurath categorised the types of informants thus:

Type I: 'Little formal education, little reading, and restricted formal contacts.

Type II: Some formal education, usually high school; wider reading, and more social contacts.

Type III: Superior education, usually university; wide reading, and extensive social contacts.

Cutting across these categories is age, which Kurath divided into two distinct types:

Type A: Aged, or regarded as old-fashioned.

Type B: Middle-aged, or regarded as more modern.

All types of informants were to be nonmobile, that is, lifelong residents of the area in which they were interviewed. Clearly, the archetypal NORM informant belongs to category IA, and it is worth noting that in the New England survey NORMs constitute the bare majority, whereas in other surveys they have constituted the greater majority. Type I informants were interviewed in every community, Type II in about 80 per cent, and Type III only in larger communities or about 20 per cent of the communities visited by fieldworkers.

The *Linguistic Atlas of the Gulf States* again made a departure from tradition. While the majority of informants were over sixty and more than 80 per cent of them were rural, almost half were women and about 70 per cent were middle class.

The SED was not at all inclined to follow the American precedent and include non-NORM speakers. Indeed, the guidelines by which fieldworkers should choose their informants have rarely been so explicit. The informants, and preferably their parents also, were to be natives of the area; they were to be small farmers, or at least associated with a farming community; and they had to be at least sixty (and most were at least a decade older).

The motivation for so consistent a choice of informants throughout the history of dialect geography seems clear. The informants should be nonmobile simply to guarantee that their speech is characteristic of the region in which they live. They should be older in order to reflect the speech of a bygone era; Kurath says, 'Since most of the [Type I] informants . . . are over 70 and not a few over 80, it would seem that we shall be able to establish the regionalism of the pre-industrial era of New England' (1949: 27). They should be rural presumably because urban communities involve too much mobility and flux. And they should be male because in the western nations women's speech is considered to be more self-conscious and class-conscious than men's; Orton says, 'In this country [England] men speak vernacular more frequently, more consistently, and more genuinely than women' (1962: 15).

However clear the motivation seems, it is nevertheless true that the narrow choice of informants in dialect geography is probably the greatest single source of disaffection for it. Readers and researchers have questioned the relevance of what seems to be a kind of linguistic archaeology. Young people who have been natives of a particular region for their entire lives have often been disturbed to discover that the speech recorded in field studies of their regions is totally alien to anything they are familiar with. The greatest proportion of the population is mobile, younger, urban and female – in other words, the diametrical opposite of NORMs. The NORM population was always rare, and it has been dwindling for generations. The classic works of dialect geography recorded the speech of the NORMs faithfully and in a sense enshrined it, but it is likely that the future of dialect studies will have to be directed towards more representative populations.

Further information

The best source of information about the breadth and extent of projects in dialect geography up to mid-century is Pop 1950. Short general histories are hard to find, but Lehmann 1962 provides an interesting perspective on it. G. Wenker's contribution to German dialect geography is described in Mitzka 1952. J. Gilliéron's monumental work, *Atlas linguistique de la France*, is published in thirteen volumes (1902–10). A useful interpretation of some of Gilliéron's research is found in Jochnowitz 1973.

The *Linguistic Atlas of New England*, a bibliophile's delight with its 734 maps in a folio format, is by H. Kurath, M. Hanley, B. Bloch and G. S. Lowman, Jr (1939–43). Lee Pederson's *Linguistic Atlas of the Gulf States* is published by the University of Georgia Press (1986–92). The best guide is Pederson's own commentary in Preston 1993b.

The volumes of *Basic Material* from the Survey of English Dialects each have H. Orton as the first editor and a different co-editor: with W. Halliday, *The Six Northern Counties and the Isle of Man* (1962–3); with M. Barry, *The West Midland Counties* (1969–71); with P. M. Tilling, *The East Midland Counties and East Anglia* (1969–71); and with M. F. Wakelin, *The Southern Counties* (1967–8).

The quotation by William Kretzschmar about computerised data handling is from his introduction to *Computer Methods in Dialectology* (1989). The conceptual innovations required for analysing language variation are discussed in Chambers 1995: chapter 1.

Kurath 1972 discusses making a questionnaire, mapping the information, selecting informants, and much else besides, from the perspective of a great contributor to the classic age of dialect geography. The questionnaires used in various surveys are published in handbooks. Wenker's original postal questionnaire is in Mitzka 1952; the American one in Kurath and Bloch 1939; the English one in Orton 1962; and the Scottish one in McIntosh 1952. A revealing view of a traditional dialect geographer's reaction to the use of tape-recording may be found in McDavid, Jr 1957. Orton 1960, from which Map 2-1 is taken, is a generally useful article on methodology. Francis 1978, a review of Orton and Wright 1974, makes several interesting points about linguistic maps, including the distinction between display maps and interpretive maps.

The selection of informants is included in most of the articles listed above and in all the handbooks as well. A highly critical view of the selection of informants in dialect geography and other aspects of traditional methodology is stated by Pickford 1956 and by Underwood 1976.

3

Dialectology and linguistics

Dialectology is to some extent an autonomous discipline, with its own goals and methods. In the previous chapter, we reviewed the most distinctive aspects of dialect geography. But we also noted its common ground with other branches of linguistic science, especially phonetics, historical linguistics and sociolinguistics. In this chapter, we look more closely at the relationship between dialectology and general linguistics.

Modern dialectologists are usually trained as linguists, and many of them contribute to the literature on phonology or syntax or other branches as well as to dialect studies. Obviously, detailed descriptions of peripheral and secondary dialects are directly relevant to theories of phonology and grammar. It is perhaps surprising, then, to discover that interchanges between dialectologists and theoretical linguists are not as common as they might be, though in recent years both groups have come to realise that the rich variability of linguistic systems can illuminate and challenge universal claims about grammar and phonology.

Dialectology took its impetus partly out of the desire to illuminate and challenge Neogrammarian principles in the nineteenth century, as we noted in 2.1 above. We begin this chapter with a closer look at the relationship between dialectology and philology, and then move on to discuss its relationship with some other important theoretical frameworks.

3.1 Dialectology and philology

Wenker's original work on German dialects was motivated in part by the claim, new at the time, made by scholars working on the history of languages, that sound change was regular. This suggestion, which some philologists had found rather startling, pointed out that if a sound change took place it would take place in all cases. That is, it would affect all words that had the sound in question, or at least all words in which the sound occurred in a particular environment. If word-initial /t/ changed to /ts/ as the result of a sound change, as we know it did during the history of the German language, it would change to /ts/ in every single case. The fact that sound change is regular in this way explains why regular correspondences are found between related languages and dialects. The German sound change /t/ > /ts/ did not take place in English, which retained the original /t/, and for this reason English word-initial /t/ regularly corresponds to German /ts/ (spelt *z*):

English	German
ten	zehn
tell	zählen 'to count'
tongue	Zunge
tide	Zeit 'time'

The claim about the regularity of sound change is thus substantially correct. Wenker's survey of German dialects nevertheless showed that the situation was actually more complex than had originally been suggested. One of the linguistic features which the survey investigated was the change of mediaeval German /uː/ to modern German /au/. This diphthongisation is thought to have started in the southeast of the German-speaking area and to have spread northwards and westwards, with dialects in the north and southwest of the area remaining unaffected by the change. We would therefore expect there to be a single isogloss bisecting the German-speaking area, dividing areas which have the original /uː/ from those which have the newer /au/. Wenker found, however, that the isogloss for /huːs/: /haus/ *Haus* 'house' did not coincide with the isogloss for /huːs/: /aus/ *aus* 'out', which in turn did not coincide with that for /bruːn/: /braun/ *braun* 'brown' and so on. There were some dialects where the sound change had not been carried through regularly, and where some words had the original vowel and other words the newer diphthong. We discuss the implications of this finding more fully in Chapter 10.

3.2 Structural dialectology

In more recent times linguistics has had a certain amount of influence on dialectology. Modern linguistic thinking, for example, indicated that it was a drawback of traditional dialectology that it tended to treat linguistic forms in isolation rather than as parts of systems or structures. We can illustrate this point in the following way. The local accents of three towns in East Anglia (see Map 11-12, p. 182) have different pronunciations of the vowel of words like *road*:

	road	nose
Lowestoft	[reʉd]	[neʉz]
Ipswich	[reʉd]	[neʉz]
Colchester	[rʌud]	[nʌuz]

This phonetic information suggests that it would be reasonable to draw an isogloss for this vowel dividing Lowestoft and Ipswich in the north from Colchester in the south. However, if we examine some further pronunciations, the picture looks a little different:

	rowed	*knows*
Lowestoft	[rʌud]	[nʌuz]
Ipswich	[rɵud]	[nɵuz]
Colchester	[rʌud]	[nʌuz]

It now emerges that it would be more revealing to draw an isogloss between Lowestoft in the north and Ipswich and Colchester in the south, because Lowestoft has two vowels at this point in its phonological system whereas the other towns have only one. Lowestoft English, in common with other varieties spoken in the northern part of East Anglia, distinguishes by means of this additional vowel phoneme between pairs such as:

nose	knows
road	rowed
moan	mown
sole	soul

(These two vowels, as the spelling suggests, were originally distinct in all varieties of English, but have become merged in most modern varieties.) In drawing the isogloss in this second way we are grouping varieties together not according to whether they are phonetically similar or not, but on the basis of their phonological systems. Equally, we are now comparing individual forms not as 'the same' or 'different' but as constituent parts of their own systems.

This structural approach has implications for dialectological fieldwork. William G. Moulton pointed out that dialect researchers should be aware of varieties as having systems, and not rely on atomistic phonetic transcriptions alone. They should investigate phonemic contrasts by asking informants whether pairs of words sound the same or rhyme. And it is certain that mistakes can occur if Moulton's recommendations are not followed. We know from our own work, for instance, that in many areas of the English county of Norfolk pairs of words such as *fool* and *foal*, *cool* and *coal* may be homophonous. However, in some of the SED transcriptions for Norfolk, words such as *fool* appear with vowel symbols of the type [ṳː] while words of the type *foal* are written [o̦ː]. This is presumably the result of preconceptions on the part of the fieldworker, and is of course misleading to workers attempting to use the published data for analytical purposes.

The systematic approach to dialect differences was fundamental to STRUCTURAL DIALECTOLOGY. Structural dialectology can be said to have begun in 1954 with the publication by Uriel Weinreich of an article called 'Is a structural dialectology possible?' The reason for the tentative nature of this title lay in the fact that linguists, at that time, tended to adhere to the view that one linguistic system should be studied on its own terms without reference to other systems. The phonemic system of a particular variety was worked out using the well-known principle of complementary distribution of phones, phonetic similarity and the existence of minimal pairs *within that variety*. It was therefore meaningless, it was argued, to compare, say, a phoneme /æ/ in one variety which was in contrast with a phoneme /aː/, as in Received Pronunciation (RP) *Sam* /sæm/ and *psalm* /saːm/, with the /æ/ phoneme of another variety where it is not in contrast with /aː/, as in many Scots varieties in which *Sam* and *psalm* are pronounced the same. The function of a phoneme was to be different from other phonemes, and each phoneme was therefore a contrastive unit. An /æ/ which contrasted with /aː/ was not the same order of entity as an /æ/ which did not. Not only were the two /æ/s not the same, they were not even comparable. And since dialectology is based on the comparison of one variety with another, there was a strong tendency for linguists to ignore dialectology (see 2.1).

Weinreich attempted to reconcile the two areas of study by showing that comparison could be not only meaningful but also revealing. His main innovation was to construct a higher-level system which could incorporate two or more dialect systems. Ipswich, for instance, has the (partial) vowel system:

/uː/   (as in *boot*)
/ou/   (*nose, knows*)
/au/   (*house*)

Corresponding to this, Lowestoft has:

/uː/   (*boot*)
/ou/   (*nose*)
/ʌu/   (*knows*)
/au/   (*house*)

We can combine the two by constructing a joint system:

$$\text{Lowestoft, Ipswich } //\text{uː} \approx {}^{L}_{I} \frac{\text{ou} \sim \text{ʌu}}{\text{ou}} \approx \text{au}//$$

Weinreich called this kind of system a DIASYSTEM. It illustrates the partial differences and partial similarities of related varieties, and points out the systematic nature of the correspondences between them. In the schema above, location of L /ou/ ~ /ʌu/ above I /ou/ is an illustration of lexical correspondences: it shows that words that have either /ou/ or /ʌu/ in variety L (= Lowestoft) will have /ou/ in I (= Ipswich). The two lexical sets of L correspond to the one lexical set of I, and given the L form we can always predict what the I form will be (although not, of course, vice versa).

A diasystem can be regarded as being merely a display device – a way for the linguist to present the facts about the relationship between varieties. Alternatively, the stronger claim can be made that the diasystem has some kind of reality in the sense that speakers and listeners may know and use such a system in their production and/or comprehension. Weinreich himself regarded the diasystem as something more than an artificial construct, and wrote that 'a diasystem is experienced in a very real way by bilingual (including "bidialectal") speakers and corresponds to what students of language contact have called "merged system"'. Weinreich also suggested that diasystems could be constructed at the lexical and grammatical levels.

3.2.1 *Inventory, distribution and incidence*

Structural dialectology, then, represented an attempt to apply some of the insights of linguistics to the dialectological work of comparing language varieties. There were, however, a number of difficulties with work of this sort, and ultimately it has to be said to have failed. For example, phonologically, varieties may differ in a number of ways. They can, first, differ in terms of phoneme INVENTORY – how many, and which, phonemes they have. The comparison of the Lowestoft and Ipswich varieties provides an example of this: Lowestoft has an additional vowel /ʌu/. A second example is one we shall be examining at greater length in later chapters: varieties spoken in the north of England, unlike most other varieties of English, do not have the vowel /ʌ/. In these accents words such as *up* and *but* have /ʊ/, and *blood* and *hood*, *dull* and *full* rhyme. Differences of this sort can, as we have seen, be handled very easily by structural dialectology. In this case it is a simple matter to construct a (partial) diasystem for short vowels incorporating both southern and northern English English varieties:

$$\text{S, N } // \text{ ɪ, ɛ} \approx \text{æ} \approx \frac{\text{S } \text{ʊ} \sim \text{ʌ}}{\text{N } \text{ʊ}} \approx \text{ɒ } //$$

The schema shows that southern (S) and northern (N) varieties have the short vowels /ɪ/, /ɛ/, /æ/ and /ɒ/ in common, but that all words that have /ʊ/ or /ʌ/ in the south have /ʊ/ in the north.

Secondly, varieties may also differ in terms of phoneme DISTRIBUTION. They may have the same inventories but differ in the phonological environments in which particular phonemes may occur. A well-known example of this in English concerns the consonant /r/. All varieties of English have /r/ in their inventories, but they differ in whether or not they permit non-prevocalic /r/, that is /r/ before a pause, as in *far*, or before a consonant, as in *farm* or *far behind*. All accents of English permit /r/ before a vowel (as in *rat, carry* and – with the exception of many South African, and black and southern American varieties – *far away*). But Scottish, Irish, a majority of American and nearly all Canadian accents have postvocalic /r/ (and are therefore said to be RHOTIC), while Australian, South African, most Welsh, most New Zealand and a majority of English accents do not (they are NONRHOTIC). There was, however, no satisfactory way of illustrating this important difference between English varieties in terms of a diasystem. It would have been possible to construct separate consonantal diasystems for each position in syllable structure, but this would be an extremely cumbersome way of illustrating the difference. And the normal type of diasystem would simply show that all varieties have /r/.

Finally, varieties may differ in terms of phoneme INCIDENCE. They may share the same inventory and yet differ in the incidence of particular phonemes in the sets of words. If we again compare northern and southern English English accents we observe that they agree in having the vowels /æ/ (as in *Sam, cat*) and /aː/ (as in *psalm, cart*) in their inventories. They do not agree, however, in the incidence of these vowels. There is a large group of words, including items such as *path, grass, laugh, dance, grant* and *sample*, in which northern accents have /æ/ but southern accents have /aː/:

	pat	*path*	*palm*
North	/æ/	/æ/	/aː/
South	/æ/	/aː/	/aː/

It is clearly an important fact that two dialects may have identical phoneme inventories and yet differ significantly because of the incidence of phonemes in lexical items. This particular difference, in fact, is probably the most important feature distinguishing between northern and southern accents, and certainly it is one of which all English people are aware. Unfortunately, however, there was again no simple way in which this type of difference could be illustrated by means of a diasystem.

3.2.2   *Lexical correspondences*

The problem of dealing with lexical correspondences – of showing which phoneme in a set of words in one variety corresponds to which phoneme in the same set in another variety – is a complex one where differences of incidence are involved. Consider the following phonological differences between RP and the English spoken in the East Anglian city of Norwich:

	RP vowels	*Norwich vowels*
dew, view	/juː/	/uː/
do, lose	/uː/	/ʉː/
school, food	/uː/	/uː/
go, load	/ou/	/ʉː/
know, old	/ou/	/ou/
home, stone	/ou/	/ʊ/
put, pull	/ʊ/	/ʊ/

It is instructive, first, to note that in attempting to present a comparison between RP and Norwich we encounter the problem discussed above of the comparability of forms from different systems. RP *do* and *school* have the same vowel, and Norwich *school* and *go* have the same vowel. But what does it mean to write /uː/ for both Norwich and RP? Is it a claim that /uː/ is the 'same' vowel in both varieties, and, if so, is this claim a legitimate one? The vowels certainly *sound* similar (approximately [uː]), but phonetic similarity alone is not enough. London and Yorkshire English both have a vowel [aː], but it would not be sensible to claim that they were the 'same' diasystemic vowel /a/, since in London this vowel occurs in the lexical set of *but, cup*, while in Yorkshire it occurs in *bat, cap*. To claim that they were the same vowel would be to fail to take lexical correspondences into account. The Norwich–RP comparison is not so arbitrary as this since the set which includes *school* has a similar vowel in both cases, even if *do* and *go* do not. But generally the lexical correspondences are very complex: Norwich /ʉː/ corresponds to RP /juː/ *and* to RP /uː/; /uː/ corresponds to /uː/ *and* /ou/; /ʊ/ corresponds to /ʊ/ *and* /ou/. RP /ou/, on the other hand, corresponds to Norwich /uː/, /ou/ and /ʊ/.

In any comparison of these two varieties, the Weinreich type of diasystem could only indicate differences of inventory. Thus, it would simply indicate, in this case, that Norwich has an extra vowel, although it is an indication of the severity of the comparability problem that it is not absolutely clear *which* of the Norwich vowels it is that is extra. The symbolisation suggests that it is /ʉː/, but alternative symbolisations are possible.

In a study of Swiss German dialects, W. G. Moulton attempted to improve on this situation. His improvement lay in developing a method of illustrating lexical correspondences based on the fact that related varieties differ, as we saw in 3.1, because they are descended from a common source as the result of different linguistic changes. In the case of English, the common source can be regarded as being Middle (mediaeval) English, where the incidence of vowels in the lexical items under comparison was as follows:

1. *dew, view*   /iu/
2. *do, lose, school, food*   /oː/
3. *go, load, home, stone*   /ɔː/
4. *know, old*   /ou/
5. *put, pull*   /ʊ/

Using the numbers 1–5 allotted to the lexical sets here we can construct, following Moulton, a more instructive diasystem by labelling the modern vowels with their Middle English sources:

$$\text{RP, Norwich } // \begin{array}{c} \text{N} \\ \text{RP} \end{array} \frac{\text{ʉː}_{1,2} \sim \text{uː}_{2,3} \sim \text{ou}_4 \sim \text{ʊ}_{3,5}}{\text{juː}_1 \sim \text{uː}_2 \sim \text{ou}_{3,4} \sim \text{ʊ}_5} //$$

This schema reveals that Norwich /uː/ occurs in words descended from both the Middle English 2 (/oː/) set (*school, food*) and from the Middle English 3 (/ɔː/) set (*go, load*).

RP /uː/, on the other hand, occurs only in items descended from the Middle English /oː/ set.

Even this schema for a diasystem, however, gives only a rough indication of lexical correspondences. It shares with Weinreich's original system the drawback that it fails to show *exactly* which lexical items have a particular vowel. And it is not able to show the *degree* to which a modern phoneme corresponds to one historical source rather than another. The above diasystem shows that some Middle English /oː/s have become /ʉː/ in Norwich and others /uː/, but not which or how many.

A diasystem of this type, as Moulton pointed out, also has the unfortunate consequence of giving the impression that RP and Norwich do not, at least in these partial systems, have a single phonological unit in common. As Ernst Pulgram has written: 'a diasystem that takes into account certain conditions which historical linguists, dialectologists, and the speakers will regard as indispensable and that then shows so little agreement between closely related dialects as to make them seem foreign to one another distorts the facts' (1964: 67). In other words, if we take lexical correspondences into account the results can approach the absurd. And if we do not take lexical correspondences into account, further potential absurdities become possible: London and Yorkshire [aˈ˕] could be regarded as diasystematically the same; and a diasystem could be constructed for totally unrelated varieties such as, say, English and Chinese. (It is possible that Weinreich would not necessarily have thought the latter absurd in the case of an English–Chinese bilingual since he does write 'a diasystem is experienced in a very real way by bilingual . . . speakers' (1954: 390).)

3.3   Generative dialectology

Structural dialectology, then, was able to handle inventory differences successfully, but it could deal with incidence and distribution differences only with difficulty. A way out of some of these difficulties was offered by GENERATIVE DIALECTOLOGY, which also had the advantage of making it easier to handle more than two varieties at any one time.

Generative dialectology involved the application of concepts and findings from generative phonology to the description and comparison of different dialects. Generative dialectology presupposed a two-level approach to phonology which posited (a) underlying forms, which were the phonological forms in which lexical items were listed in the lexicon, and (b) phonological rules which converted these underlying forms into surface forms and thus, ultimately, into their actual pronunciation. In particular, forms involved in alternations of various kinds appeared in the lexicon in only one form, the others being the result of the application of rules. This produced a simplicity of description and made possible the representation of generalisations about the way in which the language works which, it was supposed, the native speaker knows and operates with.

Generative dialectology worked on the assumption that a single underlying form can be postulated for related dialects, and that these dialects differ in (a) the phonological rules that apply to the underlying forms, and/or (b) the environments in which the rules apply, and/or (c) the order in which the rules apply.

We can illustrate this from dialects of modern Greek. Four of the phonological rules set up by Brian Newton for northern Greek dialects are:

(1) High vowel loss: unstressed /i/ and /u/ are lost.

(2) Voicing assimilation: voiceless stops become voiced before voiced stops; voiced stops become voiceless before voiceless stops.

(3) Vowel epenthesis: when the final consonant of a word-final consonant cluster is a nasal, an /i/ is inserted before the nasal.

(4) Rounding: /i/ becomes /u/ before a following labial consonant.

From the underlying form /ðik'os mu/ 'my own', we can account for four different pronunciations found in northern Greek dialects in terms of which of these rules they have, and in which order:

	Macedonia	*Thessaly*	*Epirus*	*Euboea*
underlying form:	/ðikosmu/	/ðikosmu/	/ðikosmu/	/ðikosmu/
rules:	(1) ðkosm	(1) ðkosm	(1) ðkosm	(1) ðkosm
	(2) θkozm	(2) θkozm	(3) ðkosim	(3) ðkosim
	(3) θkozim	(3) θkozim	(2) θkosim	(2) θkosim
		(4) θkozum		(4) θkosum
surface form:	θkozim	θkozum	θkosim	θkosum

Note in particular that if voicing assimilation applies *before* vowel epenthesis the output is *θkozim* (as in Macedonia), but if it applies after vowel epenthesis the output is *θkosim* (as in Epirus).

One problem for generative phonology was what exactly underlying forms should look like and how they should be arrived at. An early assumption was that it would be possible to take forms from one dialect as basic and derive all other dialects from it. It can quite readily be demonstrated, however, that this cannot be done. It is clear from the examples discussed in 3.2 that if we wished to establish a set of common underlying forms for English English, we would have to take note of the inventory difference outlined there – that northern varieties lack /ʌ/. The only way to deal with this would be to take the southern forms as basic and derive northern forms from them by means of a rule:

(i)   ʌ → ʊ

Obviously it would be impossible to do it the other way round because if we took the northern /ʊ/ form as basic there would be no way of telling which of these was /ʌ/

and which /ʊ/ in the south. For this feature, then, we must choose the underlying forms from the southern dialect.

However, if we turn to a second feature, postvocalic *r*, we find that we must choose underlying forms from elsewhere. Clearly, the rhotic forms such as /kɑːrt/ must be basic and the *r-less* forms must be derived from them by the rule:

(ii) $r \rightarrow \varnothing \, / \ ——— \begin{Bmatrix} \# \\ C \end{Bmatrix}$

It would be impossible to take the nonrhotic forms as basic, because there would be no way of predicting where *r* was to be inserted in rhotic accents.

In English English, we would therefore have to look for our underlying forms in southwestern accents because southeastern varieties are not rhotic. On the other hand, it is actually not possible to take southwestern forms as basic because of another feature, the East Anglian distinction noted above for Lowestoft and Norwich between the vowels of *moan* and *mown*, and *road* and *rowed*. To cope with this contrast, we have to have distinct underlying forms for the two lexical sets, and then apply a rule that merges them for other varieties. Since southwestern varieties do not make this distinction, they cannot be basic. East Anglian varieties, on the other hand, are not rhotic and can therefore not be basic either. Underlying forms, that is to say, cannot be taken from any one dialect, and are in fact best regarded as forms which are more abstract, in the sense that they do not necessarily occur in any one dialect.

By giving up the claim that diasystemic underlying forms must be determined by a single dialect, generative dialectology eventually avoided this dilemma. However, a number of difficulties remained. Generative dialectology could cope with inventory differences by rules such as (i), and with distribution differences by rules such as (ii). It was therefore an advance on structural dialectology. But it was not by any means an unqualified advance, for dialectology could only cope with incidence differences if they were phonologically conditioned and regular. We saw earlier (in 3.2.1) that there is an important difference in English English varieties involving the incidence of /æ/ and /ɑː/ in words such as *path, grass* and *laugh*. At first, it might seem that generative dialectology could handle this difference by a simple rule, because the vowel in question occurs, in this lexical set, before one of the voiceless fricatives *θ s* or *f*. It might be possible, then, to postulate underlying /æ/ and derive southern /ɑː/ by the following rule:

$$\text{æ} \rightarrow \text{ɑː} \, / \ ——— \begin{Bmatrix} \theta \\ s \\ f \end{Bmatrix}$$

However, this rule turns out to be much too general because even in the south of England there are many words which have /æ/ in the environment: *maths, ass, mass, raffle, cafeteria*, etc. (If we try to state the rule the other way, with /ɑː/ as the underlying vowel, there are still problems because of a number of words such as *half, calf* and *master* which have /ɑː/ even in the north.) This difference between northern and southern accents is phonologically conditioned, as the rule suggests, but it is not regular (see 8.2). The rule can therefore only work if large numbers of words are labelled as exceptions in the lexicon. The complexities increase if we attempt to deal with the set of words including *dance, plant, sample*, etc., which also has /æ/ in the north and /ɑː/ in the south, because of an even greater number of 'irregular' words, like *ant, romance, ample*, etc., which have /æ/ in both regions.

3.4 Polylectal grammars

A second related problem for generative dialectology concerned exactly what status was claimed for our underlying forms and rules and thus, ultimately, for systems, grammars or descriptions themselves. One of the motivations for generative dialectology was that it could be regarded as providing an explanation or characterisation of how speakers of different but related dialects are able to communicate. Mutual intelligibility can readily be accounted for if the linguistic systems involved are fundamentally the same and differ only in terms of a number of rules. This, however, may be seen as a claim that speakers in some sense 'know' the overall system, and can use it in their comprehension of different varieties.

There are, however, many factors which suggest that common underlying forms of the type generative dialectologists might have liked to set up have no 'psychological reality' and are simply not known by speakers. Many speakers of northern English varieties of English, for instance, hypercorrect when trying to produce statusful RP-type pronunciations and introduce /ʌ/ into their speech not only in *but* and *butter* but also in items such as *could* and *hook*. Similarly, it is obvious that many speakers from, say, the southeast of England do not 'know' underlying forms with /r/ for words like *cart* and *car* since, in attempting to imitate southwestern (or American) accents, they frequently (in spite of the potential assistance of the spelling) introduce /r/ where it does not belong, in words like *last* /lɑːrst/, *father* /fɑːrðə/, and so on. (Actors can very often be heard doing this.)

The fact still remains, though, that all speakers are able to comprehend many more dialects than they actually speak, and many speakers are to some degree bidialectal. This fact led a number of linguists in the 1970s to build on generative dialectology and to propose that it was legitimate to construct POLYLECTAL GRAMMARS – grammars that incorporate more than one variety.

We have to accept, of course, that mutual intelligibility of different dialects exists. It does not necessarily follow, however, that the polylectal grammar is necessarily the best way of accounting for mutual intelligibility. It might be, for instance, that we should assume instead that speakers simply have increasingly greater difficulties in understanding speakers who have grammars which are increasingly unlike their own, and that comprehension is achieved in a very ad hoc manner, the listener employing all the clues that he can to help overcome the dissimilarities.

There is, in any case, the interesting problem of exactly how much polylectal competence speakers can be said to have. How much do they 'know' of other varieties? There is evidence that speakers not only can understand other dialects but also, given enough information, can make predictions about what is and is not grammatical in other varieties. There are, however, limits to this kind of ability. There is evidence, for instance, that native speakers of English English, in the absence of any supplementary information, are prepared to predict that sentences such as:

(5) Look, is that a man stand there?
(6) I might could do it.

are not grammatical in any form of English (and indeed that 'not even foreigners' would say them) whereas they are actually perfectly acceptable constructions in (a) certain East Anglian, and (b) certain northeastern English, southern Scottish, and southern American varieties.

There are also limits to speakers' comprehension of grammatical forms that do not occur in their own dialects, especially out of context, but even in some cases if context is provided. It has been shown, for instance, that speakers who do not have the forms in question in their own dialects may have considerable difficulty with constructions such as:

(7) He eats a lot anymore (= 'He eats a lot nowadays' in certain US and Canadian dialects).
(8) I been know that (= 'I've known that for a long time' in certain varieties of American Black English).
(9) It's dangerous to smoke in a petrol station without causing an explosion (= '... because you might cause an explosion' in certain south Wales varieties).

There is also a problem of where polylectal grammars stop in a rather different, if related, sense. Unless a polylectal grammar covers a whole dialect continuum (see Chapter 1), it has to stop, socially or geographically, at some point. But there may well be no point at all at which it would be anything other than arbitrary to draw the line. On the other hand, there are many cases – the Dutch–German continuum, for instance – where a polylectal grammar covering the whole continuum would not be a reasonable construct since no native speaker has even receptive competence of all the varieties concerned.

The notion of polylectal grammars, while interesting, also therefore seems to be a theoretical dead-end. In more recent years, the most fruitful area of interaction between dialectology and linguistics has involved variation theory, which itself arose out of urban dialectology, the subject matter of the next chapter.

Further information

The neogrammarian hypothesis about the regularity of sound change is discussed in Bloomfield 1933: chapter 20; Anderson 1973: chapter 1, and in many other introductory texts. For a thorough, up-to-date discussion of it, see Labov 1994: chapters 15–18. In addition to Weinreich's original article (1954), the other articles on structural dialectology cited are: Moulton 1960 and Pulgram 1964. Another helpful paper is Cochrane 1959. Useful works on generative dialectology are Newton 1972, from which our Greek example in this chapter is taken; Keyser's (1963) review of Kurath and McDavid 1961; Saporta 1965; King 1969, especially chapter 3; and Vasiliu 1966. An attempt to establish underlying forms from one dialect of a set may be found in O'Neill 1963. Thomas 1967 shows, with examples from Welsh, that underlying forms have to be more abstract. Glauser 1985 looks at the geographical distribution of phonological subrules.

Polylectal grammars are discussed in Bailey 1973 and Bickerton 1975. The research on speakers' predictions of grammaticality in other varieties is cited along with similar examples in Chambers and Trudgill 1991. An important article on the limits of grammars is Labov 1973.

4

Urban dialectology

At the same time that dialectology was beginning to be influenced directly (if only slightly) by linguistics, it was also beginning to be influenced indirectly by the social sciences. Some dialectologists began to recognise that the spatial dimension of linguistic variation had been concentrated on to the exclusion of the social dimension. To some, this was felt to be a deficiency, since social variation in language is as pervasive and important as regional variation. All dialects are both regional and social. All speakers have a social background as well as a regional location, and in their speech they often identify themselves not only as natives or inhabitants of a particular place but also as members of a particular social class, age group, ethnic background, or other social characteristic. The concentration of work on the language of NORMs and the working class, it was therefore realised, had led to considerable ignorance about the dialects spoken by other social groups.

4.1 Social dialects

One of the first dialect studies to attempt to take social factors into account was the Linguistic Atlas of the United States and Canada. When work was begun on this survey in the 1930s it was very much in the mould of traditional dialectology. However, fieldworkers on the original New England section of the survey were instructed to select socially different types of informant (see 2.3.3). Taking note of the social dimension of linguistic variation in this way was an important step, but the process by which informants were classified was obviously still somewhat subjective – exactly how uneducated was 'uneducated'? – and selection was rather haphazard – fieldworkers were restricted to people they happened to be able to come into contact with. These factors did not represent any kind of problem for Kurath's survey, since its aim was for the most part to examine geographical differentiation. For other types of work, however, it does present a problem, and one we shall return to shortly.

4.2 Urban dialects

It also gradually came to be realised that the focusing of traditional dialectology on rural dialects had led to an almost total neglect, in many countries, of the speech forms used by the majority of the population, namely those who lived in towns and cities. This was of course particularly true of heavily urbanised countries such as England, where perhaps 90 per cent of the population live in towns. Linguists and dialectologists remained ignorant about the way in which most people in England (and elsewhere) speak, and have therefore been missing out on a great deal of linguistic data. The feeling therefore developed that the study of urban dialects was not only an interesting but a necessary task.

This development towards social and urban dialectology has to be seen in its historical context. The initial impetus for dialectological work, as we have seen, lay in comparative philology, and it was because of this historical emphasis that dialectologists had looked mainly to rural speech forms. Urban dialects were felt, correctly, to be less conservative. They tended to be relatively new, often resulting from immigration from surrounding rural areas, and were therefore less interesting for philologists. Similarly, in any given locality, dialectologists were not interested in any social variation present but simply in obtaining information on the most conservative variety spoken there. When the emphasis in linguistic studies changed, however, the way was open for the emphasis in dialectology also to change, to a certain extent. The trend towards the study of social and urban dialects thus reflects the growth in the synchronic approach to the study of language – an approach which showed particularly rapid development from the 1930s onwards.

Many early urban dialect studies, not surprisingly, were carried out in the manner of traditional dialectology, ignoring the social dimension, and selecting informants as available. Eva Sivertsen's book *Cockney Phonology*, published in 1960, is essentially a work in rural dialectology carried out in one of the largest cities in the world. Even if we take 'Cockney' to mean 'working-class London East End English' it is still a variety spoken by tens of thousands of people. Sivertsen, however, obtained most of her data from four speakers, all of them women over sixty living in Bethnal Green.

David DeCamp, similarly, investigated the speech of San Francisco by studying the speech of people known to him, and of people known to them. Wolfgang Viereck, in the same vein, studied the speech of Gateshead, a town of 115,000 inhabitants in the northeast of England, by investigating the speech of twelve men, ten of them over seventy. His justification for this was that he was concerned not to produce an accurate description of Gateshead dialect as it is spoken today, but to select speakers of what he considered 'pure' Gateshead dialect: dialect, presumably, from the time before it became altered by external influences. Actually, linguistic studies suggest that there is probably no such thing as a 'pure' dialect, since most varieties of language appear to be variable and to show signs of influence from other varieties.

These studies, and others like them, provide valuable records of the speech of the people who were interviewed. In a few instances, they may record obsolescent forms and rare constructions. The problem is that there is no way of knowing if what they are describing is truly the language of the town in question or simply that of an individual the investigator happens to have come across.

4.3 **Representativeness**

The usual procedure in traditional dialectology was to select NORMs, informants who were not only elderly but also uneducated and untravelled, because it was felt that this method would produce examples of the 'most genuine' dialect. As we have seen, 'genuine' is not a very meaningful notion when applied to language varieties. The original dialectologists were looking for the most conservative varieties, because of their philological interests. With the movement away from diachronic studies, however, the way was now clear for the recognition of the fact that the 'most genuine' dialect did not necessarily (indeed did not usually) mean the most 'typical'. If what one wanted was not the most old-fashioned variety available but rather an accurate picture of all the linguistic varieties spoken in a particular area, other methods of informant selection would have to be used.

This became even clearer with the advent of work on urban dialectology. The size and social complexity of urban communities mean that it is very difficult for any individual to have a reliable idea of what speech forms are 'typical', and personal contacts as a means of selecting and obtaining informants are not very reliable. What works in the village does not work in the town.

Obviously, though, it would not be sensible to arrive at a description of what is typical of the speech of a city by investigating its entire population. Linguists have therefore followed the example of social scientists, geographers, botanists and opinion pollsters and taken random samples of the population of cities in order to carry out their work. Individuals are selected at random from the total population in such a way that all members of the community have an equal chance of selection, in order that the speakers investigated should be REPRESENTATIVE of the entire population. Recordings are then made of the speech of the sample.

In Britain, as in many other countries, this process is easily carried out by taking the sample from the electoral register or some other list of the adult population of the area. The people selected are then contacted and asked to take part in the survey. As with all social surveys, there are difficulties at this point. Some of the people selected have moved away or died, and others are not willing to cooperate. The problem of refusals, however, is thought to be less serious for linguistic studies than it is for social or political surveys. People who refuse to give their views on controversial social questions may well have different views on those questions from those who agree to help, and it is therefore important to try and persuade reluctant interviewees to take part. This seems not to be the case with language. There is no reason to suppose that speakers who refuse to take part in such surveys have linguistic characteristics different from those who do. In fact, William Labov, who carried out the first major work of this type, in the Lower East Side of New York City, managed to obtain samples of speech from many people who had refused to be interviewed, by the simple expedient of speaking to them, on some pretext, on the telephone. Analysis showed that there were no differences between their speech and that of the other informants. It has since been felt, therefore, that it is not as important for linguists as for social scientists to persuade reluctant informants to cooperate, and this may in any case not be very productive since reluctant speakers are unlikely to say very much.

4.4 Obtaining data

Having secured the cooperation of informants, the next task is obviously to obtain the linguistic data required. In traditional dialectology, as we have seen, data was often obtained by asking informants to respond, most usually with one-word answers, to individual questionnaire items. In an urban situation, and given the wide social range of informants, it is especially clear that this is not a very satisfactory method. If we are after typical speech forms, it is not enough simply to obtain representative speakers. We also have to acquire representative speech. We have to ensure that speakers produce speech that is typical of the way in which they normally speak.

Now the more attention speakers pay to the way they are speaking, the more formal and careful their speech is likely to be. By asking informants, in effect, what they call something or how they pronounce a particular word, the dialectologist is directing *considerable* attention to their language. Urban dialect surveys, which have in any case been much more concerned with phonology and grammar than lexis, have therefore usually proceeded by obtaining tape-recorded stretches of quasi-conversational speech from their informants, usually by the asking of questions designed to produce large amounts of talk.

Even this is not particularly satisfactory, however. Although informants are producing connected speech rather than one-word answers, a tape-recorded interview with a stranger is still bound to direct their attention to their speech to a certain extent. Labov has labelled this problem THE OBSERVER'S PARADOX: linguists want to observe the way people speak when they are not being observed. What the linguist is hoping to study in particular is INFORMAL speech, not necessarily because it may be more 'normal' – all speakers have both informal and formal styles – but because it is generally more systematic and regular and therefore more interesting than other varieties. (It is at this level, least influenced by notions of linguistic 'correctness', that linguistic tendencies and regularities are most clearly to be found and where many linguistic changes take place.) Any observation of the way somebody speaks, however, is liable to put them on their linguistic best behaviour to the extent that they are liable to speak more as they would in FORMAL situations.

In the New York City study, Labov developed a number of ways of overcoming the observer's paradox, notably by recording conversation outside the formal context of the interview (at the beginning or end of the interview, or speech to third persons), and by directing informants' attention *away* from their speech by encouraging their emotional involvement, particularly by asking questions such as: 'Have you ever been in a situation where you thought you were going to be killed?' As we shall see in the next chapter, these methods did succeed in producing a different, more casual style of speech.

In more recent work, Labov and other linguists have overcome the problem in a number of other more sophisticated ways, especially by recording groups of speakers rather than individuals. Wherever random sampling is required, however, recording individuals in face-to-face interviews remains, for practical reasons, the normal procedure.

4.5 Classifying informants

The outcome of successful fieldwork is thus large amounts of tape-recorded speech from large numbers of people. Depending on the size of the survey area and on the particular objectives of the survey, the number of informants employed might range from, say, twenty-five to a few hundred.

In order to be able to handle this amount of data, we need to be able to quantify, measure and classify it. Classifying the informants is relatively simple, in fact. There are, for instance, few problems with grouping people together by age or sex. With an urban community, especially since one is dealing with a single geographical location, differentiation in terms of social stratification also cannot be ignored. Social class is, of course, a complex notion, but linguists have normally taken a relatively elementary approach to classifying informants, particularly as this has produced very satisfactory results, some of which we shall see in the next chapter. Speakers are generally grouped together according to factors such as their occupation, income, education and housing (see 5.1).

4.6 The linguistic variable

Quantifying the linguistic data is more difficult, particularly when it comes to handling linguistic variability. Long before the careful study of urban dialectology, it had been observed that speakers vary at some points in their linguistic behaviour. Many speakers of English English, for example, sometimes say *but* [bʌt] and sometimes [bʌʔ], and use both pronunciations in the same conversation, even in the same utterance. This phenomenon was, of course, not much of a problem for traditional dialectology since, if informants pronounce a word only once, variation can hardly show up in the data. In urban dialectology, however, with conversational data rather than responses to a questionnaire, it was impossible to ignore linguistic variation.

Where linguistic variation had been observed in the past, it had generally been referred to as FREE VARIATION. One of the achievements of urban dialectology has been to

49

show that this type of variation is usually not 'free' at all, but is constrained by social and/or linguistic factors. This insight was achieved in the first instance as a result of the development of the notion of the LINGUISTIC VARIABLE, a linguistic unit with two or more variants involved in covariation with other social and/or linguistic variables. Linguistic variables can often be regarded as socially different but linguistically equivalent ways of doing or saying the same thing, and occur at all levels of linguistic analysis. (The linguistic variable and 'free' variation are discussed in Chapter 9.)

Grammatical variables of certain types may be relatively simple to handle. One example is provided by the phenomenon of MULTIPLE NEGATION. In most English dialects we find the variable occurrence of forms such as:

(1) I don't want none.
He didn't do nothing.

alternating with:

(2) I don't want any.
He didn't do anything.

With variables of this type, it is a straightforward matter to examine the tape-recordings obtained and to count the number of type (1) and the number of type (2) forms used by informants. Then a simple percentage score of multiple negation usage for individuals, and ultimately for groups, can be calculated. As it happens, studies of this feature in a number of English dialects show that, as with many linguistic variables, a majority of speakers use both variants, but the proportions in which the variants occur correlate with social variables such as the formality of the situation and the speaker's social status. We examine this further in Chapter 5.

Phonological variability can be dealt with in the same way. For instance, in the New York City English studied by Labov, one of the linguistic variables investigated was (r). (It is usual to symbolise variables by enclosing them in parentheses.) The variable (r) is not equivalent to /r/ since it represents only postvocalic /r/, as in *car* and *cart*, except after the vowel of *her* and *bird*. That is, it covers /r/ in *far* and *farm*, but not in *fur*, *fern*, *rat*, *trap*, *carry* or *far away*.

In New York City, (r) is variable in the sense that most speakers sometimes have an *r* in words of the type *car* and *cart* and sometimes do not. The variable thus has two variants, *r* and zero, and the calculation of index scores for individuals and groups proceeds as with multiple negation. The analyst simply counts the number of *rs* speakers use, as opposed to the number they could have used, and works out a percentage score.

Variables which have more than two variants are more complicated. In a study of the English spoken in Norwich, one of the variables set up was (t). In many varieties of British English, /t/ is variably realised as either [t] or [ʔ] as in (5) and (6), except syllable-initially as in (3) and (4) where it can only be [t]:

(3) tea   [tiː]
(4) between   [bə'twiːn]
(5) bitter   ['bɪtə] ~ ['bɪʔə]
(6) bit   [bɪt] ~ [bɪʔ]

That is, the variable (t) is equivalent to syllable-final /t/.

In Norwich, this variable actually has three variants:

(t)-1 = [t]
(t)-2 = [tʔ]
(t)-3 = [ʔ]

Variant (t)-2 is a pronunciation involving simultaneous oral and glottal closure where the oral closure is released, inaudibly, before the glottal closure. In this case, the three variants can quite naturally be arranged in order, since (t)-2 is articulatorily intermediate between the two other variants. (It is also, it turns out, socially intermediate.)

Indices for variables of this type are computed in the following way. Suppose a speaker on our tape-recordings has seven instances of (t), consisting of two instances of (t)-1, three instances of (t)-2, and two instances of (t)-3. We compute the score by multiplying and adding:

$$
\begin{array}{r}
2 \times (t)\text{-}1 = 2 \\
3 \times (t)\text{-}2 = 6 \\
\underline{2 \times (t)\text{-}3 = 6} \\
7 \phantom{\times (t)\text{-}3 = } 14
\end{array}
$$

We then divide by the number of instances of (t): 14 ÷ 7 = 2. The (t) index for this speaker is therefore 2.0, and could equally well have been obtained by consistent usage of (t)-2.

Possible scores, it will be observed, range from 1.0 to 3.0. However, very often, simply for convenience and in order to have scores (as with two-variant variables) starting from 0, final indices are calculated by subtracting 1 from the answer and then multiplying by 100. Now we have scores ranging from 0 to 200. Consistent use of (t)-1 will then give 0, (t)-2 100, and (t)-3 200. And our informant, instead of 2.0, will score 100.

To arrive at scores for groups rather than individuals, two alternative methods are possible. We can either (a) calculate indices for individuals first, and then average them. Or (b) we can compute scores for the group as a whole as if it were a single speaker.

Method (a)

Speaker A		*Speaker B*		*Speaker C*	
$2 \times$ (t)-1 =	2	$4 \times$ (t)-1 =	4	$1 \times$ (t)-1 =	1
$3 \times$ (t)-2 =	6	$3 \times$ (t)-2 =	6	$4 \times$ (t)-2 =	8
$3 \times$ (t)-2 =	6	$1 \times$ (t)-3 =	3	$5 \times$ (t)-3 =	15
7	14	8	13	10	24

$$\frac{14}{7} = 2 \qquad \frac{13}{8} = 1.63 \qquad \frac{24}{10} = 2.4$$

Index: 100   Index: 63   Index: 140

A: 100
B: 63   Group index: $\dfrac{303}{3} = 101$
C: 140
———
303

Method (b)

	Instances of (t)	*(t) score*
Speaker A:	7	14
Speaker B:	8	13
Speaker C:	10	24
Total:	25	51

$$\frac{51}{25} = 2.04$$

Group index: 104

In this case the two results are not very different, 101 as opposed to 104, and it is in fact the simpler method, Method (b), which is normally used. However, Method (a) is sometimes preferred when only a small number of instances are obtained of some variable overall, in order to reduce the possible skewing effect of individuals who happen to have provided a high proportion of the instances.

    Vowel variables are more difficult to deal with than consonantal variables. Consonantal variables most often have obviously discrete variants: [r], [ʔ], and so on. Vowels do not. Variable vowel pronunciations are often ranged on a phonetic continuum of vowel quality, and there is no principled way in which the continuum can be divided up to provide genuinely separate variants. The solution to this problem is to acknowledge that any division of the continuum of vowel quality is arbitrary, but nevertheless to make such divisions, ensuring only that the division is consistently maintained.

One example from the Norwich study is provided by the variable (aː), which is identical with the phoneme /aː/, the vowel of *cart, path, palm, banana*. In Norwich the quality of this vowel varies from an RP-like back vowel, around [ɑː], to a very front vowel, around [aː], with of course an indefinite number of intermediate points. The procedure in this case was to isolate variants as follows:

> (aː)-1 = [ɑː], i.e. the RP vowel or something close to it.
> (aː)-2 = something between (aː)-1 and (aː)-3.
> (aː)-3 = [aː], i.e. the most extreme local pronunciation or something close to it.

Obviously this is a very ad hoc kind of approach, and the phrase 'something close to it' suggests a degree of vagueness. It works very well, however, if the analyst is consistent: if a particular vowel quality is recorded on one occasion as (aː)-1, then it must be recorded as (aː)-1 on all other occasions as well. (Obviously a few inaccuracies may occur, but we are normally dealing with such large numbers that a deviation in one direction is quite likely to be cancelled out by an equivalent deviation in the other.) Moreover it has to be remembered that the result of this exercise will be an index score which is simply a number showing how individuals and groups stand *relative* to each other. There is no 'right answer' to be aimed at, and no particular reason, for instance, why we should not have used four rather than three variants of (aː) – except that the analyst might perhaps have found it more difficult to discriminate between them consistently.

We shall see more of how linguistic variables are used in the next chapter.

Further information

The early works on urban dialectology cited are: DeCamp 1958 and 1959; Sivertsen 1960; and Viereck 1966. Urban dialect methodology is discussed in more detail in Milroy 1987. Labov's trail-blazing work is *The Social Stratification of English in New York City* (1966), and his extensive discussion of the observer's paradox and other important issues can best be read in his *Sociolinguistic Patterns* (1972b). Other works on urban dialectology include: Trudgill 1974a; Shuy et al. 1968; Wolfram 1969; Macaulay 1977; and Cheshire 1982. Useful discussions of problems associated with linguistic variables can be found in Hudson 1996; Lavandera 1978; Knowles 1978; and Chambers 1995.

SOCIAL VARIATION

5

Social differentiation and language

Traditional dialectology concentrated on the relationship between language and geography, and on the spatial differentiation of language. Urban dialectology has looked more to the relationships that obtain between language and social features. In this chapter we examine some of these relationships.

5.1 Language and social class

One of the variables investigated in the survey of Norwich English was (ng). This is the pronunciation of the suffix -*ing* in present participles such as *walking* and *going*, and in place-names such as *Reading* and *Woking*. In most varieties of English the final consonant of this suffix is variable, alternating between /ŋ/ and /n/. In Norwich, words like *walking* can be pronounced either /ˈwɔːkɪŋ/ or /ˈwɔːkn/. The variable thus has two variants:

(ng)-1 = /ŋ/
(ng)-2 = /n/

Using the methodology outlined in Chapter 4, consistent use of (ng)-2 will produce a score of 100, while consistent use of (ng)-1 will produce a score of 0.

A number of studies have shown that this variable correlates very closely with social class in a number of English varieties. As we saw in Chapter 4, classification of informants into social class groups is a relatively simple matter. In the Norwich study, the sixty speakers in the sample were classified into five groups, labelled middle middle class (MMC), lower middle class (LMC), upper working class (UWC), middle working class (MWC), and lower working class (LWC), on the basis of their occupation, income, education, father's occupation, housing and locality. People who fell into the two middle-class groups were, for the most part, working in nonmanual occupations, while the three working-class groups consisted mainly of people working in manual occupations. (People of the type normally referred to in Britain as 'upper class' or 'upper middle class' did not occur in the sample – which is not surprising, since there are not very many of them, and they tend not to live in places like Norwich.)

Measuring both the linguistic data and the social characteristics of the informants in this way permits the two to be correlated. In this case, the average (ng) scores obtained by the five different social class groups were as follows:

MMC	3
LMC	15
UWC	74
MWC	88
LWC	98

This correlation shows, first, that there is a very clear relationship between usage of this variable and social class membership: the (ng)-2 /n/ variant is much more typical of working-class speech. Secondly, it indicates that there is a large difference in scores between the LMC and UWC. This gap in linguistic behaviour between middle-class and working-class speakers has often been noted in British studies. Thirdly, it shows that the relationship between accent and social class is a matter of more-or-less rather than either–or. It is not the case that some groups use one variant and others the other; rather, all groups use both variants, but in different proportions. It is a matter of tendencies and probabilities.

Results of this type, showing clear quantitative correlations between pronunciation and social class, have now been produced in very many studies, and for very many variables. Scores for the other Norwich variables mentioned in Chapter 4 show the same sort of pattern, with lower-class groups tending to use more non-RP forms than higher-class groups:

	(aː) (as in *cart, path*)	(t) (as in *better, bet*)
MMC	42	83
LMC	98	123
UWC	160	178
MWC	178	184
LWC	187	187

It has to be conceded, of course, that index scores of this type not only conceal what individual speakers do, but also how exactly group scores are obtained. Nevertheless, it is clear from these figures that, for example, all groups of working-class speakers use more [ʔ] than any other (t) variant, and that middle-class speakers have a vowel in *cart*, on average, towards [ɑː], while LWC speakers, with 187 out of a maximum of 200, have a very front vowel (see 4.6).

It also has to be conceded that it was very clear *before* urban dialect studies of this type were carried out that there was a clear relationship between pronunciation and social class of the sort illustrated above. One does not have to be a dialectologist to be aware of this fact. The advantage of systematic research, however, is that we now know more exactly, and in more detail, what that relationship is, and how it operates. We see again with (aː) and (t), for instance, a sizeable gap in scores between the LMC and UWC, as we did for (ng), which points to a difference of considerable importance between middle-class and working-class speech.

The quantitative approach also makes possible comparisons between different studies and different accents. A revealing example is provided by two studies involving the variable (h). As is well known, many – perhaps most – varieties of Welsh and English English are variable in their pronunciation of /h/, with words like *hammer* and *heart* sometimes being pronounced with initial *h* and sometimes without. Since the British prestige accent, RP, retains *h*, we expect higher-class speakers to pronounce more *h*s than lower-class speakers. In two studies carried out in England, one in Norwich and the other in the Yorkshire town of Bradford, (h) was set up with two variants: (h)-1 = [h], and (h)-2 = zero. A comparison of the two studies, in which the social class groups were classified in the same way, shows that the variable functions in a similar way in both places, but at quantitatively different levels:

	Bradford	*Norwich*
MMC	12	6
LMC	28	14
UWC	67	40
MWC	89	60
LWC	93	60

The figures show that while in both areas *h*-dropping is correlated directly with social class, the percentage of *h*-dropping for any social class group is always greater in Bradford than in Norwich. Thus quantification of this kind reveals hitherto unknown linguistic differences, and leads one to seek an explanation. In this case the explanation may lie in the fact that *h*-dropping is a relatively recent phenomenon in Norwich, with rural accents in areas surrounding the city still retaining /h/, while in Bradford it is a linguistic feature of greater antiquity.

We shall discuss further how and why social class differences in language arise in Chapter 8, but it is clear that these discussions too will depend on precise quantitative knowledge of the type made possible by the development of the notion of the linguistic variable.

5.2 Stylistic differentiation

The scores given above from the Norwich study are all based on the style of speech most typical of tape-recorded interviews, in which speakers are devoting quite a lot of attention to the way they are speaking (see 4.4). We can call this variety

FORMAL STYLE. As we saw in Chapter 4, however, it is both possible and necessary in linguistic studies to extend the stylistic range in the direction of the less formal, and we can do this by diverting informants' attention away from their speech. Speech of this type, obtained by using the methods outlined briefly in Chapter 4, can be labelled CASUAL STYLE.

It is also possible, at the same time, if we are interested in a closer examination of stylistic variation, to extend the stylistic range in the opposite direction, by directing *more* attention to informants' speech. In many studies this has been done by asking informants to read aloud a passage of connected prose. Reading is a specifically linguistic activity which necessarily directs attention to language, particularly since it is often obvious that there is no other purpose to the reading other than to be recorded. It is also, of course, an activity which is associated for many people with school and linguistic 'correctness'. Relatively more formal styles of pronunciation, which we can call 'reading-passage style', are therefore obtained. Asking informants to record a reading passage also has the advantage, if the passage is prepared with some thought, of ensuring that the same particular key lexical items are elicited from all informants. On the other hand, it also has the disadvantage that in some places illiteracy or simple antagonism to reading aloud as an activity may render it impracticable.

Finally, it is possible to achieve even more formality by asking informants to read aloud from a prepared word list. Reading out one word at a time is a much simpler reading task than coping with a passage of connected prose, and informants are therefore correspondingly able to direct even more attention to their speech, rather than to what they are reading. 'Word-list style' is therefore the most formal of all.

As suggested in the previous chapter, these four styles are thought to provide, in the tape-recorded interview, analogues of how speakers behave linguistically in particular real-life social situations ranged at various points on the continuum from formal to informal. The nature of this kind of stylistic variation in pronunciation is revealed in the full class and style array for (ng) from the Norwich interviews (WLS = word-list style; RPS = reading-passage styles; FS = formal speech; and CS = casual speech):

	(ng)			
	WLS	*RPS*	*FS*	*CS*
MMC	0	0	3	28
LMC	0	10	15	42
UWC	5	15	74	87
MWC	23	44	88	95
LWC	29	66	98	100

It can be seen very clearly that the methodology does indeed produce stylistic differences of a quantitative nature in pronunciation, and that formal speech may be quite far removed from casual or everyday speech. It can also be noted that there is perfect consistency in this array. Scores increase regularly across the rows and down the columns and, although the different social class groups operate at very different levels of (ng) usage, they all agree in shifting in the same direction, as stylistic context alters. We shall discuss the link between class and style variation further in Chapter 6.

5.3 Sex differentiation

Another social feature with which linguistic differences have been found to correlate very closely is the sex of the speaker. We can again illustrate this form of correlation with figures for Norwich (ng). If we break down the (ng) formal speech scores given initially in 5.1 by the sex of the speaker, we get the following picture for average male and female scores:

	Total	Male	Female
		(ng)	
MMC	3	4	0
LMC	15	27	3
UWC	74	81	68
MWC	88	91	81
LWC	98	100	97

Again we see that a very consistent pattern emerges. In each social class group, male speakers have higher scores (more low-status /n/ variants) than female speakers.

The same sort of picture has been obtained in very many other studies, for very many variables: other things being equal, women tend on average to use more higher-status variants than men do. Indeed, this is perhaps the most strikingly consistent finding of all to emerge from sociolinguistic dialect studies in the industrialised western world. We give three further examples here.

(1) The Glasgow variable (i) deals with the pronunciation of the vowel /ɪ/ in *hit*, *fill*, *pin*, and has five variants, ranging from RP [ɪ] to a typically Scottish central vowel:

(i)-1 [ɪ]
(i)-2 [ɛ⁺]
(i)-3 [ɛ]
(i)-4 [ə⁺]
(i)-5 [ʌ⁺]

The most open and central pronunciations, being the most extreme (non-RP) Glaswegian pronunciations, we would expect to be most typical of working-class speech. Scores, ranged on a scale from 0 to 400, show that this is indeed the case, but that there is also a strong correlation with sex:

(i)

	Total	Male	Female
MMC	102	124	80
LMC	147	179	115
UWC	184	187	180
LWC	194	200	188

(2) One of the variables studied in a survey of the French spoken in Montreal was (l). This deals with the presence or absence of the consonant /l/ in the pronunciation of the pronouns *il* 'he, it', *elle* 'she, it', *ils* 'they', *la* 'her, it', *les* 'them', and the definite articles *la* (feminine singular) and *les* (plural). This variable, obviously, has two variants, (l)-1 = [l], and (l)-2 = zero. The [l] variant, as *il* [il], is socially more prestigious and is regarded as more 'correct' than the zero variant, as *il* [i]. This difference in social status stems from the relationship between this variable and social-class membership. The figures below show that the zero variant is most typical of working-class speakers:

	MC	WC
il (impersonal)	90	100
ils	75	100
il (personal)	72	100
elle	30	82
les (pronoun)	19	61
la (article)	11	44
la (pronoun)	13	37
les (article)	9	33

Analysis of scores by sex of speaker shows further that men are clearly more likely than women to use the lower-prestige variant:

	Female	Male
il (impersonal)	97	99
ils	90	94
il (personal)	84	94
elle	59	67
les (pronoun)	41	53
la (article)	25	34
la (pronoun)	23	31
les (article)	15	25

(3) Sex differentiation in language has been shown to occur even in the speech of children. In an investigation of the pronunciation of postvocalic /r/ in Edinburgh English, for example, it was shown that there was a pattern of sex differentiation even in the

speech of six-year-olds. Setting up postvocalic /r/ as the linguistic variable (r), it was noted that it has three variants in Edinburgh: [ɾ] (a tap); [ɹ] (a frictionless continuant); and zero. If we examine the first two of these, we can see that children from all three age groups studied are consistent, in that the boys favour [ɾ] and the girls [ɹ]:

	% variant			
Age	*Male*		*Female*	
	[ɾ]	[ɹ]	[ɾ]	[ɹ]
10	57	15	45	54
8	48	37	40	54
6	59	16	33	50

The variant [ɹ] is associated especially with middle-class speech in Scotland, and it is of course significant that the girls favour this particular form.

This pattern of sex differentiation, of which we have given only four examples, is so well documented that it requires further discussion and explanation. Some will be found in Chapter 6.

5.4 Other aspects of social differentiation in language

It seems that many forms of societal differentiation are potentially relatable to linguistic differentiation, and that the geographical differentiation initially studied by dialectologists is only one form of this.

5.4.1 *Language and ethnic group*

In many communities, different ethnic groups speak different languages. What is more interesting for our purposes, however, are cases where different ethnic groups speak the same language but differ quantitatively or qualitatively in their use of particular variables.

Since the advent of quantitative sociolinguistic studies, many examples of this phenomenon have been noted. A well-known and now much studied case is that of differences that can be found between the English of black and white speakers in the USA. One feature typical of Black varieties of American English is the absence of the copula *be* in certain grammatical contexts as in sentences like:

> She nice.
> We going.

In a study carried out in the Mississippi Delta area, it has been shown that, in that area, copula deletion actually occurs in both black and white speech. But if other factors such as social class are held constant, then it has been observed that these deleted forms, together with contracted and full forms of the copula, occur according to different patterns in black and white speech. The linguistic forms involved are:

	Full	*Contracted*	*Deleted*
is	She is nice.	She's nice.	She nice.
are	We are going.	We're going.	We going.

The following figures show that all three forms occur in the speech of both ethnic groups, but at different levels of frequency:

	is		*are*	
	Black	*White*	*Black*	*White*
Full	54	38	17	34
Contracted	18	60	6	45
Deleted	28	2	77	21
	100	100	100	100

As with our examples of social class and sex differentiation, these ethnic group differences are relative and not absolute. But it is obvious that black speakers, on average, show a much stronger tendency to deletion than white speakers, who, on the other hand, have much more contraction.

5.4.2   *Social networks*

Ethnic group differences in language can be considered to be a particular example of the role of social networks in affecting linguistic behaviour. It appears that people are influenced linguistically, as might be expected, much more by close friends, family members, work-mates, and members of other social networks to which they belong than by anybody else. Moreover, people who are well integrated into a particular social group may have linguistic characteristics rather different from those who are more peripheral in the group, because the influence of the group will be less strong and less consistent on the peripheral members.

In a study of the 'Jets', a teenage gang living in Harlem, New York City, Labov ascertained that there were two core groups of youths ('100s core' and '200s core', depending on which block they lived on) who were really central to the gang. There were also two secondary groups, who had lower status in the gang, and less strong links to it; peripheral members, whose social ties to the gang were weak; and 'lames', who were not really members of the gang at all, although they were acquainted with it. Labov's work with the gang involved long-term participation with the groups (see 4.4), and produced extended tape-recordings of the speech of the youths. One of the linguistic features studied in the speech of the youths was copula deletion (see 5.4.1), and figures for this phenomenon based on analyses of these recordings show that degree of adhesion to the gang is clearly reflected in linguistic behaviour:

% copula deletion

100s core	70
200s core	63
100s secondary	61
200s secondary	56
Peripheral	33
Lames	36

All the youths are of the same sex and approximately the same age and social class. Clearly the differences in their usage of copula deletion are due to their different positions in the social network.

A similar finding comes from work on the English spoken by Puerto Ricans in New York City, and a comparison of their English with that spoken by blacks in the same area. During analysis of their speech, the Puerto Rican (PR) speakers were divided into two groups depending on whether or not they had extensive social contacts with black speakers. It is clear, once again, that these contacts have linguistic consequences. For instance, one of the variables studied from the tape-recordings made was the realisation of the vowel /ai/ as in *try*, which is variably monophthongal [aː] rather than diphthongal [ai] in certain Black English and other varieties. A count of monophthongal variants of this variable shows the following percentages in the particular area of New York City investigated:

% monophthongs

Black speakers	77
PR speakers with black contacts	70
Other PR speakers	40

Those Puerto Ricans who associate frequently with blacks are also linguistically quite heavily influenced by them.

A similar kind of finding was obtained in a study of the English spoken by three teenage groups in Reading, England. Here an INDEX OF VERNACULAR CULTURE was devised to measure how fully individuals participated in the culture of the street rather than mainstream, more conventional culture. This index was based on the adolescents' status in the peer group (as with the Jets in Harlem); their 'toughness', as indicated by their fighting, stealing and other criminal activities; and their job ambitions – whether they wanted a 'tough' job (e.g. slaughterer) or not. One of the features studied, by means of long-term participant observation, was the usage of nonstandard present-tense -*s*, which is a common grammatical phenomenon in West of England dialects: *I wants, they goes, you knows.* Counting the number of nonstandard -*s* forms which were and were not used, percentage scores were calculated for four sets of boys, the sets having been established on the basis of how high their vernacular culture index was. The scores were:

Sets	%-s
A (very high index)	77.4
B (high index)	54.0
C (moderate index)	36.6
D (low index)	21.2

Obviously, the extent to which the boys identify themselves with the street culture has an effect on the extent to which they use nonstandard grammatical forms.

Perhaps the most interesting study involving language and social networks, however, is an investigation of the English spoken in Belfast. Partly because of the difficulties of carrying out research during the disturbances in Belfast, random sampling procedures were not applied in this study. Rather, three separate working-class inner-city communities were investigated by making contact with a core-member (who was, crucially, *without* institutional status) in each community, and then following up with further contacts made through him or her. The three areas were: The Hammer, a Protestant area in West Belfast; the Clonard, a Catholic area in West Belfast; and Ballymacarrett, a Protestant East Belfast area. The three areas are socially different in a number of important ways. The Hammer has lost its traditional industry, has much unemployment, and is currently undergoing redevelopment. As a consequence, its social networks appear to be less dense, and indeed to be somewhat disintegrated. The Clonard community is similar in that it has lost its industry and has high unemployment, but here the younger women do form a relatively homogeneous network in that many of them share a common employment. Ballymacarrett, on the other hand, still has its traditional local industry, and its network ties are fully maintained. (For further information on Ballymacarrett, see 10.2.2.)

The linguistic consequences of these differences in the nature of the networks in the communities can be illustrated in the following way. One of the variables studied in Belfast was the vowel /æ/ of *bag, hat, man*. Middle-class Belfast speech has this as approximately [a]. In working-class speech, on the other hand, this vowel is currently being backed, raised and rounded in most environments giving, in its most advanced form, pronunciations such as *fast* [fɔ·əst], *man* [mɔ·ən]. (This does not occur before velar consonants, where there are instead traces of an earlier tendency to raising: *bag* [bag] ~ [bɛg].) Fig. 5-1 shows the degree of backing of /æ/ in nonvelar environments in the three communities, by sex, age and style. High scores indicate strong tendencies to backing of /æ/.

At first sight, Fig. 5-1 might appear to convey a somewhat chaotic picture. It is noticeable, however, that in the socially stable Ballymacarrett area there is clear and regular sex and style differentiation. In the two less stable areas there is much less

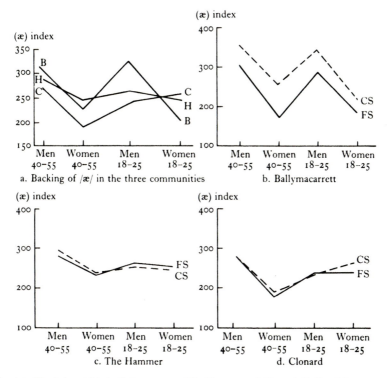

Fig. 5-1. The (æ) variable in Ballymacarrett, The Hammer and Clonard, Belfast (after Milroy 1980). FS = formal speech; CS = Casual speech

style variation, and it is often irregular. And sex variation is less significant, particularly in The Hammer. We can note especially, however, that for younger people in the Clonard, sex differentiation is the 'wrong' way round. Notice, too, that the younger Clonard women score higher than the Ballymacarrett women, although for the men the reverse is true. We can suggest, then, that this linguistic change is at its most advanced in the stable Ballymacarrett area, with the socially less cohesive areas following behind – with the important exception of the young Clonard women who, again as a result of their dense social network relationships, are also at a relatively advanced stage. The degree of backing of this vowel reflects, to a certain extent, the degree of social cohesion.

5.4.3 *Individual characteristics*

So far we have been examining the linguistic behaviour of social groups, although we have also distinguished between members of broader social-class groups in terms of their degree of adherence to particular social networks. It is clear that

individuals also differ in many other ways, and that these differences can often lead
to differences in linguistic behaviour of people who might objectively appear to fall
into the same social category.

One such feature that has been investigated is SOCIAL AMBITION. In a study of the
English spoken in Articlave, a village near Coleraine in Northern Ireland, the speech
of ten individuals was investigated. Although their educational and occupational background was noted, all the informants were also rated by all the others in terms of
how keen they were thought to be 'to get on in the world'. This was found in many
cases to correlate more closely with their usage of certain linguistic variables than other
more objective indices such as occupation and income. For example, average scores
for the use of (ng) (calculated as for Norwich – see 5.1) correlated with four groups
of speakers established on the basis of their degree of social ambition as follows:

	Group	*(ng) index*	
1.	Not ambitious	89	(4 informants)
2.	Quite ambitious	55	(2 informants)
3.	Ambitious	42	(1 informant)
4.	Very ambitious	5	(3 informants)

Because of the small number of informants in each group, these results can be only
suggestive, but they do compare very interestingly with less regular scores for groups
based on education:

	Group	*(ng) index*	
1.	Primary school	75	(4 informants)
2.	Secondary school	5	(2 informants)
3.	Grammar school	59	(3 informants)
4.	University	35	(1 informant)

These results show that our understanding of the social correlates of linguistic variation can depend upon very subtle social factors, like individual ambition, as well as
upon the more obvious factors of social differentiation, like age, sex, social class and
ethnic background.

Further information

The results from the Bradford survey are from Petyt 1985. A useful survey and bibliography
on early work on language, sex and gender is Thorne and Henley 1975. See also Trudgill
1983 and Coates 1986. For more recent discussions, see Holmes 1992: chapters 7 and 12, and
Chambers 1995: chapter 3. The Montreal data in this chapter are from Sankoff and Cedergren
1971. The Edinburgh data can be consulted further in Romaine 1988. A classic source on

American Black English is Labov 1972a. The Mississippi Delta data in this chapter are from Wolfram 1971. Labov's study of the Jets is published in Labov 1972a. The work on Puerto Rican English in New York City is from Wolfram 1974. More recent work includes Butters 1989; Baugh 1983; Montgomery and Bailey 1986; and Bailey et al. 1991. The work on Reading English is from Cheshire 1982; the data cited above come from Cheshire 1978, which appears in Trudgill 1978; this collection also includes Douglas-Cowie's article on, 'Linguistic code-switching in a Northern Irish village: social interaction and social ambition'. The Belfast study is reported in a number of places, but most accessibly in Milroy 1984, which is also an important contribution to sociolinguistic methodology.

6
Sociolinguistic structure and linguistic innovation

Dialectologists long ago established that language varies from place to place. Sociolinguists have emphasised that language can also vary from person to person in the same place. For both dialectologists and sociolinguists, it is not the mere fact of linguistic variation that is important. What is important is that that variability correlates with other factors, such that certain variants are more closely associated with one village than another, or with labourers more than managers, or with people speaking to close friends rather than to strangers, or with some other factor.

In Chapter 5 we saw that social groups tend to alter their speech in more formal styles (5.2). Moreover we noticed that all groups tend to alter it in the same direction. In the main example, the index for the (ng) variable in Norwich increased for all working-class and middle-class groups as the formality of the speech situation increased from casual style to word-list style. The fact that style shifts are always in the same direction, no matter which social group is involved, proves that there is a relationship between the two types of variation. It should be possible, then, to explain one in terms of the other. In this chapter, we will consider some of these correlations and their social significance.

6.1 Indicators and markers

One plausible explanation for linguistic variability focuses on the fact that whenever there is class differentiation in a linguistic variable, it is the variant used by the higher classes that is ascribed more status or prestige than the other variants. As a result, in situations in which attention is directed towards speech, speakers of all classes will tend to increase their use of the higher-status variants. Stylistic variation, by this explanation, is a direct result of social-class variation. Differences in social class give rise to the assigning of value judgements to particular linguistic variants, and formal situations lead to a greater use of the highly valued pronunciations.

This explanation would lead us to expect all linguistic variables to be associated with class and style profiles of the type illustrated in Fig. 6-1, which is a graphic representation of the Norwich (ng) scores tabulated in 5.2. Fig. 6-1 is an example of what is known as SHARP STRATIFICATION. It shows very clearly, by the sharp break on the

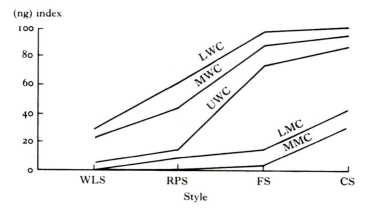

Fig. 6-1. Norwich (ng) by class and style (after Trudgill 1974a)

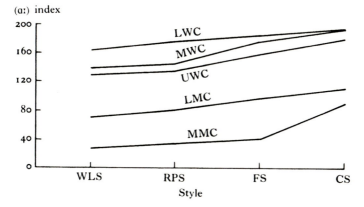

Fig. 6-2. Norwich (aː) by class and style (after Trudgill 1974a)

graph between the LMC and the UWC, the linguistic correlation with the principal social groups in Norwich. (A graph with less sharp discontinuities between classes shows what is called a *gradient* of FINE STRATIFICATION.)

However, when we look at other variables we discover that in fact not all variables which are subject to class differentiation also exhibit stylistic variation. For example, the Norwich variable (aː), introduced earlier in 5.1, undergoes little or no stylistic variation, as Fig. 6-2 shows. The variable is correlated with social class variation, as shown by the space separating the lines for each social class, but there is very little stylistic variation, especially for the working class. That is, the lines are relatively level instead of rising in the less formal styles. This point is emphasised by comparing Fig. 6-2 with Fig. 6-1.

Variables of the type illustrated by (ng), which are subject to stylistic variation as well as class, sex and/or age variation are referred to as MARKERS. Variables of the second type, illustrated by (aː), which are not involved in systematic stylistic variation, are called INDICATORS.

The question of why some variables are markers and others are indicators now arises. It seems clear that, if a variable is merely an indicator in a particular speech community, then it plays a less consequential role in the marking of class differences in that community than does a variable which is a marker. In other words, speakers appear to be less aware of the variable that is an indicator than they are of the variable that is a marker. In order to consider why they are more sensitive to the social implications of some variables than of others, we must look at such factors as pronunciation and orthography, linguistic change and phonological contrast.

6.1.1 *Overt stigmatisation*

One obvious indication that a variable is a marker rather than an indicator is that it is the subject of unfavourable comment in the community. Variables which are often mentioned in the Norwich community include (h), (t) and (ng), all of which are markers. Why are these variables subject to overt criticism while others are not? One of the main reasons seems to lie in the divergence between pronunciation and orthography. The low prestige variants of the three Norwich variables – zero, [ʔ] and [n] – can all be, and often are, characterised as 'dropping your *h*s, *t*s and *g*s'. These characterisations are commonly given by schoolteachers, but they are also given by other members of the community. (The 'dropping your *t*s' label is perhaps a bit more puzzling than the other labels, because a /t/ is in fact still present, even though it is realised as [ʔ]. Many British speakers, when they hear (t)-3, will nevertheless maintain that there is 'no *t*' there. This is apparently due to a tacit awareness of the large phonetic difference between the [t] and [ʔ] allophones.)

6.1.2 *Linguistic change*

This explanation alone, however, cannot be sufficient to account for all variables which become markers. A comparison with other markers which do not fit into this category suggests that a second factor in a variable becoming a marker in a community is that the variable is involved in an ongoing linguistic change. By contrast, variables which are indicators, like (aː), appear to be relatively stable. Speakers, then, seem to be more aware of the social significance of forms that are participating in a linguistic change. This is perhaps not surprising when one considers that variables involved in a change are manifested by the occurrence of different variants from people of different ages within the same social group. The variation within neighbourhoods and within families inevitably draws attention to the variable.

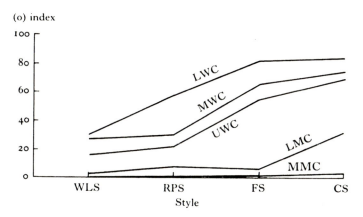

Fig. 6-3. Norwich (o) by class and style (after Trudgill 1974a)

An example of a marker which fits this category is Norwich (o), for which the vowel quality in words like *top, hot, box* and so on has two variants: (o)-1 = [ɒ], which is the low back rounded vowel of RP; and (o)-2 = [ɑ], which is the typical local unrounded vowel, similar to the standard North American realisations of this vowel. Fig. 6-3 shows that (o) is a marker, with quite strong stylistic variation. It also reveals that there is class differentiation with this variable, and the large gap between the LMC and the UWC provides another example of sharp stratification. Unrounded vowels in *top, hot* and *box* are clearly a working-class feature in Norwich.

The variable (o) is not the subject of any overt comment in Norwich, so its status as a marker cannot be explained in this way. The explanation apparently lies, instead, in the fact that (o) is involved in a current linguistic change, with the higher status RP variants very much on the increase (see 6.3.2 for a fuller discussion of variable (o)).

6.1.3 *Phonological contrast*

Studies of urban dialects show, however, that there are still other markers which are neither the subject of overt comment nor the focus of an ongoing linguistic change. One of these is the Norwich variable (yu), which involves the vowel sound in words like *tune, due, view, music* and *cue*. Historically, words like *rude* and *rule* were once pronounced [rjuːd] and [rjuːl] in most, or perhaps all, English dialects. In modern English, however, [j] no longer occurs after [r] and the pronunciation is now [ruːd] and [ruːl]. Similarly, in words like *lute* and *Luke*, the [j] following [l] has been lost in most modern dialects, and in words like *super* and *suit* it has been lost, or is rapidly being lost, after [s] as well. In many North American accents, this process has been extended even further, to include the [j] after [t], [d] and [n], as in *tune, due* and *news*. In an area of eastern England which includes Norwich (Map 6-1), the loss of [j] before [uː] has been extended still further, to include environments following any

73

Map 6-1. /j/-dropping in eastern England

consonant. Besides the environments above, in this region pronunciations such as [puː] 'pew', [muːzɪk] 'music' and [kuː] 'cue' are not uncommon. The Norwich variable (yu) therefore has two variants: (yu)-1 = [juː], as in pronunciations of *view* in RP and most other standard varieties of English; and (yu)-2 = [uː], as in [vuː] 'view'.

As might be expected from the fact that it is also the RP pronunciation, the [juː] variant is most frequent in middle-class speech in Norwich. There is clear class stratification of this variable, and it is also involved in stylistic variation, indicating that it is a marker. However, it is not the subject of any overt comment and it does not appear to be involved in a linguistic change. We therefore require an additional explanation to account for its status as a marker. One possibility arises from the fact that, unlike (aː), (yu) has variants which are phonological rather than merely phonetic. Minimal pairs such as the following depend for their differentiation upon the presence of [j]; in the region shown on Map 6-1, they are often homophonous:

cute – coot

beauty – booty

Hugh – who

feud – food

The actual number of minimal pairs may not be very large, and genuine confusion in context is quite unlikely, but it seems reasonable that by virtue of the involvement of (yu) in a phonological contrast, it may draw more attention than variables which are simply phonetic. Consequently, variables of this type will tend to show the characteristics of markers.

6.1.4 *Stereotypes*

Awareness by speakers of linguistic variables is obviously a feature which admits of degrees of more or less. It is also a feature which can change in the course of time. As a result, linguistic variables can move from the category of indicator to the category of marker, and vice versa. Variables may, for instance, start as indicators if they occur as the result of a linguistic change that only some social groups participate in. The development of the glottal stop allophone of /t/ in British English is an example of this development. The allophone appears to have begun amongst lower-class groups, and thus to have led to differentiation between higher- and lower-class speakers. Initially, this change must have been relatively unobserved. Variable (t) was thus an indicator, and its diffusion throughout the community would have been of the type referred to as CHANGE FROM BELOW, meaning not a change originating with a lower social class – although this is often the case – but a change from below the level of conscious awareness. Subsequently, as usage of the new variant increases and if factors such as those we have just outlined come into play, awareness of class differentiation will increase and the indicator will become a marker. This has, of course, actually happened in the case of (t).

There is also a third possible stage. At this stage, awareness of particular variants becomes even higher, and speakers become especially conscious of them. Their social and regional connotations become a part of common knowledge, and speakers are able to report on them without difficulty (although not necessarily accurately). Currently, (t) and (h), particularly the latter, are approaching this stage in Britain. Clearer examples, though, might be the well-known New York City pronunciation of words such as *bird* as 'boid' (actually [bɔɪd]), or the aristocratic English pronunciation *off* /ɔːf/ rather than /ɒf/. Forms of this type can be referred to as STEREOTYPES.

If very stigmatised forms become stereotyped in this way, it may only be a matter of time before they disappear altogether, as the New York [ɔɪ] pronunciation appears to be doing (see 10.2.3 for further discussion of this variable). When changes of this kind take place, reversing as they often do the original direction of a linguistic change, they can be called CHANGES FROM ABOVE, i.e. from above the level of conscious awareness.

6.2 The study of linguistic change

If we wish to study linguistic changes in progress, whether they be changes from above or below, then the most satisfactory method would obviously be to investigate a particular community and then return, say, twenty years later and carry out a further investigation. This we could call the study of linguistic change in REAL TIME. It is obviously not very convenient, however, to have to wait twenty years if we want to find out what is going on right now. An alternative, and a more immediate method is instead to investigate linguistic change in APPARENT TIME. This simply means that, in investigating a particular community, we compare the speech of older people with that of younger people, and assume that any differences are the result of linguistic change. (It is also advisable, if possible, to check any such findings against earlier dialect records, if any, to ensure that the differences are not actually age-grading differences of a type that are repeated in every generation – for fuller discussion, see 10.1.)

Many studies have made use of this technique, and it is possible to use it even in studies which use the methods of traditional dialectology. This can be illustrated from a study of the dialect of the Norwegian town of Tønsberg which was carried out using one-word responses to a questionnaire, but which was not confined simply to elderly speakers. One of the features investigated in this study was final unstressed vowels of infinitives (and a number of other words), which in middle-class Oslo speech and standard Norwegian Bokmål have -/ə/, but in other – for the most part lower-status varieties – have -/æ/ or -/ɑ/. Responses to the Tønsberg questionnaire, tabulated word by word and informant by informant, as in Table 6-1, show that a change is taking place. This evidence suggests that /æ/ is giving way to /ɑ/, which is in turn giving way to /ə/ – but of course it is only suggestive.

Information from studies of linguistic change in apparent time becomes more persuasive, of course, if larger numbers of informants are used. In a study of the English of the southern Appalachians, in the USA, for example, a total of fifty-two informants were recorded, and were divided into five age groups. Using this method, a number of very interesting findings about changing usage of linguistic forms were obtained. One linguistic form that seems to be disappearing from Appalachian English, for instance, is the use of perfective *done*, a feature that does not occur in standard English. Examples of this usage are:

Table 6-1. *Endings of selected infinitives in Tønsberg Norwegian*

	Male speakers				Female speakers		
Standard form:	*gjøre* 'do'	*stjele* 'steal'	*drepe* 'kill'		*dette* 'fall'	*drepe* 'kill'	*love* 'promise'
	Age				Age		
	78	æ	æ	æ	76	æ	æ	æ
	74	æ	æ	æ	49	æ	æ	æ
	52	æ	æ	æ	46	æ	ə	ə
	52	æ	æ	æ	46	ɑ	ə	ə
	46	æ	æ	æ	43	ɑ	ə	ə
	27	ɑ	ɑ	ɑ	26	ə	ə	ə
	20	ɑ	ə	ə	19	ə	ə	ə
	17	ɑ	ə	ə	76	ə	ə	ə
	78	ɑ	ə	ə	17	ə	ə	ə
	17	ɑ	ə	ə	17	ə	ə	ə
	16	ɑ	ə	ə	16	ə	ə	ə

We thought he was done gone.

The doctor done give him up.

I done forgot when it opened.

In this sort of construction, *done* is an aspect marker which is essentially completive in function, emphasising the completed nature of the event in question. In the tape-recordings made during this survey, only 65 uses of this form were recorded in all – a fact that emphasises the difficulty of eliciting syntactic features in empirical studies. It is of interest, however, that these forms were distributed across the age groups as follows:

Age group	*Number* *of speakers*	*Occurrences* *of 'done'*
8–11	10	6
12–14	10	7
15–18	10	5
20–40	9	14
40 +	13	33

In this case it was of course not possible to set up *done* as any kind of linguistic variable, since it is not a form which is involved in alternation with other forms that could be considered to be equivalent ways of doing or saying the same thing (see 4.6).

In sociolinguistic studies where linguistic variables are employed (as they are also in the Appalachian study for other linguistic forms), the study of change in apparent

Table 6-2. *Age group differentiation in Eskilstuna*

Age group	% -t	% dom
16–30	92	100
31–45	85	100
46–60	81	99
61–75	80	90
76 +	76	83

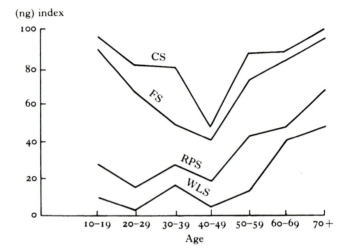

Fig. 6-4. Norwich (ng) by age and style

time becomes even more revealing. In a study of the Swedish spoken in the town of Eskilstuna, for instance, two of the variables studied were:

1. The past-participle form of some verb classes, which has two variants, one in -*t* and one in -*i*: *köpt* ~ *köpi* 'bought'.
2. The form of the third-person plural pronoun, which has two variants: *dom* and *di*.

The variants of these variables are distributed across age groups as in Table 6-2. The figures suggest that *köpi* will very soon have been entirely replaced by *köpt*, which is actually the standard Swedish form. Similarly, *dom* will very soon have ousted the older *di* form.

6.2.1 *Patterns of age differentiation*

If we correlate linguistic variables not only with age group but also with social class or style, we obtain the type of graphic pattern shown in Fig. 6-4. This is

a representation of style and age variation for the Norwich variable (ng). The curvi-
linear pattern shown in Fig. 6-4 is typical, it seems, of linguistic variables that are not
involved in linguistic change, and it requires some explanation. Why exactly is it that
the highest scores are found for the youngest and oldest speakers, while it is middle-
aged speakers who have the lowest scores? We can probably account for this by supposing that for younger speakers the most important social pressures come from the
peer group, and that linguistically they are more strongly influenced by their friends
than by anybody else. Influence from the standard language is relatively weak. Then,
as speakers get older and begin working, they move into wider and less cohesive social
networks (see 5.4.2), and are more influenced by mainstream societal values and,
perhaps, by the need to impress, succeed and make social and economic progress.
They are also, consequently, more influenced linguistically by the standard language.
For older, retired people, on the other hand, social pressures are again less, success
has already been achieved (or not, as the case may be), and social networks may again
be narrower. (We also have to acknowledge, in looking at this pattern, that in modern
Britain education is not a variable that is independent of age, in that most younger
people have, on average, more education than most older people.)

We cannot assume that the pattern of covariation with age found in Norwich will
necessarily be found everywhere else, especially if social conditions are radically different. The increase of standard forms that goes with adulthood has, however, been
documented in a number of investigations. A study of the English of black speakers
carried out in Washington, DC, for example, shows exactly this. Three of the variables studied were:

1. /d/-deletion: the absence of /d/ word-finally in words such as *coloured*
    ['kʰəlɪ], *applied* [ə'pʰla], *discovered* [ts'kəvɪ].

2. Cluster-simplification: this involves the pronunciation of words such as
    filled, sinned, licked, missed as /fɪl/, /sɪn/, /lɪk/, /mɪs/ rather than /fɪld/,
    /sɪnd/, /lɪkt/, /mɪst/.

3. -*s* absence: the absence of third-person singular present-tense -*s* as in *he*
    go, she want, it work.

When the 47 informants were divided into three age groups, children, adolescents and
adults, the covariation of the above variables with age was as in Table 6-3. Here the
same process of decreasing use of low prestige forms with the achievement of adult
status is clear.

This, then, is the normal pattern of age differentiation. If a linguistic change is taking place, however, a different pattern is found. One such is illustrated in Fig. 6-5.
This shows age-group differentiation of the Norwich variable (e) by style. The variable (e) deals with the vowel /ɛ/ where it occurs before /l/, as in *tell, well, bell*. The
variable has three variants:

Table 6-3. *Age differentiation in Washington, DC*

%	Children	Adolescents	Adults
/d/-deletion	33	26	21
Cluster simplification	53	51	46
-*s* absence	77	58	48

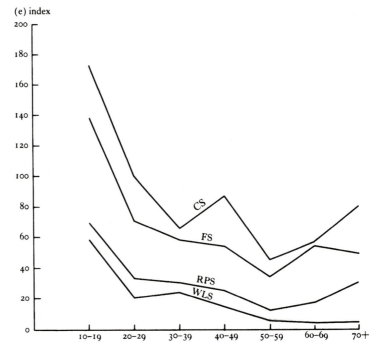

Fig. 6-5. Norwich (e) by age and style

(e)-1 = [ɛ]
(e)-2 = [ɜ]
(e)-3 = [ʌ]

The variant (e)-1 is the /ɛ/ vowel as in RP, while (e)-3 is a vowel very much retracted and lowered from that point, the most extreme Norwich pronunciation of *hell* being identical with *hull*. Fig. 6-5 shows that, while the right-hand side of the graph follows the normal kind of pattern, the left-hand side certainly does not: usage of (e)-3 is very much on the increase, with speakers under thirty showing a very high level of centralised vowels. Very clearly, a linguistic change is currently taking place.

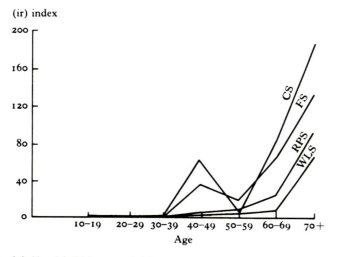

Fig. 6-6. Norwich (ir) by age and style

Conversely, if particular linguistic forms are dying out, we would expect graphs showing their covariation with age to differ from the normal in the opposite way, with the
left-hand side of the curve relatively flattened out. This is demonstrated in Fig. 6-6
which shows scores for the Norwich variable (ir), which covers the vowel of *bird,
further, fern,* whose pronunciation ranges from an RP-like [ɜː] to local pronunciations
such as [bɐːd], [baːd], [baˤd], [bɐd] 'bird'. These local forms are now dying out, and
Fig. 6-6 suggests that it will not be too long before this particular relic form has disappeared altogether.

6.3 Mechanisms of linguistic change

The Norwich variable (e), as we have just seen, is undergoing change,
and pronunciations such as *hell* [hʌɫ] are very much on the increase. It is therefore
interesting also to examine the social-class differentiation of this variable. The CS scores
for (e) by social class are:

MMC	2
LMC	42
UWC	127
MWC	87
LWC	77

For the three working-class groups, the class differentiation is the 'wrong' way round.

This is very suggestive of how linguistic changes spread through a community. We
shall deal with this at greater length in Chapter 10, but we can suppose here that this
particular innovation is being introduced into Norwich English especially by the upper
sections of the working class (see 10.2.1).

We can also suppose that ongoing linguistic changes may often be reflected in unusual patterns of social-class differentiation. This is at least partly confirmed by the Norwich variable (ī), the vowel of *ride, night, by*, which has four variants: 1 = [aɪ]; 2 = [ɐɪ]]; 3 = [ɐi]; 4 = [ɔi]. Class differentiation for this variable is:

	FS	CS
MMC	64	77
LMC	120	159
UWC	160	180
MWC	194	205
LWC	183	189

This suggests that in this case it is the MWC who are spearheading the introduction of the (ī)-4 variant into the speech community. This is confirmed by the following figures for the percentage of informants in each social class who used at least one instance of (ī)-4 = [ɔi]:

	%
MMC	17
LMC	25
UWC	37
MWC	95
LWC	62

6.3.1 *Stylistic variation*

It emerges that unusual patterns of style differentiation can also be indicative of a linguistic change in progress. A very well known example of this is provided by Labov's original New York City study of the variable (r). Fig. 6-7 shows an unusual cross-over pattern for this variable, with the LMC using higher percentages of postvocalic /r/ than even UMC speakers in the formal styles. Labov refers to the sociolinguistic structure displayed by this sociolinguistic marker as HYPERCORRECTION. (This systematic hypercorrection – sometimes called Labov-hypercorrection – must be distinguished from individual hypercorrection of the type discussed in 3.4.) We can explain this pattern by supposing that in those situations where LMC speakers are devoting considerable amounts of attention to their speech they, as it were, overdo things, and surpass even higher-class speakers. This large amount of stylistic variation can be ascribed to the LINGUISTIC INSECURITY of the LMC, who are not so socially secure as the UMC, and who are not sufficiently distant from the working class to be confident of not being identified with them. In situations where they are monitoring their speech very closely, they therefore make strong attempts to signal their social status by using linguistic prestige features such as postvocalic /r/.

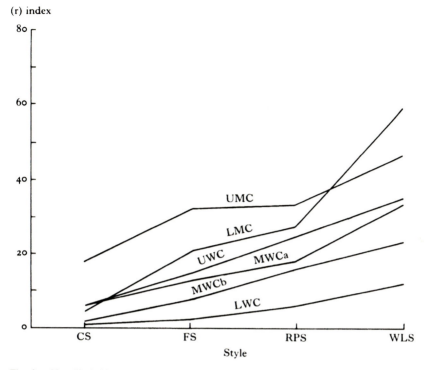

Fig. 6-7. New York City (r) by class and style (after Labov 1966)

We can also suppose that it may often be the case that it is the second-highest-status group who are the most influential in introducing prestige features into a community. In this case, the LMC are clearly in the vanguard of a change that is taking place in the usage of /r/ in New York City, a form which has only been a significant feature of New York English since World War II. This will happen, however, only where the prestige feature is geographically external to the community. We would not therefore expect to find this process occurring in England, where RP speakers are found in all areas. In England, only forms which occur in RP have high prestige, and forms that were most typical of LMC speech would not, by definition almost, be very prestigious.

6.3.2 *The role of sex*

Unusual patterns of sex differentiation are also an indication that a linguistic change is in progress. We saw in 5.3 that the normal pattern is for women to use, on average, fewer low-status forms than men. The FS scores for the Norwich variable (o) show an interesting divergence from this pattern:

	Male	Female
MMC	1	0
LMC	11	1
UWC	44	68
MWC	64	71
LWC	80	83

This shows that, for the three working-class groups, sex differentiation is the 'wrong' way round – and this is indeed a sign that a linguistic change is taking place. What is in fact happening is that the more typically local pronunciation of words like *log* as [lɑg] is giving way to the more RP-like [lɒg]. However, this seems to be taking place not so much as a result of the influence of RP but rather as the result of the influence of the working-class accents of areas bordering on the Norwich region – a case of the geographical diffusion of a linguistic innovation. Indeed, what we know of the relationship between sex and language tells us that if a linguistic change is taking place in the direction of the prestige variety it will be spearheaded by middle-class women, while changes away from the prestige norm (such as the increase of (e)-3 or (ī)-4) will have working-class (particularly UWC or MWC) men in the vanguard. In the case of (o), it seems, we have both types of change going on at once: imitation of RP and of neighbouring working-class accents in this case lead in the same direction.

This brings us to further examination of the questions we raised in 5.3. Why does sex differentiation in language occur, and why do men and women play different roles in the spreading of linguistic changes? There is no single or widely accepted explanation for why this should be, but a number of factors have been proposed:

1. In our society, women have fewer opportunities, still, for achievement, and are therefore more likely to signal their social status by how they appear and behave (including linguistically) than by what they do.

2. Women tend, perhaps as a result of fewer occupational opportunities, to participate in less cohesive social networks. They are therefore less susceptible to peer pressure than men, and at the same time are more used to finding themselves in situations that are 'formal' in the sense that they are not particularly well-acquainted with the people they are talking to. Formal speech styles therefore result.

3. In societies where gender roles are sharply differentiated, as they tend to be in ghettoes and enclaves of many kinds, women typically have greater mobility than men. (This may be a natural result of the previous factor.) Their movements are less circumscribed than men's for shopping, work or recreation, and they are more likely than men to act as arbiters with outsiders such as landlords and teachers. As a result, women have more

social contacts beyond the community. In order to fulfil their roles, they must master a wider repertoire of linguistic variants.

4. Women's traditionally greater role in child socialisation leads them to be more sensitive to norms of 'accepted' behaviour.

5. Linguistic sex differentiation is a reflection of a much wider tendency for men to be relatively more favourably regarded than women if they act tough, rough and break the rules. Women, on the other hand, are encouraged to a much greater extent to be correct, discreet, quiet and polite in their behaviour. Pressures on women to use 'correct' linguistic forms are therefore greater than those on men. (This also manifests itself in different attitudes towards swearing by men and women.) Men, on the other hand, appear at some level of awareness to be more favourably disposed than women to low-status speech forms. This may well be because of the connotations of roughness, toughness and 'masculinity' associated with working-class language (and other forms of behaviour).

6.3.3 *Covert prestige*

We find here a conflict between PRESTIGE – status as it is more usually regarded as reflecting mainstream, predominantly middle-class and overt societal values – and COVERT PRESTIGE. Labov first introduced the notion of covert prestige by pointing out that while even speakers who use high proportions of stigmatised linguistic forms such as /t/ = [ʔ] will tell you (and believe) that such forms are 'bad' and 'inferior', we have to suppose that at some level they *want* to use them. They must be favourably disposed to these forms, if only covertly, and to want to talk as they do, or they would not do so. This, then, is prestige in the sense of being favourably regarded by one's peers, and of signalling one's identity as a member of a group.

We have some evidence from the Norwich study on the different effects of covert prestige on men and women. As part of the study, speakers were asked to say which of two pronunciations of particular words they themselves used, for example [bɛtə] or [bɛʔə] 'better'. It was then possible to check with the tape recordings made to see how accurate were their perceptions of their own speech. Not surprisingly, many people claimed to say [bɛtə] when they actually said [bɛʔə]. More surprisingly, there were many informants who did the reverse, and claimed to use a lower-status form than the one they actually did use. There is no suggestion that people were being deceitful here. They reported themselves as using forms they *believed* they used, and they believed they used them because they were, at least subconsciously, favourably disposed towards them. It was therefore of considerable interest to note that the vast majority of those who 'downgraded' their linguistic performance by inaccurately claiming usage of, for example [ʔ], were men. Men, this suggests, are indeed much more influenced than women by the covert prestige of low-status linguistic forms.

Table 6-4. *Stress assignment in Trondheim Norwegian*
% nonstandard forms

Age	Male	Female
18–36	64	59
37–62	63	24
63–82	64	7

This situation, however, is not immutable. Society changes, values change, and, with them, linguistic behaviour changes. There was some evidence, for example, from the Norwich survey that younger women were beginning to be more influenced by covert prestige than older women, and a number of them also 'downgraded' their linguistic behaviour. Some interesting evidence on this point comes from a survey of Norwegian spoken in the town of Trondheim. One of the variables analysed in Trondheim was stress assignment in loanwords such as *avis* /ɑv'iːs/ 'newspaper', *generasjon* /ɡɛnɛrɑʃ'uːn/ *'generation'*. In standard Norwegian varieties, words of this type are stressed on the final syllable. In lower-status Trondheim speech, however, they are stressed on the first syllable: *avis* /'ɑːvis/, a well-known and indeed somewhat stereotyped feature of lower-class speech in many parts of Norway. In Trondheim, first-syllable stress in items of this type is much more common with working-class than with middle-class speakers. Covariation with sex and age is, however, of considerable interest, as Table 6-4 shows.

This result is striking. While men have remained very constant in their use of nonstandard forms, women have increased their nonstandard usage very considerably indeed, to the point where, for younger women, it is now very little different from that of the men. This is best regarded not so much as a linguistic change but as a change in the linguistic behaviour of women which reflects a change in their values and attitudes and which we may expect to see repeated in many other linguistic communities.

Further information

Discussion of INDICATORS, MARKERS, STEREOTYPES, HYPERCORRECTION, SHARP STRATIFICATION and FINE STRATIFICATION can all be found in Labov 1972b. The term 'Labov-hypercorrection' and the distinction between that and individual hypercorrection are made by Wells 1982: volume 3. For further information on *rude, tune, suit*, see Hughes and Trudgill 1996. The Tønsberg data are from Gulbrandsen 1975. The Appalachian study is Wolfram and Christian 1976. The Swedish work is discussed in Nordberg 1972. The Washington, DC, data are taken from Fasold 1972. Correlations of language with sex make a large literature; some general references are listed at the end of the previous chapter. The notion of covert prestige is discussed in Labov 1966: 108, and in Trudgill 1972. The Trondheim data are discussed in articles by Ulseth (n.d) and by Fintoft and Mjaavatn 1980.

SPATIAL VARIATION

7
Boundaries

Traditional dialectology focused attention on regional differences in speech, and out of that came the construct known as ISOGLOSSES, the lines marking the boundaries between two regions which differ with respect to some linguistic feature (for instance, a lexical item, or the pronunciation of a particular word). In this chapter we will take a closer look at some isoglosses in order to determine their function and their usefulness in dialectology.

7.1 Isoglosses

The term 'isogloss' was first used by J. G. A. Bielenstein, a Latvian dialectologist, in 1892. He apparently modelled his new word on the meteorological term *isotherm*, a line drawn between two locations with the same average temperature. Isogloss literally means 'equal language' (Greek *iso+gloss*). Presumably, the word is intended to convey the fact that a line drawn across a region will show two areas on either side which share some aspect of linguistic usage but which disagree with each other.

Dialectologists have used the term in two slightly different ways, with the result that the isogloss has been represented graphically in two different ways. Although it is always possible to transliterate one representation into the other, someone who is not aware of both is likely to be confused upon first encountering the unfamiliar one.

The hypothetical situation shown in Maps 7-1 and 7-2 illustrates the two uses. Assume that, in a survey, the speakers in a certain region are found to differ with respect to some linguistic feature such that some of them (*a–g*, *i* and *k* on the maps) have the feature symbolised △, whereas others (*h*, *j*, *l*, and *m–p*) have ○ instead. The usual way of representing this situation graphically is shown in Map 7-1: a single line is drawn between the locations of any two speakers exhibiting different features. The alternative representation is shown in Map 7-2: here a line is drawn linking the locations of speakers who share the feature △ and a second line is drawn to link those who share the feature ○, when those speakers are contiguous to the other group, that is, when they are at the interface between the two regions. Such double lines are sometimes called HETEROGLOSSES. Clearly, if one is provided with the information given on Map 7-1, it would be a simple task to convert it into Map 7-2, and vice versa.

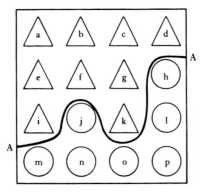

Map 7-1. A single line A separates the region where feature △ is found from the region where its counterpart ○ is found. Line A is an ISOGLOSS

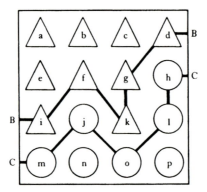

Map 7-2. Two lines separate the regions where △ and ○ are found. The lines link speakers with feature △ (line B) and those with feature ○ (line C). The two lines form a HETEROGLOSS

Nevertheless, the two representations are slightly different in what they express. In particular, heteroglosses are neutral with respect to any claim about the linguistic feature that occurs in the region between the speakers who were actually surveyed. That is, assuming that there is another speaker of the same language located between speakers *f* and *j* (and, of course, that this speaker was not included in the population sampled in the survey), the heteroglosses simply leave this speaker unclassified. The other system, with its single isogloss, cuts arbitrarily through what is in fact unknown territory, and in this respect is less precise. This is apparently the main reason that some dialectologists prefer heteroglosses.

The distinction between isoglosses and heteroglosses does not, however, carry much weight. Trivially, the two are exactly equivalent if there is not in fact any speaker in between *f* and *j* (and the others). To create such a situation, a particular survey would

have to be exhaustive for the region being surveyed, and that kind of survey is seldom
– and in dialectology, perhaps never – done. Much more significant is the fact that
the heterogloss, while it is more precise at the interface, is exactly as imprecise everywhere else. That is, consider the possibility that yet another speaker exists in the region
shown, this time located between *c* and *d*, and assume further that he has the feature
○, unlike his neighbours *c* and *d* but exactly like his neighbour to the south, *h*. (Such
possibilities, as we shall see later when we deal with a real situation, are by no means
unusual, and in fact are highly likely.) In this case, both the isogloss and the heterogloss
make the same arbitrary – and this time, quite wrong – claim, namely, that speakers
like the one between *c* and *d* do not exist. It is no doubt because the two representations of dialect boundaries are virtually equivalent that they have both remained in
use, rather than one supplanting the other. The single-line isogloss shown in Map 7-1
has been much more common.

7.2   Patterns of isoglosses

Certain patterns of isoglosses have recurred time and again in various surveys. Their recurrence is itself an interesting fact about dialects, indicating something
of the nature of the linguistic situation that exists in the region, and allowing certain
conclusions to be drawn.

7.2.1   *Criss-cross*

One such recurrent pattern looks at first glance as if it is really the absence
of pattern, since it shows up as a welter of isoglosses that crisscross one another, almost
chaotically. This was the pattern that led the earliest dialectologists to abandon certain strong tenets about the regularity of language variation, which had brought about
their predictions that isoglosses would behave more systematically. Instead of deline-
ating well-defined dialect areas which were separated from one another in terms of
major sound laws and lexical sets, isoglosses were usually found in an astounding profusion, making a wild variety of combinations in the dialectal elements predominant
from one place to the next.

A classic example is the set of isoglosses widely believed to separate Low German
from High German, which run east and west across Germany and Holland on a line
(roughly) just slightly north of Berlin. Perhaps the best-known features of this split
are the reflexes of Pre-Germanic *p, *t and *k, which remain stops in Low German
but have developed into fricatives and affricates in High German. Hence the contrast between Low German [dorp] 'village' and High German [dorf], and [dat] 'that'
opposed to [das], and [makən] 'make' opposed to [maxən]. For part of their length,
these isoglosses seem to be reasonably well-behaved, running more or less parallel to
one another and occasionally even coinciding, as shown in Map 7-3. While it is true
that they deviate to some extent, crossing one another and cutting into the opposite

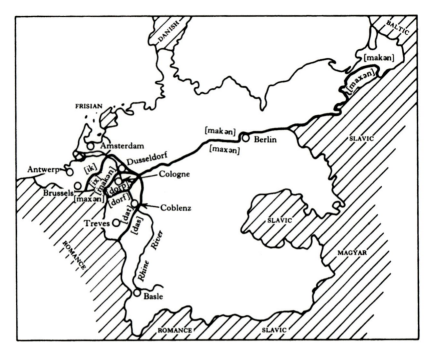

Map 7-3. Features separating Low German and High German form nearly coincident
isoglosses for much of their length, but then they diverge at the Rhine valley
(after Bloomfield 1933). This extreme divergence is known as the RHENISH FAN

territory at various points, they still might be construed as regular (in a loose sense) if
it were not for the notorious RHENISH FAN. The metaphor of the 'fan' aptly describes
what happens to these various isoglosses at the point where they meet the Rhine River.
Suddenly at that point they all seem to go their separate ways, splaying out like the
spokes of a fan. As a result, it is impossible in the Rhenish area to make any useful
generalisations about High and Low German. In one village, speakers say [dorp] like
Low Germans but [maxən] like High Germans, while villages to the south may be
characterised by [maxən] and [dorf] but [dat] (see also 3.1).

The Rhenish fan has become an instructive example for dialectologists because
it presents them with a clear and dramatic case of isoglosses going their separate
ways, without respect, as it were, for the philologist's sound laws (see 2.1). Looking
back at the several isoglosses from the perspective that the Rhenish fan provides, it
becomes obvious that much the same variety of the possible combinations of dialect
features really exists all along their length, throughout Germany and Holland. The essential difference between the area of the fan and the other areas is that the isoglosses
are more widely separated at the fan. Nevertheless, they are more or less separated
everywhere.

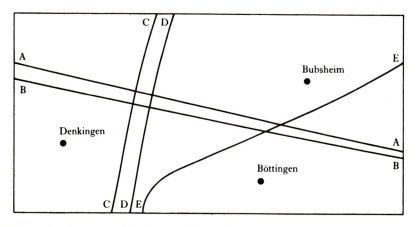

Map 7-4. Isoglosses around the German villages of Bubsheim, Denkingen and Böttingen. Isogloss A has [ɛːnt] 'end' to the north, [aynt] to the south; B has [bawn] 'bean' to the north, [bɔːn] to the south; C has [faːrb] 'colour' to the west, [farb] to the east; D has [aːlt] 'old' to the west, [alt] to the east; and E has (mɛːyə] 'to mow' to the west, [mayə] to the east (after Bloomfield 1933)

The pattern of criss-crossing isoglosses separating even contiguous villages from one another and apparently describing a bewildering variety of dialect feature combinations is now recognised as a typical pattern for any region that has a long settlement history. The isoglossic mesh is the cartographic counterpart of Edward Sapir's principle that linguistic variety increases as one gets closer to the original settlement or *Heimat*. Since the first dialect atlas projects were carried out in regions with long settlement histories, we have abundant examples of this pattern. Map 7-4 shows a typical pattern at closer range, again using German data. The villages of Bubsheim, Denkingen and Böttingen are contiguous to one another and only a few kilometres apart. Yet, as Map 7-4 shows, the three villages have apparently unique combinations of linguistic features. Although they can sometimes be paired with one another in terms of shared features, there is no obvious coherence to the pairing of the villages and the distinctiveness in other respects. Bubsheim differs from the other two by features A and B, but shares feature E with Denkingen and features C and D with Böttingen, and so on. This kind of fine distinction in a region always indicates a long settlement history.

7.2.2 *Transitions*

The converse is true as well. Now that we are beginning to get dialect research in more recently settled regions, like inland North America and Australia, it is becoming apparent that dialect features tend to be shared over relatively great distances when the settlement history goes back only one or two centuries. Work on the Linguistic Atlas of the United States and Canada provides a case in point. The survey was begun in New England and then extended to the southern Atlantic states, two of the longest settled regions in North America, and the published results of these surveys were not at all out of the ordinary when compared with the results that had been found in the European surveys. However, when the research was extended inland, into the much more recent settlements in the midwest and California, isoglosses just seemed to dwindle and disappear. (An example of a midwestern transitional region is discussed in 9.3 below.) The major dialect areas identified in the Atlantic seaboard surveys seem to melt into one another as one moves away from the coast.

7.2.3   *Relic areas*

Another common pattern of isoglosses that has emerged from dialect atlases is in some ways the antithesis of the helter-skelter pattern discussed above. Instead, in this pattern one finds a particular isogloss delimiting areas in more than one part of the survey region, with no continuity. In other words, a linguistic feature exists in two or more parts of the region but those parts are separated from one another by an area in which a different, or opposing, feature occurs. Such a pattern indicates a late stage in the displacement of a formerly widespread linguistic feature by an innovation. In earlier times, the feature which now occurs in isolated areas was also found in the in-between areas. Its status is now that of a RELIC FEATURE, and the in-between areas show the progress of the innovation. Rhotic (or *r*-ful) dialects are linguistic relics in England, as shown in Map 7-5. Nonrhotic or *r*-less dialects have been displacing them since the seventeenth century. Among the linguistically most conservative population in England, represented by the NORMs of the SED, both rhotic and nonrhotic dialects are found throughout the country. The fact that the rhotic dialects are relics is indicated on Map 7-5 not by the predominance of nonrhotic dialects, but by the discontinuity of the regions where rhotic dialects are found. A century or so earlier, they covered even more of the country and the three areas probably formed part of a continuous network. The innovating feature, in this instance an innovation more than three centuries old, has pushed into the region and left the older feature in a scattering of isolated areas (see also 11.2).

7.3   **Bundles**

As implied throughout the preceding discussion, each isogloss plots a single linguistic feature. It is worth emphasising this point, because people sometimes use the word 'isogloss' in casual usage as if it meant the whole set of features that separate a dialect area. Needless to say, the significance of a dialect area increases as more and more isoglosses are found which separate it from adjoining areas. Thus, for example, the isoglosses running more or less together throughout Germany in Map 7-3 reveal a more significant division than the few features separating Bubsheim and Böttingen in Map 7-4. The coincidence of a set of isoglosses is called a BUNDLE.

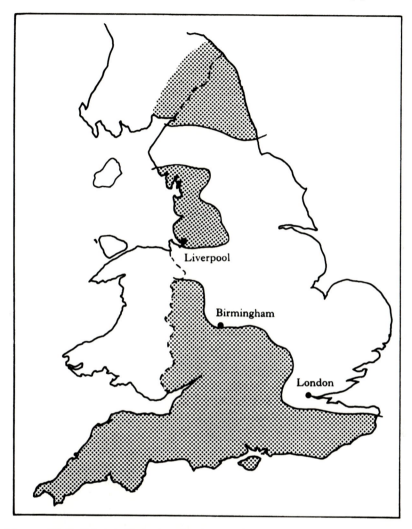

Map 7-5. Rhotic dialects in England are found among the most conservative speakers
(NORMs) in the rural south, around Liverpool in Lancashire, and in Northumberland
(after Trudgill 1974c). The discontinuous distribution of the rhotic areas indicates
that rhotic dialects are RELIC features in England

Perhaps the most striking example of a bundle that has emerged so far in dialectology comes from the French survey of Gilliéron and Edmont. Among the nine bundles
which have been extracted from their materials, one has a particular prominence in
both the number of isoglosses which come together and their closeness throughout
the entire area. This bundle runs east and west across France, as shown in Map 7-6.
Unfortunately, it is impossible to be certain just how many isoglosses are represented

95

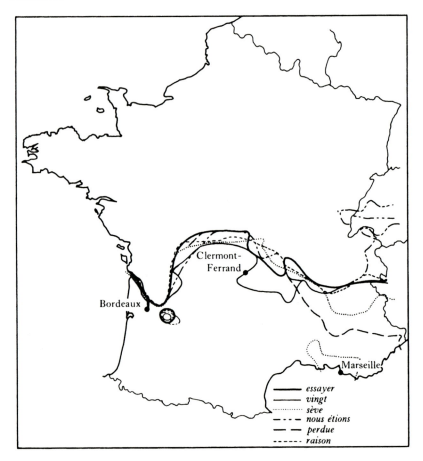

Map 7-6. Several isoglosses coincide, more or less, to divide France into the venerable dialect areas known as *langue d'oc* and *langue d'oil* (after Jochnowitz 1973). The coincidence of isoglosses is called a BUNDLE

by the bundle, because several of the features that are represented by a single line are really four or five isoglosses, bringing together four or five separate items that are comparable. The bundle marks the major dialect division in France and documents the dialect split between *langue d'oil* in the north and *langue d'oc* in the south (see 2.1). We return to this remarkable linguistic bundle later on (in 7.5), in the discussion of cultural correlates and dialect areas.

7.4 Grading of isoglosses

It is undeniable that some isoglosses are of greater significance than others, in the sense that some mark distinctions 'felt' to be culturally important while others do not, some persist while others are transitory, and the like. It is equally obvious that some bundles are more significant than others, in the same sense. Yet in the entire history of dialectology, no one has succeeded in devising a satisfactory procedure or a set of principles to determine which isoglosses or which bundles should outrank some others. The lack of a theory or even a heuristic that would make this possible constitutes a notable weakness in dialect geography.

In attempting to determine the linguistic significance of particular isoglosses there might at first seem to be an obvious way to approach the problem, namely, by categorising isoglosses according to the type of linguistic feature they describe and then grading them according to our knowledge of linguistic structure, or according to empirical observations about the persistence of different categories and the like. While it is true that isoglosses can be so categorised, it turns out that they cannot successfully be graded in those terms beyond a few fairly superficial observations, as we shall see.

The categories described here are given in order of increasingly more abstract levels of linguistic structure.

First, LEXICAL ISOGLOSSES describe contrasts in the words used by different speakers to characterise the same object or action, like the use of the terms *dutch cheese* in the northeastern region of North America and *cottage cheese* in the American midland, or *brose* in Scotland and *gruel* or *oatmeal* in adjacent parts of northern England.

Second, PRONUNCIATION ISOGLOSSES, sometimes considered together with lexical isoglosses, include most of the examples discussed so far in this chapter, such as [dat] and [das] for German 'that', Bubsheim [mayə] 'to mow' versus Böttingen [mɛːyə], and the like; a well-known example from North America is the contrasting pronunciation of *greasy* which has [s] in the north and [z] in the midland and south.

Clearly both of these types of isogloss involve the lexicon, but the former involves a difference in formatives from one dialect to the other while the latter involves a contrast in the phonemic representation of the same formative. It seems a safe assumption to rank lexical differences as more superficial than pronunciation differences because the former are more likely to be subject to self-conscious control or change by speakers than the latter. The two North American examples cited above may be instructive: while both were among the set of isoglosses on which the distinction between American northern and midland was based, the contrast between *dutch cheese* and *cottage cheese* has all but disappeared in the intervening decades, with *cottage cheese* now in widespread use throughout the entire area by manufacturers and their customers alike; the contrasting pronunciations of *greasy* persist, however, and when the unfamiliar pronunciation is drawn to the attention of speakers in either region, it is invariably considered to be quite strange if not merely 'wrong'.

In phonology, there are also two types of isogloss. The first is PHONETIC, involving contrasts in the phonetic output of two regions as the result of a more general or an additional phonological rule in one of them. In Canadian English /aj/ and /aw/ have a noticeably high onset in words like *wife, mice, south* and *mouse*, that is, before voiceless obstruents, a feature that is attributed to the rule of Canadian Raising rather than to a phonemic difference.

Opposed to these are dialects which differ in their phonemic inventories, which results in a PHONEMIC ISOGLOSS. Two well-known examples from England which will be discussed in some detail in the next chapter are southern /ʊ/, in words like *put*, *butcher* and *cushion*, and /ʌ/, in *putt*, *butter* and *blushing*, etc., whereas in the north both sets of words have /ʊ/, and /ʌ/ does not exist; and the southern contrasts between *laugh*, *bath* and *basket*, with a long vowel, and *lap*, *bat* and *battle*, with a short vowel, whereas in the north both sets of words have a short vowel (see 3.2.1). In Canada, eastern New England and western Pennsylvania (and increasingly elsewhere in the United States), words like *cot*, *bobble* and *tot* have the same vowel as *caught*, *bauble* and *taut*, although in virtually all other parts of the world where English is spoken the two lists are distinguished by having different vowels. Where the distinction has been lost, the dialects lack the second phoneme – an inventory difference.

There are thus two kinds of phonological isoglosses, phonetic and phonemic, and it might be tempting to rank them impressionistically, as we did with the lexical isoglosses, by attributing more significance to the phonemic type, since it has greater structural significance. However, it is quite useless to do so because particular cases seem to give equivocal evidence. For example, of the two distinctions cited for Canadian English above – the phonetic raising in *wife* and *mouse*, and the phonemic merger which makes *cot* and *caught* homophones – it is the phonemic one that proves to be less persistent, being levelled or 'corrected' by Canadian emigrants to the United States much more readily and consistently than the phonetic one. In the two cases of southern English vowel contrasts opposed to a single vowel phoneme in the north, the phonemic contrast for *butcher* and *butter* almost invariably develops in the speech of a northerner transplanted to the south, but the one for *bath* and *bat* seldom does, even though the northern dialect already has a long low vowel in certain words like *father* and *lager*.

The remaining types of isogloss can be grouped together under the heading 'grammatical isoglosses', with two subtypes. One is MORPHOLOGICAL, involving paradigmatic, inflectional and derivational differences between regions. An example is the occurrence of *holp* as the past tense of *help* in the American south (though its use is restricted to NORMs there), in contrast to *helped* elsewhere.

A SYNTACTIC ISOGLOSS involves some aspect of sentence formation, like the use of *for to* in many parts of the English-speaking world as a complementiser, as in 'John went downtown for to see his friend'; by contrast, no standard dialect of English, in any part of the world, includes *for to* among its complementisers.

Impressions as to how these grammatical isoglosses should be graded relative to one another or the other types are lacking. There is, however, abundant evidence in sociolinguistics that grammatical variables stratify speech communities much more sharply than do phonological and lexical variables. That is, phonological and lexical variables often occur in the speech of almost everyone in the community, but most grammatical variables are more restricted, occurring in the speech of one class but seldom or never in the speech of other classes. For example, the well-studied (ng) variable occurs in the speech of virtually everyone in English-speaking communities; it is a marker only in terms of its frequency, because it occurs less frequently in the speech of the middle class, usually only in casual speech. By comparison, the best-known grammatical variables – *ain't* for *isn't*, *hisself* for *himself, come* as the past tense instead of *came, youse* [jəz] for plural *you* – mark their users as working class in most English-speaking communities. They are almost nonexistent in middle-class speech.

Facts like these suggest that the major division among the different structural categories of isoglosses comes between grammatical isoglosses and lexical/phonological isoglosses. In other words, two regions with grammatical isoglosses at their borders will be regarded as sharply different dialect areas, much more so than regions separated by few grammatical isoglosses or by phonological and lexical isoglosses.

In passing, it is worth mentioning the possibility of SEMANTIC ISOGLOSSES as a separate subtype. These might be construed as involving contrasts in meaning from one region to another, perhaps including differences like the use of the verb *fix* in Britain to mean 'make fast, make firm' as opposed to its use in North America, where its primary meaning is 'repair' (although it may have the other meaning as a secondary one for some speakers). However, this type of isogloss is probably subsumed by the category of lexical isoglosses, since it is at least arguable that the dialect contrast comes down in the end to the use of a different word in one region. Thus, in the example given, the contrast might better be seen as involving not the two meanings of *fix* but the use of two different words, *repair* and *fix*, with the same meanings in the two regions.

Assuming, then, that the structural significance of the isogloss types is agreed to be in the order in which they were just discussed, it is fairly easy to devise a system for grading them. Unfortunately, it is much more difficult to find any real use for such a system, or to take it very seriously. Nevertheless, one could begin by indexing each type, with the most superficial type being valued as '1' and the deepest type as '6', as follows:

LEXICAL	1.	lexical
	2.	pronunciation
PHONOLOGICAL	3.	phonetic
	4.	phonemic
GRAMMATICAL	5.	morphological
	6.	syntactic

Now, for any linguistic survey, a score can be determined for any bundle by adding up the index value of each of the isoglosses. For the bundle between Bubsheim and

Böttingen in Map 7-4, the three pronunciation isoglosses give a score of six (= 3 × 2). The single phonetic isogloss between rhotic and nonrhotic dialects in Map 7-5 is scored three. Ostensibly, two regions with a number of dialect differences of the type shown at the top of the scale could be demonstrated to be closer linguistically than two other regions with fewer but more highly ranked differences. However, such a conclusion depends upon some empirically indefensible assumptions regarding the rank order of isogloss types, and there is no reason, given the present state of research into isoglosses, why some other researcher could not claim that their rank order is exactly the opposite to the one posited here. Furthermore, the procedure outlined here implies that a given survey will exhaustively identify all of the isoglosses in a region. Other-wise, assigning an index score to two or more bundles and comparing them is merely deceptive, if one of the bundles is missing a highly valued isogloss or two.

Because of considerations like these, the grading of isoglosses in terms of their struc-tural significance fails. However, in spite of its results, the idea seems to be promis-ing and it has an initial appeal for many dialectologists. It may yet turn out to be an appropriate direction to pursue, perhaps when structural significance is better under-stood and types of isoglosses have been more thoroughly investigated.

7.5 Cultural correlates of isoglosses

The previous section has shown how isoglosses are felt to have varying 'strengths' in delimiting dialect areas. In a broad sense, isoglosses may be thought of as one aspect of the local culture of the region which they delimit, in so far as a dis-tinctive regional speech contributes to a sense of community. Dialectologists have occa-sionally noted that their isoglosses correlate fairly closely with some other aspect of local culture. In so doing, they have been able to add a linguistic dimension to the social history of that region.

A fairly simple example is provided by the distribution of certain place-names in Massachusetts, when viewed in the light of the findings of the *Linguistic Atlas of New England* (*LANE*). The *LANE* survey found three principal dialect areas converging in the state of Massachusetts, as shown in Map 7-7. The most important bundle is the one which runs vertically through the state, dividing it into eastern and western dia-lect areas. Among the isoglosses in this bundle are the following: *stoneboat* in the west and *stone drag* in the east both describe an unwheeled cart onto which rocks are loaded as a field is being cleared; *bellygut* in the west describes a ride face down on a sleigh, which is *belly bump* in the east; and the unstressed vowel in words like *towel* and *funnel* is [ə] in the west and [i] in the east. The eastern section is then subdivided by a second bundle, which includes the following isoglosses: in the northern region, a 'pancake' is referred to as a *fritter* but it is a *griddle cake* in the south; the term *swill* for 'pig feed' is found throughout the area but only in the north does it exist

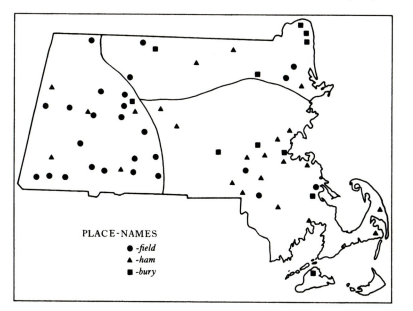

PLACE-NAMES
● *-field*
▲ *-ham*
■ *-bury*

Map 7-7. The state of Massachusetts, showing the major isogloss bundles which divide it into three regions, and the occurrence of certain place-names prior to the American Revolution (after Green and Green 1971). Each of the regions shows a preference for a different type of place-name

alongside the synonym *orts*; and the act of hauling supplies is called *teaming* in the north and *carting* in the south.

The three regions thus delimited have been found to correspond fairly well to the distribution of certain place-name types which were predominant in the region prior to the American Revolution. As Map 7-7 shows, the western region preferred place-names ending in *-field(s)* (Chesterfield, Newfields, and the like), and nineteen towns were so named, contrasted to only eight in the other two regions. The northeastern region is somewhat equivocal, although its five uses of names ending in *-bury* (Newbury, Salisbury and so on) represents a high proportion. In the southeast, *-ham* is relatively frequent by comparison with the other two regions (Oakham, Stoughtonham and so on). Thus the three areas can be shown to cohere not only with respect to a number of dialectal features but also with respect to local tendencies in the choice of place-names.

More striking yet is the bundle of isoglosses dividing France into southern and northern regions shown in Map 7-6 above. Although it is only one of nine such bundles which have been extracted from Gilliéron's massive data, it is widely held to be the most significant, and its significance derives in large part from the cultural correlates which can be shown to correspond to it, albeit roughly. Not only does the bundle describe the location of important linguistic differences, but it also describes the location of venerable social and cultural differences.

Essentially, the bundle corresponds roughly to the French layman's notion of where the 'Provençal' or 'southern' territory begins, and citizens to the south of the line consider themselves southerners. In France, this popular feeling of allegiance is fairly strong, and it is sometimes attributed to an ancient ethnic split between (as A. Brun put it) 'partially Romanised Celts in the north and thoroughly Romanised non-Celts in the south' (quoted by Jochnowitz 1973: 156).

In these historical circumstances, it is not surprising to find the same sort of rough correspondence between the isogloss bundle and a number of nonlinguistic boundaries. In agriculture, the bundle roughly describes the division between biennial and triennial rotation of crops, whereby a single crop is raised in alternate years in the south and the field lies fallow in between, but in the north the fields are sown with two different crops in successive years and then lie fallow in the third. Similarly, the bundle approximates an old split in legal practice that existed in France at the time of the fall of the Roman Empire, when Roman law ceased to hold in the nation, and only ended at the time of the institution of the Napoleonic Code in 1804. During those intervening centuries, the north adhered to a system of common law, probably introduced by the Frankish invaders, in which the law was established as a growing body of precedent. The south, on the other hand, retained the legal traditions of Rome, with a written code that was judged more or less immutable. The actual line which marked the legal split was itself not well defined, but it was in the same general area as the bundle. Finally, in architecture, the roofs of houses in southern France are typically flat, in the Mediterranean style, but in the north they are steeply pitched. Since there is no correlation between rainfall levels and roof style, the difference is adjudged to be stylistic rather than merely functional. Although the flat style has spread northward along the Rhone Valley and thereby pushed its way into the northern speech area – the opposite direction, one notes, to the spread of linguistic features in recent centuries – elsewhere the occurrence of roof styles correlates closely with the major linguistic bundle which divides France.

There is of course no necessary relation among things like roofs, legal systems, crop rotation and place-names. They have been brought together in this section simply because they are among the means that human beings use to impress their individuality upon their surroundings. In the uniqueness of their approach to such things, the people of a particular region are able to create a sense of place and a sense of community. Language, it turns out, is another of these artifacts, and its regional variety contributes to the sense of community. As such, it would be surprising to discover that language did not correlate with other aspects of culture. The study of regional variety in language can thus be seen as one dimension of social history.

7.6 **Isoglosses and dialect variation**

Throughout this chapter, we have concentrated on the traditional uses of the isogloss in dialectology. It serves as a marker of dialect variation, separating regions where people who speak the same language differ from one another. Linguistically, those differences (as noted in 7.4) may be found at any structural level: lexical, pronunciation, phonetic, phonemic, morphological or syntactic. Geographically, where people differ with respect to one feature, they are likely to differ on others as well. Thus, isoglosses are said to bundle (as in 7.3), and the more bundling, the more distinctive the dialects on either side. Patterns are discernible for, say, ancient cleavages or relic forms (in 7.2), and significant dialect differences between two regions are often reflected in other cultural differences as well (in 7.5).

In discussing the geographic distribution of dialect features from this point on, we probe beneath the abstraction of the isogloss in an effort to discover the linguistic and social factors that hold at dialect boundaries.

Further information

Isoglosses and the other linguistic phenomena which comprise boundaries have not yet received a full, book-length study. However, certain aspects of them are dealt with in most introductory works. Among these, we recommend the following: Bloomfield 1933: chapter 19; Kurath 1972, especially chapter 2; and Palmer 1936: chapter 7. While none of these sources is at all comprehensive, all of them offer different emphases and perspectives, and for that reason are worth looking into.

Bloomfield's chapter is a good source of information on the Rhenish fan (Map 7-3) and is the best source on the villages of Bubsheim, Denkingen and Böttingen (Map 7-4). The distribution of rhotic and nonrhotic dialects in England (Map 7-5) is discussed in Trudgill 1974b. The isoglosses separating *langue d'oil* and *langue d'oc* in France (Map 7-6) are described and discussed in Jochnowitz 1973. The various linguistic features which exemplify the structural categories of isoglosses come from many sources, but most of them are at least mentioned in the following: for American features, see Kurath 1972; for England, see Wakelin 1972; and for Canadian features, see Chambers 1973. The correspondence between New England dialects and place-names (Map 7-7) is found in Green and Green 1971. The correlation between the Franco-Provençal isogloss bundle and several nonlinguistic boundaries is discussed in detail in Jochnowitz 1973. Theoretical considerations of the isogloss in relation to dialect variation may be found in Chambers 1993, and a spirited defence of the uses of the isogloss is presented by Kretzschmar 1992.

8
Transitions

As we have seen, isoglosses serve a number of descriptive purposes in dialectology. Sometimes the patterns they form are recognisable types, as in the criss-cross of old, established regions and the insularity of relic areas. They bundle together at more significant dialect junctures, and they sometimes correlate with other aspects of regional culture whose distribution can be plotted geographically.

Yet the isogloss, as any dialect geographer nowadays would surely agree, represents a very abstract conceptualisation of the way in which dialect regions meet. Neighbours who speak the same language normally interact with one another to some degree, no matter how insular their occupations or how difficult the terrain between them. Interaction, even for the most isolated people, stimulates bonds of various kinds, such as sharing tips about egg production or showing off a new sun hat or using local words for discussing local events. Neighbours seldom differ absolutely in any respect. In order for dialect regions to abut as abruptly as the isogloss implies, they would have to be separated by an unbridgeable abyss.

Maintaining the isoglossic abyss depends upon looking at only one question and counting only one response to it. Amalgamating answers for several questions or counting more than one answer introduces variability, and variability causes the isogloss to vanish.

In this chapter, we consider the linguistic variability that underlies the isogloss and is literally hidden by it.

8.1 Gradual and abrupt transition

Faced with what seems to be an endless variety of speech from region to region, dialectologists naturally raise their eyes from the minutiae of their data and pose more general questions. One of the key questions has to do with the way in which dialect areas abut with one another. Is there a limit to the kinds of variation that can exist between one speaker and his neighbour? If so, what is it? How do neighbours accommodate one another at a speech boundary? How *real* is such a boundary, or in other words, to what extent (if any) does it influence the daily affairs of the region or affect the behaviour, consciously or – more likely – subconsciously, of the people in the speech community?

The drawing of an isogloss on a map clearly implies that one variable gives way to another variable at some particular point in space. This remains true whether the isogloss is represented by a single line or a double one (as in Maps 7-1 and 7-2 above), and whether or not the isogloss is described by listing the variables on each side or by citing only one variable (as in the fairly common practice of stating that an isogloss shows, for example, 'the southern limit' of a particular variable, without mentioning what is on the other side).

As obvious as the assumption of geographical abruptness may seem, it has seldom – perhaps never – been the subject of professional scrutiny or debate. Indeed, it seems quite clear that it is not an assumption that can bear much scrutiny. Part of the conventional wisdom of philology is that variation is not abrupt (see 1.3). The point that speech variation ranges along a continuum rather than existing at polar extremes has now been reinforced by careful studies of creole communities (see 1.4) and urban socioeconomic groups (see 5.1). Most dialectologists agree that variation in speech is gradual, not abrupt, although one still occasionally hears a version of the old anecdote about the dialectologist who is told by the farmer's wife, 'Oh no, sir. If you want someone who speaks that way, you must go to that farmhouse over there.' In fact, most discussions of dialectology in textbooks deal with isoglosses and dialect continua side by side, without mentioning their incompatibility.

To give such discussions their due, it should be mentioned that there is a sense in which isoglosses and continua are not incompatible. Isogloss bundles, as we saw in the last chapter, are made up of lines that occur in the same vicinity but are hardly ever contiguous. In moving from the region on one side of a bundle to the other, then, one would have the impression of a continuum, since first one feature and then another and eventually another would vary from site to site. Thus the notion of a bundle, which is based on the notion of the isogloss, can be reconciled with geographic gradualness.

The rest of this chapter is devoted to a critical study of two 'isoglosses' in England, which will demonstrate that isoglosses – and by implication, bundles – are overlaid on linguistic variability. The kind of variation that is found in transition zones is, as we will see, regular and systematic. To proceed, we begin with an overview of the variables which form the basis for that conclusion.

8.2 Introduction to the variables

The two best-known differences between the English spoken in the south of England and in the midlands and north involve what we will call (u) and (a). These symbols are taken from the orthographic representations in Middle English (ME), where the features are also represented as *ŭ* and *ă*, or 'short *u*' and 'short *a*'. In the seventeenth century, both of these phonemes underwent a linguistic change in the region of London. ME *ŭ*, phonetically [ʊ], developed an unrounded variant, [ʌ], in certain words. The variation was first noted by an orthoepist in 1580, and by 1640 was a commonplace observation. Although the variation apparently never became rule-governed, certain phonological environments inhibited it: thus, the rounded [ʊ] usually occurs after labials other than /m/, and before /ʃ, l/, as in *push, pull, bush, bull, full* and *wool*. However, the occurrence of either variant, [ʊ] or [ʌ], is not predictable anywhere today, and all standard accents of English have contrasting pairs like *put* and *putt, butcher* and *butter*, and *cushion* and *cousin*.

Similarly, ME *ă* became lengthened in certain words, beginning probably a few decades later than the development of ME *ŭ*. This change seems to have become rule-governed, affecting virtually all words in which [a] occurred before /f, θ, s/, that is, the anterior fricatives, such as *laugh, path* and *glass*, and also, but evidently somewhat later, affecting many words in which it occurred before clusters of a nasal plus obstruent, such as *advantage, demand, dance* and *branch*. However, if these changes ever were rule-governed, the rule did not persist, and words of recent origin, like *cafeteria*, have the short vowel.

Both of these innovations began diffusing from London over three centuries ago and they are now general throughout the south of England. However, their northward progress has been notably slow. Map 8-1 represents by means of an isogloss for the words *some* and *chaff* the distribution of the northern pronunciations of these two words, which represent (u) and (a) respectively. The pronunciations shown on the map are those of the most conservative linguistic group, the NORMs of the SED. In what follows, we concentrate on a small area along the frontier of these two innovations, at the easternmost end where the map shows the isoglosses beginning at The Wash and cutting into East Anglia.

8.3 The transition zone for (u)

The SED materials provide occurrences of a considerable number of instances of words which have the unrounded vowel [ʌ] in southern English (and elsewhere throughout the English-speaking world) but which retain the rounded vowel in the north of England. The following list was culled from the records and forms the database for the discussions which follow:

> *brother, brush* (3 occurrences), *bump, bunch, butter, clump, come, cousins, cud, cutter, cutting* (2), *does, done, dove* (2), *dozen, drunk, duck* (2), *dull, dung* (2), *dust, dustpan, enough, funnel, gull, gums, gutter* (2), *hub, hundred, hungry, lump, mongrel, muck, mud, mushrooms, must, other/ tother, pluck* (2), *puddles, puppies/pups, rubbish* (2), *sawdust, shovel, shut, slugs, stubble, stump, sun, thumb, thunder, tuft, tup(hog), truss, tussock, uncle, up, us.*

Map 8-1. England, showing the southern limit of [ʊ] in *some* (solid line) and the short vowel [a] in *chaff* (broken line) (after Wakelin 1972: 87)

Even though no individual informant volunteered every one of these items during his interview, all volunteered two-thirds or more, making a large enough sample for reasonable confidence. To determine the area to be investigated, a continuous group of speakers with [ʊ] in all of the words of the list was identified to form the northern edge of the territory, and a second group of speakers with [ʌ] in all the words was identified to form the southern edge. On Map 8-2, the first group is identified by the index 100 (that is, 100 per cent [ʊ]) and the second by 0. The main interest, of course, is in the speakers located in between these two groups. In the most literal interpretation of what an isogloss is, one would predict that there would be no speakers there at all, but that prediction is so patently unrealistic that it is doubtful that anyone really

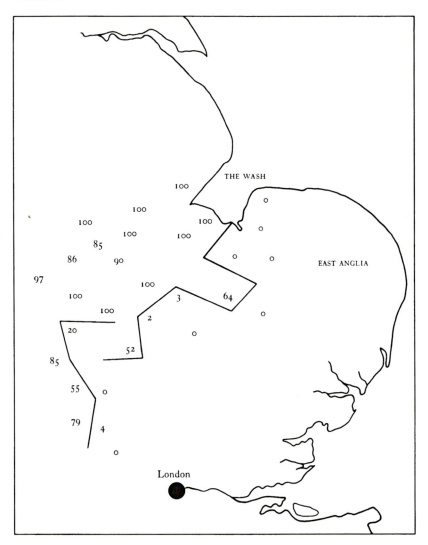

Map 8-2. East Anglia and the east midlands, showing occurrences of (u). Each number is an
index for one SED informant, showing the percentage of words with [ʊ] in a list of
sixty-five items such as *brother*, *gutter*, *rubbish* and *us*. The solid line is an attempt
to reduce the variability to an isogloss

holds to it. In fact, as Map 8-2 shows, there are many speakers in between the two
groups, with a range of indices for the occurrences of [ʊ] in the data from 97 per cent
all the way down to 2 per cent.

Structurally, the linguistic difference between speakers at the top of the scale (100)
and those at the bottom (0) is that the latter have one vowel phoneme /ʌ/, which the

former do not have. What can be said of those in the middle? Their vowel system apparently cannot be described in terms of phonemes at all, and instead we shall say that they have a variable, (u), in their vowel system. Since in this case the speakers with the variable are located between speakers who do not have variables, it seems likely that the variable is a transitional development marking the restructuring of the vowel system. Their indices make it possible to rank them along a continuum between 'more northern' (closer to 100) and 'less northern' (closer to 0), and it is surely no accident that, as the map shows, any line drawn from a site indexed at 100 to a site indexed at 0 will generally cut through sites in which the index decreases from north to south (except at the easternmost edge where there are apparently no transitional lects; but see the next section). The indices, though static, chart the progress of a sound change.

The actual data for each speaker affords an opportunity to underline the speciousness of isoglosses. As has been pointed out several times, an isogloss describes the boundary of only a single linguistic feature. In the case of (u), a description in terms of isoglosses would require the drawing of some sixty-five lines – one for each *occurrence* of each word in the data listed above. Yet it seems quite clear that the whole set of data is involved in the linguistic change, and that it is a single change that is taking place. An attempt even to make a minimal improvement by permitting isoglosses to be drawn for each *word* in the list rather than each occurrence of each word must fail, for the data shows that for most words which have been elicited more than once, individual speakers in the transitional area are likely to have variable pronunciations, saying, for example, [dʊk] 'duck' on one occasion and [dʌk] on another.

This kind of individual variety obviously cannot be accommodated by an isogloss. Moreover, any effort in the direction of redefining the notion of the isogloss to make it more general seems likely to fail. If, for example, we were to make an arbitrary but not unreasonable assumption that any neighbouring speakers whose indices differ by 50 per cent or more belong on opposite sides of an isogloss, then we would have a heuristic for constructing an isogloss even in the presence of linguistic variables. However, the heuristic fails, as Map 8-2 shows. Instead of a single line, it results in a series of discontinuous lines. In the open section of Map 8-2, the neighbouring indices are 100, 52 and 20, in which the middle figure cannot be assigned a place along the isogloss with respect to the other two. If one tries to patch up the heuristic by making the differential 30 instead of 50, which would fill in the gap in this case, the result is chaos, since many of the formerly well-behaved sections of the old line become completely boxed in now. In any event, the very acknowledgement that transitional dialects exist would seem to render the isogloss obsolete, because they can no more be assigned an absolute place on one or the other side of a line than can an individual speaker who has a variable pronunciation of a single word. Rather than attempt to 'regularise' the variability, a more fruitful approach to the problem of transition would seem to be to seek generalisations and systematicity in the variability itself.

8.4   **Mixed and fudged lects**

Looking more closely at the transitional LECTS (or varieties), we note a discrepancy in the phonetic range used by speakers. The quantification shown in Map 8-2, in which the indices tabulate the percentage of 'northern' pronunciations, is based on occurrences not only of [ʊ], the high front-rounded lax vowel, but also of [ʏ] and [ʉ], which are more open and more close realisations of that vowel. The decision to group all three together in the quantification seems noncontroversial, since they are minimally different phones. However, the phonetics that are *not* included in the quantification – that is, the phone types that do not count in determining the percentage for any speaker – divide into two groups. One of them, obviously, is [ʌ], the mid-central unrounded vowel, along with its open and close realisations, [ʌ̞] and [ʌ̝]. The other is [ɤ], a higher mid-central unrounded vowel, which also shows up in a more close realisation, [ɤ̝]. Grouping them together as 'non-ʊ' forms (so to speak) is clearly justified, but separating them is useful in showing up a distinction in transitional types.

Lects which mix the vowels [ʊ] and [ʌ] are to some extent expected, perhaps even predictable, in an area intermediate between one which uniformly has [ʊ] and one which has [ʌ]. Such lects also fit readily into the concept of a dialect continuum. If we distinguish among them in terms of whether they are 'more northern' or 'less northern', again arbitrarily but not unreasonably choosing the midpoint on the continuum, 50, as the dividing line, we can plot the distribution of such MIXED LECTS in the region as in Map 8-3. Structurally, mixed northern lects have a phoneme /ʊ/ with a fairly complex allophony which includes [ʊ], [ʌ], and the variable (u). Mixed southern lects have phonemes /ʊ/ and /ʌ/ which are neutralised by the occurrence of (u) in the allophony. A comparison of Map 8-3 with Map 8-2, on which the actual indices are recorded, will show that the two apparent discrepancies in the distribution of mixed lects, where mixed northern lects interrupt what would otherwise be a wide band of mixed 'non-ʊ' lects, are the result of two speakers whose indices are close to the middle of the continuum, at 52 and 64.

Turning now to the set of lects which have [ɤ], we should perhaps ask first how such a phonetic realisation arises when it is not found at either of the poles on the continuum. It is, however, very closely related to both of the other phones, being central and unrounded like [ʌ] but higher, midway between it and [ʊ]. Impressionistically, it might seem to be a nearly perfect realisation of (u), combining some properties of both of the other phonetic realisations. In other words, it is a fudge between the contending phone types of this change in progress, a way, as it were, of being at neither pole on the continuum or conversely of being at both poles at once. The distribution of the FUDGED LECTS is shown on Map 8-4. There are two clusters: at the western edge of the map, two sites which otherwise belong clearly in the northern dialect area (indexed as 86 and 90, on Map 8-2) include a few occurrences of the fudge; more significantly, the four Norfolk sites, all indexed at 0 and thus clearly in

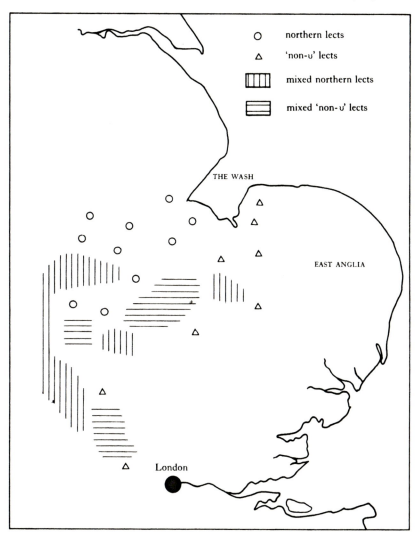

Map 8-3. The distribution of mixed lects in the transition zone

the southern dialect region, show a marked tendency toward the fudge, with two of the sites actually preferring it to [ʌ] by a slight margin. Structurally, it is more difficult to determine how fudged lects should be placed on the continuum, but by the very nature of the fudge, it seems reasonable to consider it a more neutral realisation than either of the other phones and thus to place fudged lects nearer the middle than mixed lects. Table 8-1 arranges the continuum graphically and summarises the varieties found in the region.

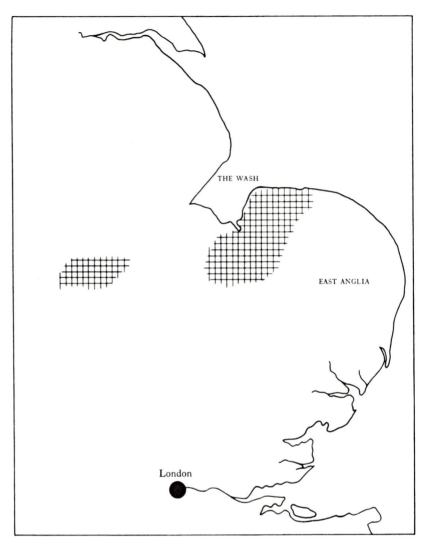

Map 8-4. Distribution of fudged lects, showing concentrations in Leicestershire to the west and Norfolk to the east

Map 8-5 shows the geographic distribution of the lectal types listed in Table 8-1. Since we know that the change in progress is moving from south to north in this case, we can identify the line to the north as the BEACH HEAD of the innovation and the line to the south as its BASE. In between is the transition zone, a kind of linguistic no-man's land in which the variable (u) is, for the time being at least, pervasive.

A number of questions arise from Map 8-5. One would like to know, first of all, if the geographic distribution of the lectal types is accidental or integral. Do fudged lects

Table 8-1. *Summary of lectal types for (u) arranged on a continuum.*
Note that the 'Phonemic structure' refers specifically to the set of
words considered as the data base in this section

Index	Type	Phonemic structure	Phonetics
100	Pure	/ʊ/	[ʊ]
	Mixed	/ʊ/	[ʊ, ʌ]
	Fudged	/ʊ/	[ʊ, ɣ]
⁻50			
	Fudged	/ʌ/	[ʌ, ɣ]
	Mixed	/ʌ/	[ʌ, ʊ]
0	Pure	/ʌ/	[ʌ]

always occur at the beach head, as they do here? Are fudged and mixed lects always distinct from one another, as in this case? Are these types of lects always found in transition zones? We will find some answers – at least tentative ones – by turning now to a second case, variable (a).

8.5   The variable (a)

The variable (a) is phonologically more complicated than (u) because of certain ancillary developments that have taken place in some areas. The original change involved vowel lengthening, which resulted in ME *ă*, phonetically short [a], showing up as long [aː] before the anterior fricatives. As we shall see, that is still the most common phonetic realisation of the innovation. However, in certain dialects one or both of the phones from ME *ă* has undergone a quality change as well. Thus long [aː] is sometimes backed to [ɑː], and short [a] is sometimes fronted to [æ]. Both developments have occurred in RP and elsewhere. Where either development is found, the character of the innovation is altered from a length distinction to a quality distinction, and vowel length is predictable by a late rule.

The SED records include fewer words which are susceptible to this change than there were for (u), largely because the environment of the change is more restricted and thus encompasses a smaller data base to begin with. Nevertheless, there are enough instances to ensure a reliable result. The list is as follows:

> *after*(birth), *after*(noon), *ask, basket, chaff, grass* (3 occurrences), *haft, last, laugh/laughing* (2), *master, past, pasture, path, shaft* (4), *shaft*(horse)/ *shafter.*

This list will be referred to as Data 1, to distinguish it from a second set of words, called Data 2, which is not susceptible to this change. Because of the phonetic complexity of the innovation, the second list is necessary to establish whether the change is one of length or quality for any given lect. Data 2 includes the following words:

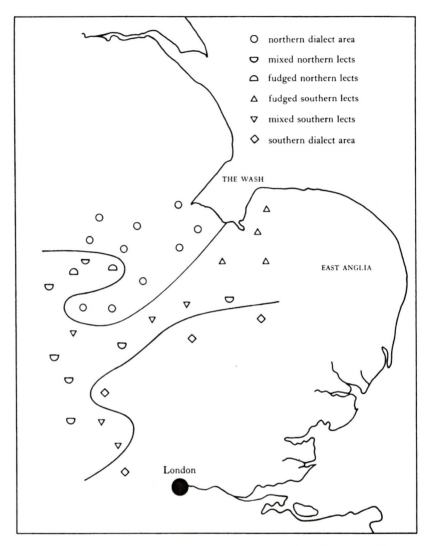

Map 8-5. The elements of a transition zone, showing the distribution of lectal types. The northern line marks the beach head of the innovation; the southern line its base

ant, ant(hill), axle, bag, bat, panting, sack, scratch(ing), stacks.

None of the words in Data 2 is known to have undergone lengthening as a result of this or any other innovation, in any region.

The transitional nature of the same general area discussed for (u) can again be established by a simple quantification based on Data 1, by determining the instances of short

[a] in the list for each speaker and taking a percentage. Hence a speaker who has only [a] in Data 1 (as in Data 2) will have an index score of 100, and a speaker who has some other vowel in all the words in Data 1 (in contrast to Data 2) will have an index score of 0. As before, the southern limit of the lects scoring 0 will establish the base of the innovation. As Map 8-6 shows, the beach head can be readily located, just as it was for (u). However, the base is more complicated. Several lects are indexed at 0, but among them there are three different types. First is the expected contrast in terms of length, [aː] in Data 1 opposed to [a] in Data 2, represented by the lects in Map 8-6 pushing northward into the east midlands. The other two also show consistent contrasts between the vowels of the two sets of data. One of them, located in Suffolk in East Anglia, also has [aː] in Data 1 but has [æ] in Data 2, indicating that the contrast is in vowel quality. The other, immediately to the north in East Anglia, typically has [ɑː] in Data 1, a difference in both length and quality from [æ] in Data 2, although there are some instances as well of [aː] in Data 1 and various other reflexes, as we shall see. Most significantly, there is a consistent contrast in vowel quality between the two sets. (There is a strong suspicion, based partly on earlier records made in Norfolk and partly on informal observations in the area, that the typical vowel of Data 1 should be [aː], not [ɑː], and therefore the apparent contrast between the two regions of East Anglia is not real. However, these phonetic details do not materially affect the exposition here and will not be pursued.) Structurally, then, both types of lect located in East Anglia share the quality contrast.

In the transitional zone are found lects of various types, including mixed lects precisely with the properties that we might expect. Again taking the index score of 50 as a dividing point, there are lects which belong to the northern dialect area by virtue of a preponderance of the vowel [a] in Data 1 (and, of course, also in Data 2), but with some occurrences of [ɑː] as well and even a few of [aː]. These are shown on Map 8-7 forming a kind of linguistic fringe along the beach head. Complementing these are mixed lects which predominantly have [aː] in Data 1 as opposed to [a] in Data 2, but also have occasional neutralisations, with the short vowel occurring in Data 1 as well. On Map 8-7, these appear at the apex of each of the base regions.

There is also evidence of fudging, which in this situation is considered to be the occurrence of 'half-long' vowels, usually either [ɑˑ] or [aˑ]. One of the areas where fudged vowels occur is in the northernmost lects of East Anglia, which, as we have seen, all have the index 0. Since the innovation is signalled by vowel *quality* in this region, instances of half-long vowels are relatively insignificant.

Several lects remain unaccounted for. These cluster in a kind of corridor between the two base regions already identified and also, at the northern end, come up against mixed lects of both kinds (see Map 8-7). Surrounded by such diversity, it is difficult to guess what their properties might be. In fact, they reflect the diversity in an

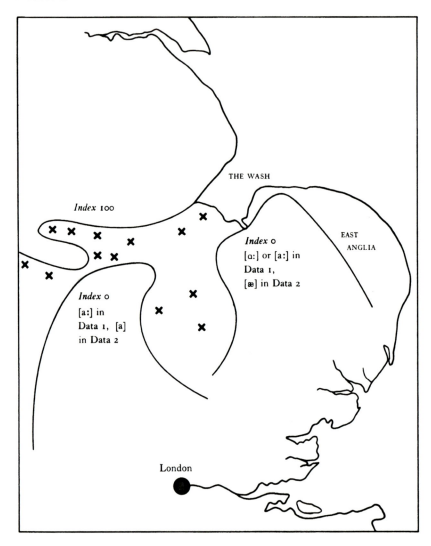

THE WASH

Index 100

EAST
ANGLIA

Index 0
[ɑ:] or [a:] in
Data 1,
[æ] in Data 2

Index 0
[a:] in
Data 1, [a]
in Data 2

London

Map 8-6. Variable (a) in East Anglia and the east midlands. The northern line is the beach
   head of the innovation (index 100) and the two southern lines (both index 0) are its
   base. In between, X marks the occurrence of transitional lects

interesting way. Though they belong with the southern group – their indices are less
than 50 – they are mixed lects, with [a] as well as [a:] in Data 1, and they are also
fudged lects, with [aˈ] showing up as well. A similar kind of SCRAMBLING occurs in
the vowel of Data 2, which elsewhere is very straightforward. Here, however, it usually occurs as [æ], as in the base lects to the east, but also occurs as [a], as in the lects
on the three other sides.

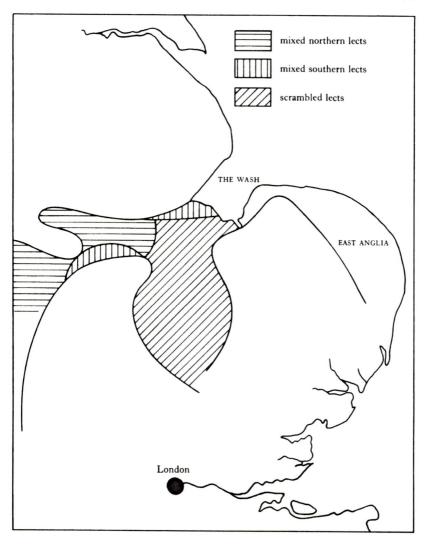

Map 8-7. The transition zone for (a) in East Anglia and the east midlands

The transition zone for (a), then, is much more diverse than for (u). Table 8-2 summarises the lectal continuum in the region.

In spite of the diversity, it is interesting to note that the transition zone for (a) has exactly the same components as the one for (u). Here, as there, we find mixed lects and fudged lects intervening between areas which lack the variables. The so-called SCRAMBLED LECTS for (a) are not really different in kind from what we have already seen, since they are merely a combination of mixed and fudged lects. Their occurrence

117

Table 8-2. *The lectal continuum for (a) in East Anglia and the east midlands*

			Phonetics	
Index	Type	Phonemic structure	Data 1	Data 2
100	Pure	/a/	[a]	[a]
	Mixed	/a/	[a, aː, ɑː]	[a]
50	Mixed	/aː/; /a/	[aː, a̠ː, a]	[a]
	Scrambled	/aː/; /æ/	[aː, ä, aˑ, æː, a]	[æ, æ, a]
	Fudged	/ɑː/; /æ/	[ɑː, ɑˑ, ɑ, aː, aˑ]	[æ]
0	Pure	/aː/; /æ/	[aː]	[æ]
	Pure	/aː/; /a/	[aː]	[a]

answers one of the questions which closed the previous section, by proving that mixed and fudged elements can co-occur in a single lect. The fact that phonetic fudging is a property of lects well away from the beach head in the transition zone for (a) answers another question by proving that fudging can occur anywhere in the zone and is not restricted to the beach head. And once again we have seen that the isogloss is simply inapplicable to the linguistic situation.

8.6 Transitions in general

The analysis of transitions presented above can only scratch the surface of that topic. The very fact that the two variables used as case studies share so many similarities suggests the limits of the analysis. Both are in the same region, involve notably slow changes in progress, and are restricted to the linguistic behaviour of NORMs. Research into transitions will profit from cross-linguistic studies, a range of variables that includes stable, nonchanging ones and dynamic ones which are sweeping through a region, and of course a broader population sample.

We believe that transitions point the way to a deeper understanding of geographic variability than any other theoretical device posited so far. The discovery of mixed and fudged lects makes a plausible entry into figuring out how neighbours accommodate one another in an area of variability, and the reasonably coherent spatial patterns of the lects ranged side by side along a continuum raise anew the prospect that linguistics and geography can find some fecund common ground.

8.7 Dialect variation and mapping

One clear advantage of the abstractness of isoglosses is cartographic. Maps are two-dimensional, and isoglosses are too. Drawing a single line on a map to mark the boundary between dialect regions is not only conceptually simple but also cartographically straightforward.

The discovery that dialect variation is multidimensional makes it harder to represent on maps. In attempting to capture the dynamism of linguistic change and diffusion, dialectologists must face the fact that maps are not intrinsically well suited as graphic devices for representing dynamism.

In the analysis of (u) and (a) in the preceding sections, we found that the speakers of pure northern lects and pure southern lects were separated by speakers of transitional lects. No isoglossic line could divide the speakers meaningfully, or, from another viewpoint, the isogloss shattered into two or more lines and still left some speakers in between, uncontained by the lines. To represent the dialect situation on the map, we had to add more information. In Map 8-2, the discontinuous lines were surrounded by numbers in the range 0–100 representing the percentage of northern vowels in each speaker's responses to the word list. Making sense of the map required interpreting the significance of the numbers in order to infer the dialect gradation.

Further analysis then showed that the numbers alone were not entirely meaningful because the transitional lects were made up of two kinds, mixed and fudged. In Map 8-5, the numbers were replaced by symbols for the kinds of lects identified in a key. Again, the dialect situation had to be inferred by interpreting the symbols and observing their coherence – how identical symbols tend to cluster.

Drawing inferences from dialect maps gets more complex as the dialect situation adds dimensions. Eventually, we will have the wherewithal to create multidimensional displays involving stereoscopy or holography, but for the time being the best we can do is superimpose visual devices on flat planes. Those visual devices must be adapted to the purpose in each case. The examples that follow provide interesting and instructive attempts at mapping variability in other situations.

8.7.1 *A relic feature in the west midlands*

Relic features, as discussed in 7.2 above, are features of accent or dialect that are receding from general use in the community and occur only in isolated enclaves. Macaulay (1985) looked at one relic feature in terms of its dynamics. He then applied the same methods of analysis and presentation as in our study of (u) and (a) and discovered a kind of anti-transitional pattern.

Macaulay collated words with final velar nasals in the west midlands, where some speakers pronounce a velar stop after the nasal, that is [ŋg], in words like *among*, *string, tongue* and *wrong*. Instead of revealing a progression from 100 per cent to 0 across the region of variability as in the transition zone, Macaulay's results, as shown on Map 8-8, reveal a kind of nesting of frequencies, with the categorical users (100 per cent) surrounded by a region of relatively high frequency users (70 per cent), who are in turn surrounded by a band of infrequent users (25–60 per cent).

The pattern in Map 8-8 appears to be the cartographic snapshot of a relic area, where a formerly widespread feature survives in isolation. The pronunciation [ŋg] was once

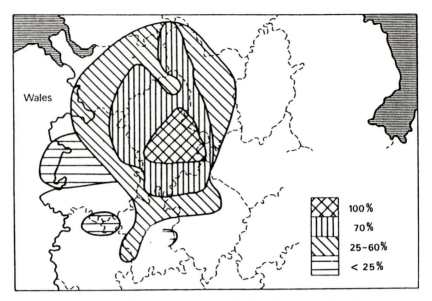

Map 8-8. Final velar stops in the west midlands of England (Macaulay 1985: 184)

predominant throughout the region, but it is being supplanted by [ŋ], the standard pronunciation. Macaulay's map gives a view of the way the old feature is receding. Presumably, in the course of time, the percentages will decrease from the core outwards as fewer speakers retain the old feature. The size of the relic area will shrink, and eventually disappear.

It is instructive to compare Map 8-8 with the more familiar static views in traditional dialectology as shown, for example, in Map 7-5 above. Here, in Map 8-8, the encroachment of the standard is made visible in the layers of diminishing frequency of the recessive velar stop pronunciation. Macaulay's map thus captures the dynamism of the linguistic change taking place in the west midlands.

8.7.2 *The interplay of social and geographical variation*

The dimensions of variability are not only linguistic, as in the cases we have looked at so far. They can also be social, with the usage of young people differing from old, or women differing from men, or middle class differing from working class.

Attempting to represent linguistic variability when there is both a geographical dimension and a social dimension obviously overburdens the graphic resources available in map-making. One or another of the dimensions must be stylised or distorted, but of course it is crucial that the stylisation or the distortion be rationalised in some way and made explicit in order to maintain legibility.

One cartographic solution is demonstrated in a later chapter, in 11.6.1, in a study of the diffusion of the variable (sj) in southern Norway. This variable is undergoing rapid change. Socially, the age of speakers is the crucial determinant: young people often use a retroflex fricative where their parents used a palatal fricative and their grandparents used a palatalised fricative. Geographically, this linguistic change is not taking place uniformly throughout the region but is radiating outwards from the urban areas in the west. There is thus both a social dimension to the variability and a geographic dimension. The cartographic problem is to represent both the age difference and the diffusion pattern.

In this case we have chosen to keep the geographical aspect intact and show the age variation indirectly. Showing the social dimensions of the diffusion requires three maps, one each for the oldest speakers (Map 11-9), the middle-aged speakers (Map 11-10), and the youngest speakers (Map 11-11). What is directly represented in all three maps, of course, is the land mass of southern Norway with its urban areas and coastal fretwork. Superimposed on this in all three maps is the range of the linguistic variation for different age groups. In order to grasp the rapidity of the diffusion, readers must visualise these three maps stroboscopically, as successive images of a changing landscape. This is best done by concentrating on the location and density of particular hatching patterns from the first map to the second and third. Nevertheless, it can only be done inferentially – the age gradation is not directly represented. In effect, the cartographic representation for this study required a choice as to which dimension would be shown directly and which would be shown inferentially. Because we are more interested in geographic diffusion in that section than in age-group differences, our choice was clear.

8.7.3 *Mapping social variation directly*

Sometimes it is the social dimension that is more important or more interesting, and in these cases a different choice would be made. Map 8-9 provides an example. The survey region represented in the map is the Canada–United States border in the Niagara region, with the city of Niagara Falls in Ontario indicated by a grid on the left and the American conurbation of Buffalo in upstate New York shown as a grid on the right. Separating these two regions is the Niagara gorge, including the famous Falls. Even though the gorge is only a few hundred metres wide at most, it is also the international border between Canada and the United States. Not surprisingly, dialect differences across the border are often sharp.

Those differences are not always straightforward, however. American features and Canadian features are undergoing changes such that young people in both places share more features than did their parents or grandparents. Sometimes American usage changes in the direction of Canadian usage but more often Canadian usage changes in the direction of American usage. Map 8-9 shows an instance of the latter.

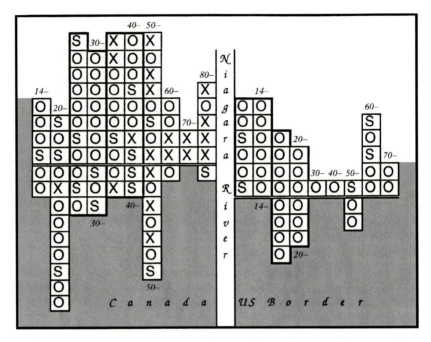

Map 8-9. Lexical choices at the Canada–US border at Niagara: O = *couch*, X = *chesterfield*, S = *sofa* (detail from Chambers 1995a)

In the northern United States, the most common term for a long, upholstered seat that holds three or four people is *couch*. In Canada, the most common term used to be *chesterfield*, a word that was peculiarly Canadian with this meaning. Since the 1950s Canadians have begun using *couch*, like the Americans. Among Canadians under 50, *couch* is now the most common term. (For more detail on this variable, see 10.2.3 below.)

These social dimensions are represented as directly as possible in Map 8-9. Actually, Map 8-9 is properly a cartogram rather than a map, that is, it is a stylised representation of the geographic space. Obviously, it completely ignores physical details such as the width of the Niagara River, the exact location of the Falls, and the mileage between the urban centres on both sides of the river. All that is left of the geography is the proximity of the two regions shown here as grids, and their east-west orientation. (Map 8-9 is actually a detail from a larger cartogram with ten other regions represented similarly as grids and oriented by proximity and direction.)

The map slights the geographical dimension, so to speak, in favour of the social dimension. Each square in the grid represents one person who answered the dialect questionnaire. The double line that bisects the grids represents women in the squares above and men in the squares below. The grids are organised from left to right by age, with the youngest (14–19) on the left and the oldest (over 80) on the right.

When the configuration of the grids is understood, it becomes relatively easy to interpret (or 'read') the cartogram. You can see at a glance that the US word for a long, upholstered seat is overwhelmingly *couch* (represented as O on the cartogram): everybody in the Buffalo grid says *couch* except for five people who say *sofa* (S). Nobody in that grid says *chesterfield* (X). To find people who do say *chesterfield*, you have to look at the Canadian grid, and there it is found mainly among the older people, that is, by the people represented in the squares on the right: it is used by the majority of people over 70, and then by a minority of middle-aged people, but among the people under 30 it is almost never used. Although there are a few people who use *sofa* (more here, as it happens, than in any other part of Canada), the term preferred by the young people is clearly *couch*, as it also is across the border.

The principal linguistic interest in this case study lies clearly in the social change in the use of the lexical variants. Young Canadians tend to use the word *couch* as their American neighbours do. They do not use the word *chesterfield*, as most of their elders do. In making this lexical change, they have eliminated a distinctive Canadianism from their dialect.

The cartographic display emphasises the social dimension of the change, making it the focal point. Geographic detail is minimal. In this case, as in the southern Norway diffusion, there were too many variables to represent all of them on the map, but in this case we elected to put the emphasis on the social dimension rather than the geographic one. Until we acquire the technological resources to manipulate multidimensional media, the mapping of spatial and social variables will require us to make choices along these lines on our dialect maps.

Further information

The study of (u) and (a) in this chapter was undertaken specifically for the first edition of this book by J. K. Chambers. The data comes from the records of the SED as compiled in Orton and Tilling (eds.) 1969–71. Map 8-1, which is also based on SED records, follows the map shown in Wakelin, 1972. Map 8-8 and the analysis of east midlands [ŋg], also based on SED records, are by Macaulay 1985. The case of *chesterfield* is discussed in detail by Chambers 1995a and the cartographic representation in Map 8-9 is part of the methodology discussed in Chambers 1994. For a discussion that complements the material in this chapter, see Kretzschmar 1996a, which provides a historical perspective on transitions as well as a method for quantifying features in transition zones.

MECHANISMS OF VARIATION

9
Variability

'Everyone knows that language is variable', said Edward Sapir in 1921. However, throughout the history of linguistics, linguists have tended to act as if language were not variable. Most linguistic theories have started from the assumption that variability in language is unmanageable, or uninteresting, or both. Consequently, there has been a tendency to abstract away from the variable data that linguists inevitably encounter in order to begin the analysis at some more homogeneous 'level'. The analysis of linguistic variability is much more recent, and more and more linguists are coming to see that variability is not only interesting but also that it can be made manageable and integrated into linguistic theory. The main impetus has come from urban dialectologists, and the movement has gradually been joined by mathematical linguists who see linguistic variability as a testing ground for probability theory, by sociologists of language who meet complex variability situations in language planning and multilingual literacy programmes, by linguistic philosophers who are seeking to model variability with many-valued logics and 'fuzzy' categories, and, perhaps belatedly considering their long confrontation with variability, by dialect geographers. This chapter outlines some of the main thrusts in the attempt to integrate the analysis of variability into linguistic theory.

9.1 The variable as a structural unit

A fundamental paradox of linguistic theory is summed up in the question posed by Uriel Weinreich in the title of a well-known article: 'Is a structural dialectology possible?' If one were to apply only common sense, this would seem like a question that does not need to be asked at all. In so far as 'structural linguistics' is a theory of language, how can it help but encompass a 'structural dialectology'? And yet the answer to Weinreich's question, as we have seen in Chapter 3, is not at all straightforward, and few dialectologists have been satisfied with the framework outlined by Weinreich in that article, or, for that matter, with any other framework that can be described as 'structuralist'.

9.1.1 *Variability as accidental*

One reason for the dissatisfaction felt by dialectologists, probably the main one, is the peripheral status (at best) that variability has had in such theories. When it has been considered at all, variability has usually been categorised either as the result of DIALECT MIXTURE or as FREE VARIATION. In the dialect mixture hypothesis, the variable element of a person's speech is assumed to be the result of two or more coexistent dialects which the person controls. It is not unusual, of course, for people raised in one location or one social class to retain their 'home' dialects in some circumstances long after they have changed their location and their status and, with them, their accents. However, there is no clear connection between this kind of 'mixture' and the occurrence of variable features in speech. An obvious objection to the consigning of variables to dialect mixture of this sort is the fact that people who are known to be bidialectal actually do control the two dialects, using one of them in special circumstances, such as when visiting a speaker with a similar 'home' background and using the other for daily social and business affairs. There may even be INTERFERENCE between the two dialects, such as the use of a particular vowel sound from the home dialect in the adopted dialect, and this particular feature may even be a true variable in the sense that the quality of the vowel varies between the one found in the home dialect and the one found in the adopted dialect. Even so, it is merely arbitrary to ascribe this feature to a mixing of two dialects rather than to consider it simply a feature of that person's adopted dialect, with exactly the same status as any other comparable feature.

The free variation hypothesis maintains that the variable elements in speech are the unpredictable occurrences of some linguistic feature which for some reason or other has two or more possible realisations. When a reason is offered, it usually involves the notion that the varying feature is undergoing a change and its representation in the grammar is thus unsettled. In fact, the variables that have been studied so far suggest that there is no such thing as *free* variation, and that features which vary are conditioned, sometimes by a complex of linguistic and social factors. Most linguists would now agree with the criticism of the psychologist Fischer: 'Free variation is of course a label, not an explanation. It does not tell us where the variants came from nor why the speakers use them in differing proportions, but is rather a way of excluding such questions from the scope of immediate inquiry' (Fischer 1958: 47–8).

9.1.2 *Variability as essential*

The alternative to ignoring variability in language or to assigning it a peripheral and accidental status is, of course, to incorporate it. The variable thus becomes another structural unit, equivalent to structural units like the phone, phoneme, morpheme, and others that linguists have posited.

A reasonable claim for dialectology is that dialects may differ from one another at any significant level of linguistic analysis, or, in other words, in terms of any structural unit. In this respect, the variable clearly deserves status as a structural unit. We have already seen dialect differences at several levels, including (Chapter 8) groups of lects that differ by having two phonemes /ʊ/ and /ʌ/ where another has only one, /ʊ/, and both contrast with a third group which has a variable (u). At the phonemic level, lects with the variable (u) may be classed with one or another of the invariant groups only by quantifying the occurrences in some speech event and making an arbitrary quantitative threshold to determine the classes. Such a procedure may seem artificial or abstract, but on the other hand phonemicisation is a relatively abstract level of analysis, and the realisation of a phoneme as a variable is no more (or less) abstract than the realisation of a phoneme as one of two or more predictable allophones.

The really radical departure from traditional structuralist theories is not in the abstractness but in the fact that variables can only be integrated with other structural units by quantification, whereas the venerable assumption of virtually all linguistic theories has been that structural units are *qualitatively* distinct from one another. Lects may differ quantitatively when a variable is involved. That is, lects may be distinguished not only by the presence or absence of a variable, but also by the frequency with which a particular variant occurs.

An obvious example of variation in terms of the frequency of a variable is found in the tendency of virtually all English lects, including standard ones, to simplify final consonant clusters. This variable, which will be symbolised as (CC̲), is realised by variant pronunciations of such words as *post* and *hand*, which are heard as *pos'* and *han'*. In the standard accents of England, the United States, Canada, Australia and so on, the final consonant can be deleted only in casual speech, and even then almost exclusively only before a following consonant, so that *post card* and *handful* are heard as *pos' card* and *han' ful*. In these dialects, then, (CC̲) is highly constrained.

It is not nearly so tightly constrained in other lects where it has been studied carefully, such as the black vernacular of New York City and Detroit and the rural vernacular of northern England. In northern England, thirteen of the seventy-five informants interviewed by the SED turned out to have a constraint on the variable similar to that of the standard dialect, namely, a restriction on (CC̲) to the environment immediately preceding another consonant. However, any similarity ends there, because the frequency of its occurrence, even in this restricted context, is many times that of the standard lects, and in fact it is realised no less than 62 per cent of the time in the speech of any informant, with most of the speakers clustering around 80 per cent. Thus the rural northerners of England may be said to have the same variable, (CC̲), as speakers of standard English dialects, and for some of them it has the same linguistic constraint, occurring only in the environment of a third consonant, but in its frequency it proves to be a much more salient feature of northern speech.

9.1.3 *Variable constraints*

The conditioning factor on the variable discussed above is not unlike the kind of linguistic conditioning that has traditionally been posited for allophonic variation. What distinguishes the two cases is, of course, the fact that the condition specifies an environment where more than one variant is found, whereas in allophony it specifies an environment where a single variant – an allophone – occurs. Moreover, what is significant in lects with a variable is not simply the fact that variation occurs there but the frequency with which it occurs, as we saw in the contrast between rural vernacular and standard dialects. It is not uncommon for a variable to have more than one of these conditioning factors, which are called VARIABLE CONSTRAINTS. When there is more than one variable constraint, each of them will be ranked as 'stronger' (permitting a higher frequency of some variant) and 'weaker'. The studies of black vernacular in New York City and Detroit and rural vernacular in northern England have all shown the deletion of a consonant when a vowel follows, as in *firs(t) answer* and *poun(d) of tea*, to be much less frequent than when a consonant follows. Other variable constraints involved in determining the frequency of variability can be ranked relative to these two, as we shall see. For now, the important point is that such variable constraints participate in determining linguistic variability, thus refuting the hypothesis that such variability is free.

Two other factors that impinge upon variability in language, already introduced in Chapter 5, are STYLE and CLASS. Inclusion of these nonlinguistic factors constitutes a radical departure for most structuralist theories, although they were always known (or at least believed) to play a role in linguistic behaviour. Both style and class exist as continua that must be partitioned, with some degree of artificiality, in order to be studied linguistically. Nevertheless, the difficulties inherent in the partitioning have been satisfactorily overcome in numerous studies of urban dialects, and by now their inclusion in theoretical discussions is hardly controversial.

Such factors not only *can* be incorporated in linguistic theory, but they *must* be incorporated if the variable is accepted as a structural unit. The study of variability thus combines linguistic and nonlinguistic elements. In theory, we can distinguish the linguistic variable itself, which is realised linguistically by its variants in the context of variable constraints, and the factors such as style and class, which define the social context in which the speech event takes place. However, it is only in the presence of the latter that the linguistic variable becomes meaningful, because it is dependent upon them and correlated with them. In practice, the distinction between the linguistic and nonlinguistic aspects of variability cannot be made, because the most compelling proof of the structural significance of the linguistic variable consists in showing that the variable alters in an orderly way when one or more of the independent social variables change.

Table 9-1. *The possible lects in a speech community*
in which (X) implies (Y). The variable is present
(+) or not (ø)

	Variable	
Lect	(X)	(Y)
1	ø	ø
2	+	ø
3	+	+

9.2 Implicational scales

One device for representing variability is to arrange the variable elements on a SCALOGRAM, a matrix that presents an implicational array. The use of a scalogram depends upon a particular relationship between variables. To be arranged on a scalogram, the variables must be implicationally related to one another. That is, for two variables (X) and (Y) which co-occur in some speech community, it must follow that (Y) implies (X), but not vice versa. In other words, if some speakers in the community have (X) and some have (X) and (Y) but none has only (Y), then there is an implicational relationship between (X) and (Y).

The simple scalogram shown in Table 9-1 lists the possible lects that will be found in that community. On the assumption that a speaker can either have (+) or not have (ø) a variable, there are three possible lects. The fourth logical possibility (only (Y) and not (X)) is ruled out by the implicational relationship between the variables.

The theoretical significance of implicational relationships lies in the elegant manner in which they capture systematic constraints. If features are organised systematically, their occurrence cannot be random or arbitrary. Dialects, of course, are systems. As such, their features should occur with constraints – they should be rule-governed, or dependent, or otherwise restricted in their privileges of occurrence. In our simple example in Table 9-1, with two hypothetical variables (X) and (Y), the *logical* possibilities if those two features occurred independently of one another would be four lects. But the variables are not independent; they are implicational. Of the four possible lects, only three actually occur.

Obviously, the more variables that are implicational, the tighter the constraints on the system. In a celebrated instance from anthropological linguistics, Berlin and Kay (1969) discovered that the colour terms found in the languages of the world exist in implicational relationships. Languages can have as few as two basic colour terms and as many as eleven. If those colour terms occurred randomly, there would be 2,048 possible combinations. But the colour terms are not random. Instead, they are implicational;

for example, a language only has a term for *red* if it also has a term for *white* and *black*. The actual combinations of basic colour terms found in the languages of the world are only twenty-two.

9.2.1 *Default singulars in Alabama*

The discovery that dialect data can be arranged implicationally has emerged from a number of different studies. For instance, Feagin (1979) found several examples of implicational relationships among syntactic variable constraints in her careful study of the grammar of Anniston, Alabama, a small southern city in the United States.

Among the structures she analysed were sentences in which the subjects and verbs do not agree, as in

> I seen three rats, but they was all too far off to shoot.

Here, the subject pronoun *they* is third-person plural, but the form of the copula is *was*, which occurs in standard dialects only with singular subjects. Nonagreement structures like these occur in vernaculars all over the world. They are sometimes referred to as 'subject/verb nonconcord' or 'invariant *was*', but we prefer the term 'default singulars' because it captures the essential fact that when agreement is not salient it is the singular form that fills the verb slot.

Although structures like these are well known in vernacular dialects, few dialectologists have collected as many authentic examples from so many respondents as Feagin did. When she analysed her corpus, she discovered that her working-class subjects tended to use default singulars more frequently than people of other classes, but she also discovered an interesting linguistic constraint. Default singulars occurred more often after certain constituents in subject position than after others. Specifically, the frequency of default singulars increased with the types of subjects shown from (A) to (E) in the following examples (slightly simplified from Feagin's originals):

(A)   They was all born in Georgia, mama and my daddy both.
(B)   All the student teachers was comin' out to Wellborn.
(C)   We was in an ideal place for it.
(D)   You was a majorette?
(E)   There was about twenty-somethin' boys and just four girls.

When the subject NP is expletive *there*, as in (E), the default singular is very common, in fact nearly categorical. It is also common after the second-person pronoun *you* as in (D), but it is less common with first-person plural *we* as in (C) and with overtly plural full NPs such as *all the student teachers* in (B). Least frequent is its occurrence with *they*, the third-person plural pronoun in (A).

These constraints form a continuum for the frequency of default singulars, with each step from (A) to (E) representing an increment in frequency. More than that, the

Table 9-2. *Default singulars in Anniston, Alabama (based on Feagin 1979: 201), shown as a scalogram in which they occur (+) or do not occur (ø) with types of subjects*

	Default Singulars with				
	they	NPpl	we	you	there
Lect 1	ø	ø	ø	ø	+
2	ø	ø	ø	+	+
3	ø	ø	+	+	+
4	ø	+	+	+	+
5	+	+	+	+	+

continuum turns out to be implicational. That is, if a person is heard using a default singular with first-person plural pronouns as in (C), then it is predictable that that person will also use them with the subject-types listed below them, but not vice versa. People draw the line at different points, but their use falls into one of the possible lects on the scalogram in Table 9-2.

To some extent, the scalogram in Table 9-2 can be explained. Expletive *there* is receptive to nonagreement because it does not encode singularity or plurality but is invariant in form; in standard dialects, agreement is based on the NP that follows it (as in *there was one*, but *there were many*) and all standard dialects tolerate default singulars after *there* in casual speech. The second-person pronoun *you* occurs with *was* presumably because of the analogical force of standard *I was* and *it was* on either side of *you were* in the paradigm. For the other three cases, no ready explanation comes to mind, but evidently the saliency of the plurality increases from *we* to NPpl to *they*.

It is worth emphasising the relative orderliness that implicational relationships such as this one impose upon dialect variation. If people varied randomly in their use of default singulars with particular subject-types, the number of lects would multiply. As it happens, there are only five lects, and they fall along a neat continuum.

9.2.2 *(CC) in northern England*

A second example of an implicational relationship comes from phonology, from the arrangement of the variable constraints on the rule of final consonant cluster simplification (CC), introduced in the preceding section. As mentioned there, the tendency to simplify clusters (as in *pos'* and *han'* for *post* and *hand*) is found in many dialects when the cluster precedes a consonant (as in *pos'card* and *han'ful*), but is not as common when a vowel follows (as in *post office* and *handout*). In the dialects that have been studied most carefully for this variable, the two linguistic environments are in fact implicational, in the sense that any speaker who permits deletion before a following vowel will permit it before a following consonant but not vice versa.

Table 9-3. *A scalogram of the variable constraints on (C$\underline{C}$) in northern England, showing the range of lects found there (from Chambers 1982)*

Variable constraints			before pause	
Lect	before C	before V	preceding sonorant	preceding obstruent
1	+	+	+	+
2	+	+	+	ø
3	+	+	ø	ø
4	+	ø	ø	ø

The implicational relationship becomes more interesting when we add a third possible context, namely, before a following pause (that is, at an utterance boundary). In the study of the rural vernacular of northern England, based on the data from the SED records, words before a pause are quite plentiful because they were elicited by a set questionnaire which naturally favoured one-word or very short answers rather than discourses. Indeed, the responses before a pause were so plentiful that they could be further subdivided according to whether the deletable consonant (the second in the cluster) was preceded by a sonorant (the *n* in *hand*) or an obstruent (the *s* in *post*), which were also found to be significant variable constraints in the black vernacular of Detroit. As in the Detroit dialect, these two environments in the northern England dialect turned out to be ranked with the preceding sonorant favouring deletion more than the preceding obstruent. Moreover, in northern England there were some speakers who deleted final consonants occasionally after sonorants (and before a pause) but never after obstruents (in the same environment). In other words, these two variable constraints are also implicational, in the sense that any speaker who permits deletion after an obstruent will also permit it after a sonorant but not vice versa.

These two environments thus form a hierarchy within a hierarchy, since they are only quantifiable, given the data available, in the context of a following pause, which is itself an environment less favourable for deletion than the context of a following vowel, which is in turn less favourable than a following consonant. The implicational array for the lects of northern England with respect to the variable (C$\underline{C}$) is shown in Table 9-3. The symbol '+' here indicates that a variable constraint applies in a certain lect and 'ø' indicates that it does not. The array shows that speakers vary in a well-defined manner, such that any speaker who permits variability in a certain environment will also permit it in any environment shown to the left of it in Table 9-3.

Once again, the hierarchy of variable constraints on (C$\underline{C}$) seems to be susceptible to at least a partial explanation. The key to understanding (C$\underline{C}$) apparently lies in the first variable constraint, the environment before a consonant, which as we have seen is very widespread in English and occurs (however infrequently) in several standard dialects as well as nonstandard ones. By contrast, the other constraints apply only to nonstandard dialects. The occurrence of a final cluster before another consonant creates a triconsonantal sequence, and triconsonantal sequences tend to undergo simplification by various phonological devices in every language which has them (and many, like Japanese and Dakota, do not allow them at all).

There is a universal tendency, then, to simplify such sequences of consonants. Thus it should not be surprising to find the same tendency in both standard and nonstandard dialects of English. However, one important difference between standard and some nonstandard dialects is that the latter have apparently extended the simplification to apply not only to triconsonantal sequences but also to biconsonantal sequences. As a result, the other variable constraints describe the possible environments for the extension of the rule to simplification of biconsonantal clusters. Precisely why these extended environments should arrange themselves in the order shown in Table 9-3 is much harder to explain, and in fact there is evidence of panlectal disorder with respect to these constraints, with the environment before a pause apparently outweighing the environment before a vowel in the black vernacular of New York City, although Detroit vernacular ranks the variable constraints the same as northern England. By contrast, there is no disorder anywhere with respect to the environment before a consonant, which is part of a universal tendency and apparently initiates the tendency to simplify consonant clusters in English.

Here again, as in the earlier example of default singulars, the implicational relationship among variable constraints imposes a relative orderliness on the variability that is found in the speech community. Far from the random babble that might occur if individuals differed from one another without limit or constraint, the lects are ranged along a continuum in which each one differs from the one before it in a well-defined way. The discovery of such orderliness is pleasing, but it is not surprising. Languages exist partly, perhaps mainly, so that people can communicate with one another, and the communicative function of dialects will obviously be enhanced by orderly relationships in the variability that is found in any community.

9.3 Handling quantitative data

One of the fundamental implications of accepting the variable as a structural unit is the necessity of dealing with linguistic data quantitatively, but handling quantitative data raises several interesting problems.

QUALITATIVE differences are absolute. One dialect has a feature that is absent from the other. We have noticed, for instance, that some accents have one or more phonemes which are lacking in others. Southern England English has /ʊ/ and /ʌ/ where northern England has only /ʊ/ (discussed in 8.2), and northern American English has /ɑ/ and /ɔ/ where Canadian has only /ɑ/ (mentioned in 7.4.1). Elsewhere, we saw that working-class speech may include a second-person plural pronoun *youse* [jəz] which is missing from middle-class speech in that community. Differences like these are qualitative. The phonemic inventories have an additional member, and the pronoun paradigm has an additional distinction. They differ from one another absolutely.

Differences can also be relative, and we have also seen numerous examples of these throughout this book. Relative differences are QUANTITATIVE. Everyone in a speech community might occasionally say *walkin'*, *talkin'* and *singin'* as variants of *walking*, *talking* and *singing*. What distinguishes certain accents from others is not the fact that the variant forms occur in a person's speech but how frequently they occur. Similarly, in the study of default singulars in Anniston, Alabama (9.2 above), we noticed that one feature of the local dialect was the use of sentences such as *There was three explosions* and *We was playing ball*. People there sometimes say *There were three explosions* and *We were playing ball* as well. The way people in Anniston differ from one another is in the frequency with which they say one or the other. Another distinction, as we saw earlier, has to do with the relative frequency of the two types of sentence. The type *There was . . .* occurred much more frequently than the type *We was . . .* in the speech of everyone in the community. Obviously, that fact only emerges upon determining the frequency with which they occur.

Determining the frequency of features requires a quantitative method of some kind. In simple cases, it might be done by calculating the percentage of a particular variant in the set of all possible contexts where that variant might occur. For example, the frequency of sentences with default singulars could be determined by counting all the sentences with copula verbs after plural subjects in a large speech sample, and then calculating the percentage of those sentences with default singulars. In any event it can only be determined in quantitative terms.

Methods of quantifying data are extremely important for linguistic research that studies variability. In Chapter 4 we discussed index scores, the means by which one determines the proportion of variants in a sample of speech. That method was developed by sociolinguists, and is one among many other quantification methods used by them.

Dialectology shares many of its quantification methods with sociolinguistics, but it has necessarily developed some methods of its own as well, particularly suited to its own requirements, and it is on these that we will focus in the next section.

9.4 Quantifying geographic variables

Dialectologists are particularly interested in discovering the spatial patterns underlying the variables they are studying. To uncover those patterns, researchers have applied many different statistical and mathematical models to their data. Doing so not only allows them to handle more data but also introduces a greater measure of objectivity into the analysis.

Needless to say, the development of computerisation allows data-handling on an entirely different order from what was previously possible. It has also, in its first decades, introduced into the field a profusion of methodologies, and with such profusion comes the potential for confusion. Most dialectologists discovered the statistical applications they use by consulting with statisticians and computer scientists rather than with other dialectologists. As a result, there is no consensus as to which programs are most suitable for dialect data or how best to apply them. The field is going through a protracted period of discovery. It is an exciting time, in which the singleness of purpose easily outweighs the methodological pluralism, and the analytic depth is adequate reward for the constant learning task.

To some extent, the current methodological confusion is terminological rather than substantive. The statistical applications dialectologists are using almost invariably belong to the class of multivariate applications. Though multivariate programs have developed independently to some extent in different research centres and often have different names – correspondence analysis, for instance, is known as dual scaling in some places and canonical correlation analysis in others – the basic methods have more similarities than differences.

Our discussion in this section will focus on two historically important cases as prototypes. Dialectometry (9.4.1) is a pioneering effort at quantifying geolinguistic variables that actually predates the microchip revolution, and multidimensional scaling (9.4.2) describes the statistical application in the forefront of the field. In both instances, we will introduce sufficient detail to make the methods coherent but our emphasis will be on the goals and methods that are generally shared by all researchers involved in quantifying geographic variables.

9.4.1 Dialectometry

The term *dialectometry* is now quite commonly used as the generic term for all kinds of quantitative analyses of dialect data. It is well suited for that use, of course, because it literally means 'the measure of dialect'. A few years from now, it may be so widely accepted in this general sense that it could stand as the title for this whole section in place of the more cumbersome title 'quantifying geographic variables'. As it comes into more general use, it will pay tacit homage to the man who coined it, Jean Séguy. In this section, we use it in its restricted sense, for the innovative *dialectométrie* that Séguy pioneered.

Séguy was director of the *Atlas linguistique de la Gascogne*, one of the regional surveys comprising the Nouvel atlas linguistique de la France. He supervised fieldwork in the Gascony region in 1947–51, and he and his associates published the first volume of *Atlas linguistique et ethnographique de la Gascogne* in 1954. In the next decade and a half, they published four more volumes, eventually dropping ethnography from the title and concentrating on the linguistic aspects. In all respects, the first five atlas volumes perpetuated the Gilliéron tradition – handsome, solid folios of maps plotting single answers in exquisite detail.

However, Séguy was increasingly dissatisfied with traditional analytic methods, and he harboured an ambition to improve on them. His goal was to reveal the dialect regions of Gascony in a more objective way – to let the regions reveal themselves, so to speak. He sought to do it by assigning numerical weights to his data in a consistent and objective manner. As far as possible, he tried to replace the dialectologist's subjective judgements of significance or strength with calculations derived from quantifying the data.

Séguy's basic concept was simple, and it anticipated the essential feature of all the statistical analyses of dialects that would come after. Séguy and his research team compared the responses in each pair of contiguous sites for all items in the survey data, counting the number of items on which the neighbours *disagreed*. By counting disagreements in this way, they were actually constructing a dissimilarity matrix, which is the basis for all multivariate statistics. The number of disagreements between any two neighbours was then reduced to a percentage, and the percentage was treated as an index score indicating the *linguistic distance* between any two places.

Séguy's method still required some judgements as to where to set thresholds and cut-off points and how to interpret significance and meanings. No method can ever completely remove the dialectologist from the analysis. For example, the Gascony data consisted of more than 400 items, and they fell into the usual types in, of course, different proportions: 170 lexical variables, 67 pronunciation, 75 phonetic/phonological, 45 morphological, and 68 syntactic. If the distance metric was calculated on all items without distinction, lexical variants would automatically carry more weight than the other types in the calculation of linguistic distance simply by virtue of their larger representation in the database. So Séguy neutralised the differences by calculating a percentage for each type rather than for each item. The distance metric was determined as the mean percentage for the five variable types. Thus morphological variables weighed the same as lexical variables, and so on. This seems a reasonable decision in light of the fact (discussed in 7.4 above) that no one has succeeded in demonstrating which types might be more salient in determining dialect differences.

Séguy and his associates set about calculating the linguistic distances between neighbouring sites for each variable, and then for each variable type, and then for the composites. They plotted them on the base map, and published them in 1973 in volume 6 of the *Atlas*. The dialectometric maps took up only the last ten pages of a folio that included more than 450 maps altogether. Séguy also included a brief explication of his method under the heading 'Dialectométrie' along with sundry other notes in the *Notice explicative*, a typescript monograph attached to the volume.

Map 9-1 shows a detail from Séguy's dialectometric display map. The dialectologists have superimposed on the map of southwestern Gascony a grid of lines connecting all neighbouring sites. Written on each line is the distance metric – the number that indicates how dissimilar the speech is in the two places connected by the line.

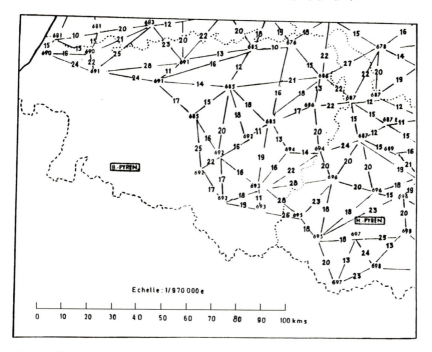

Map 9-1. Southwest Gascony showing linguistic distances between neighbouring survey sites (detail from Séguy 1973, map 2524)

The lower the number, the fewer the dissimilarities in the speech of the people who were interviewed in the two communities.

Looking at the distance metrics on the map, it is fairly straightforward to make a basic inference about the relative variability: where neighbours are very similar they belong to the same speech community, and where they differ greatly they form transition zones between communities.

Dialectometric maps obviously require a large format when there are numerous sites in order to accommodate the numbered links between all sites. But the numbers succeed in providing a numerical scorecard for dialect gradience. With careful browsing, readers can discern regional contrasts. On Map 9-1, beside the Bay of Biscay on the west coast it is possible to pick out a group of sites marked by low linguistic distance, in the range of 10–15 per cent; this region must include many dialect similarities. In the lower central region, site 693 is linked to its neighbours on three sides by low scores in the range 11–19 but to its neighbours on the east by higher scores of 22–28. This difference can be explained (in part, at least) by the fact that the places with high scores are found across the departmental boundary in Hautes-Pyrénées.

Differences like these have dialectological significance, and identifying them directs researchers and students to seek an explanation in social, historical or physical terms.

The display maps thus provide a convenient summary for a wealth of data and a productive model for further work.

Séguy and his associates went a step further and derived interpretive maps from the display maps by an objective formula. Based on the range of gradations in the whole region, they clustered the distance metrics into four significant degrees: (1) under 13 per cent, (2) 14–17 per cent, (3) 18–23 per cent, and (4) over 23 per cent. Each degree was then represented on the interpretive map by particular line-types (unmarked, dotted, light, heavy). The pattern of lines divided Gascony into regions of greater dialect diversity and regions of relative homogeneity. They tried more general clustering as well, but with less confidence. Of his most general map, Séguy expressed doubts. 'Ce "gradient de la gasconicité" est une tentative aventurée', he said – its 'Gasconicity' is risky (1973: Map 2526).

Despite the modesty of this inaugural publication on *dialectométrie*, Séguy's initiatives slowly found an audience. For one thing, Séguy and his associates – 'mes élèves-camarades', he calls them in his dedication to volume 6 of the *Atlas* – presented their innovations at conferences, giving them a prominence they were not given in print. For another thing, the timing was propitious. Not only did dialectometry lend itself readily to the burgeoning technologies of the day, notably the mainframe computer, but it also presented one of the first real alternatives to the isogloss and other entrenched methods. Several dialectologists recognized in the dialometric display a visual analogue for the dynamics of dialect gradation in space, or at least a first approximation of it.

Eventually dialectometry attracted proponents all over the world. It has now been taken up productively in distant centres – by Goebl in Austria, Thomas in Wales, Viereck in Germany, Kirk in Britain, Ogura in Japan, Cichocki in Canada, Kretzschmar in the United States, among others. For the most part, these researchers work independently of one another. In time, this research community will undoubtedly cohere, and particular methods and techniques will diffuse to a greater extent than they have so far.

Dialectometry is now entrenched, and it is not too soon to ask larger questions of it. What does it reveal about regular inhibitors and promoters of diffusion, about limits on differences and similarities among neighbours, and about common or universal patterns of gradience? The answers to those questions will require a comparative dialectometry, and a theoretical sensitivity commensurate with the data-handling and map-making that have so far provided the focus of activity.

9.4.2 *Multidimensional scaling*

Another method of analysing geographic variables quantitatively is to submit them to multivariate statistical programs. Multivariate analyses calculate relationships between the rows and columns of a matrix. The results of dialect surveys form a natural matrix, with the individuals (the respondents in the survey) as columns and the variables (the choices of, say, lexical items or verb forms) as rows. (Table 9-4 below is an example.) With the almost unbounded data-handling capabilities of computers, the matrix being analysed can be huge.

Statistics originated to estimate significance (as in t-tests) and to test hypotheses (as in chi-square). Multivariate statistics do neither: they are fundamentally descriptive devices, used as a means of reducing volumes of complex data to a set of comprehensible relationships. The relationships expressed with multivariate statistics might be descriptions, synopses, correlations, or, for that matter, linguistic distances.

As already noted, multivariate analyses are usually based on a dissimilarity matrix not unlike Séguy's distance measures. Once dissimilarities are calculated, they may then be represented graphically by a procedure called scaling. The basic principle of multivariate scaling is straightforward: if two individuals A and B are found to be twice as dissimilar as B and C, then A will be placed twice as far from B as C is. However, the graphic relationship is not quite so straightforward, because the points being scaled are multidimensional.

Here, Séguy's mapping method in dialectometry makes an instructive contrast to multidimensional scaling. Séguy, as we saw in the last section, uses the map of Gascony and then states the linguistic distance between the places on the map with a number. Whether the linguistic distance is large or small, the actual space between the places remains the same, because it represents geographic distance. In other words, in Séguy's system, geographic distance is represented spatially on the map but linguistic distance is only asserted (as a number) but not represented spatially.

In multivariate scaling, linguistic distance (or whatever the statistical measure is) *is* represented spatially. A, B and C will be placed not only a certain distance apart based on their dissimilarities (and regardless of their geographic proximity) but perhaps also on different planes, depending upon the dimensions of their dissimilarity. (This is illustrated graphically below, in Fig. 9-1.) Those dimensions must then be interpreted.

Incidentally, the difference between Séguy's method and the scaling method makes a perfect illustration of the theoretical choice discussed in 8.7 above. When the variables to be mapped include more than two dimensions, one of those dimensions must be represented indirectly. Either the geographical dimension is represented directly (as in Séguy's method) or the other dimension, which might be social, cultural, linguistic or something else, is represented directly and the geography must be inferred (as in the scaling method).

One clear advantage of multidimensional analysis is that the investigator's categorisations of the variables do not pre-judge the analysis or affect it in any other way. The statistical program searches the matrix for dissimilarities wherever they may be found and scales them independently for each dimension. Multivariate scaling often reveals correlations in the data that the investigator had not previously recognised. Indeed, with very large databases, it is expected to.

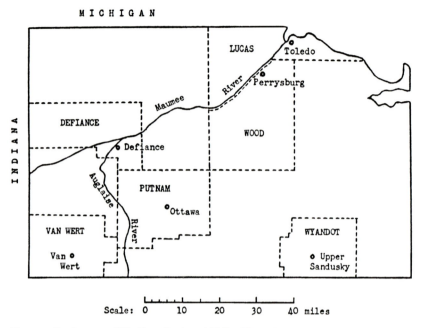

M I C H I G A N

Map 9-2. Northwestern Ohio (from Davis and McDavid 1950)

9.4.3 *A transition zone in Ohio*

Even relatively small databases can be profitably scaled in this way, especially when there are minute variations or complex combinations, as in most dialect survey data. A classic example of complex variation in a small database was provided by Alva Davis and Raven McDavid, two of the principal fieldworkers for the Linguistic Atlas of the United States and Canada, in an article that appeared in *Language* in 1950. It is interesting in its own right, but it also makes a useful exemplar for multidimensional scaling.

As the atlas fieldwork in the United States moved away from the Atlantic seaboard into the more recently settled inland states, dialect patterns became less coherent (as discussed in 7.2.2 above). One of the first inland surveys took in the Great Lakes region in the states of Ohio, Michigan, Indiana, Illinois and Wisconsin. While fieldwork was still being carried out there, Davis and McDavid were struck by the amount of variability in the ten records collected from five towns in northwestern Ohio. The reason for the variability was, they said, that the region was 'a transition area', meaning that it 'has undergone influence from two or more directions, so that competing forms exist in it side by side' (1950: 264). The purpose of their article was to illustrate the phenomenon of a transition area.

The region had been settled relatively recently, starting in the 1840s. The five towns where the ten dialect records were collected are shown on Map 9-2: Perrysburg, Defiance,

Table 9-4. *Nine variables used by ten informants in northwestern Ohio (based on Davis & McDavid 1950)*

	P1	P2	D1	D2	V1	V2	O1	O2	US1	US2
1. hay cock (N)		x	x	x				x		
hay doodle (M)			x		x	x	x	x	x	x
2. pail (N)	x	x		x			x		x	
bucket (M)			x		x	x		x	x	x
3. swill (N)	x	x		x						
slop (M)			x	x	x	x	x	x	x	x
4. johnnycake (N)	x	x	x	x						
corn bread			x		x		x	x	x	x
corn pone (M)					x	x	x		x	x
5. cherry pit (N)	x	x		x	x		x	x		x
cherry seed (M)			x			x	x		x	
cherry stone								x	x	
6. baby creeps (N)	x		x	x					x	
baby crawls (M)		x	x		x	x		x	x	x
7. greasy (N: s, M: z)	z	z	z	z	s	z	z	z	z	z
8. with (N: θ, M: ð)	ð	ð, θ	ð	ð	ð	ð	θ	ð	θ	ð
9. dived	x			x	x		x	x	x	x
dove (N)		x	x	x			x			

Ottawa, Van Wert and Upper Sandusky. They are all within about 80 miles of each other at the furthest. Two informants were chosen from each community: one of them, a NORM, is identified throughout as the first informant (P1, D1, O1, V1, US1), and the other, a more educated, more socially active man, as the second informant (P2, D2, O2, V2, US2). The ten men ranged in age from 73–94, were unacquainted with one another, and all but one of them were interviewed by McDavid in 1949.

From the dialect records, Davis and McDavid culled 56 variables (39 vocabulary, 10 pronunciation, 7 grammar), most of which have variants that are identifiably Northern and Midland, the two dialect regions on the Atlantic seaboard of North America that supplied most of the migrants to these inland states. Table 9-4 lists a sample of nine of the variables, with their variants in the left column identified where applicable as Northern (N) or Midland (M), and their occurrence in the field records of the ten informants (P1, P2, D1, etc.) indicated by x for the lexical and grammatical variants (1–6, 9), and by the phoneme for the pronunciation variants (7–8).

Finding a pattern in the distribution of variants in Table 9-4 is, as Davis and McDavid point out, very difficult. Comparing pairs of speakers from the same location, where one might reasonably expect similarity, is often puzzling. The two from Perrysburg, for instance, usually make the same choices, but they differ on the verb for describing a baby's movements (*creep, crawl*) and on the past tense of the verb *dive* (*dived, dove*). The two from Van Wert likewise have much in common, but they differ on the name for the cherry stone (*pit, seed*) and on the voicing of the medial fricative in *greasy*. The two from Defiance have much less in common, and the two from Ottawa still less. Generalisations like these are, of course, little better than impressions.

The heterogeneity of data in such a relatively compact region is truly remarkable. It provides, exactly as Davis and McDavid intended, a prototypical illustration of a transition area. 'This sampling of what happens in a transition area reveals the complexity to be found even in a limited section of the so-called "General American" speech area', they concluded. 'The distribution of forms closely reflects the settlement history, but one is at a loss to give convincing reasons for the restriction of some items and the spreading of others' (1950: 272). They offered their article as an illustration of 'the problems of dialect formation in this country, where speech mixture must have been the rule from the earliest colonial times' (ibid.).

However, this article by Davis and McDavid attracted attention not only as an illustration of a transition area but also for the challenge it posed for dialectologists intent upon discovering in it some semblance of geolinguistic coherence. Two years later, in 1952, *Language* published a response by David Reed and John Spicer, who were fieldworkers for LAUSC in California. Because they worked in a region even more recently settled than Ohio where NORMS were few, Reed and Spicer regularly confronted variability not unlike that in northwestern Ohio. Their purpose in responding to the first article was to demonstrate that 'the speech patterns of transition areas grow much clearer when viewed as quantitative rather than qualitative phenomena' (1952: 348). They ran the Ohio data through a statistical analysis of covariance and showed that there were in fact broad patterns of geolinguistic coherence in the sense that the speech of subjects who lived closer to one another resembled one another more than it did those who lived further away.

Reed and Spicer's reanalysis was one of the first applications of statistics to dialect variables. The covariance program they used has now been supplanted many times by better statistical tools, and the mapping schema they adapted, with iso-lines marking quantitatively similar speakers like isotherms on a weather map, poses almost as many problems of interpretation as it solves. Nevertheless, their article is remarkably prescient. Their approach was decades ahead of its time in the questions it asked and the solution it sought. Today, dialectology has been largely reformed as a quantitative discipline in much the terms Reed and Spicer envisaged.

9.4.4 *Correspondence analysis of the matrix*

The data from northwestern Ohio make an inviting display, when converted into a matrix as in Table 9-4, for multivariate analysis. The statistical

program we will apply to it, correspondence analysis, searches for degrees of association between the rows and the columns in the matrix. The program scans the rows (the
linguistic data) identifying and keeping track of dissimilarities among the columns (the
informants) and computing resemblances in terms of distance metrics. Correspondence analysis makes literally thousands of comparisons (and does so in a matter of
seconds) in order to extract the dominant relationships in the matrix and plot them in
multidimensional space.

It is worth emphasising that a clear advantage of this kind of analysis is its relative
objectivity. The dialectologist does not affect the analysis by submitting geographical,
social or linguistic information of any kind. What is submitted to the statistical program is simply the data matrix, in this case Table 9-4. The matrix gives no indication,
for instance, that D1 and D2 both live in Defiance whereas US1 and US2 live in Upper
Sandusky. It does not state that, say, O1 is a NORM whereas O2 is better educated and
middle class. It also does not indicate that, say, *greasy* with [z] and *bucket* are both
midland responses that should in some sense be associated with one another. If these
associations fall out of the data, it is because they are inextricably woven into it.

Correspondence analysis presents the correlations it finds on multidimensional
scales, as described earlier. Fig. 9-1 shows one set of correlations – the most relevant
one for our purposes. The most obvious observation about Fig. 9-1 is that the column
headings (P1, P2, D1, etc.) of Table 9-4 appear on the graph in a particular configuration. The column headings, as we know, represent the ten informants. Their location
on the graph, as we also know, is determined by their dissimilarities to one another.
The more dissimilar they are, the greater the distance between them, and vice versa.

The informants form three clusters on the graph: P1 and P2 are very close to one
another at the top, five others (V1, V2, O2, US1 and US2) are distant from P1 and
P2 at the bottom, and three others (D1, D2 and O1) are spread along the space between
them.

The three clusters are distributed differently in the quadrants of the graph. P1 and
P2 occupy the upper-right quadrant, and the five most distant informants occupy the
lower-right quadrant. These placements indicate that the multivariate analysis has discovered significantly different – in fact, opposed – patterns of variant choices by these
two groups of informants. In order to discover exactly how they are opposed, we must
scan the data matrix. What we find when we look at the individuals who have been
clustered by the statistical program is a contrasting pattern of choices. For example,
where P1 and P2 choose *pail*, the others (V1, V2, O2, US1 and US2) choose *bucket*,
and where P1 and P2 choose *swill* (as the name for pig food) the others (V1, V2,
O2, US1 and US2) choose *slop*. The two groups differ in their choices often enough
that the scaling puts them in diametrically different quadrants.

Closer inspection of the data in Table 9-4 (and the other variables in the database)
shows that P1 and P2 tend to choose Northern variants (*pail, swill*, among others) and

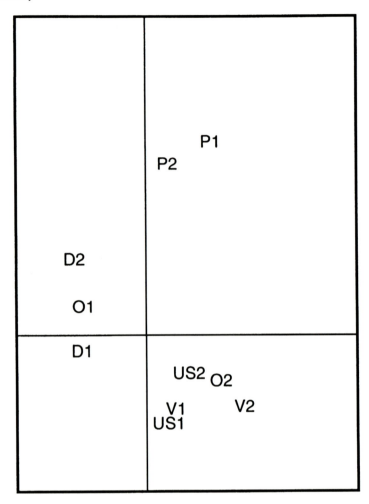

Fig. 9-1. Multidimensional scaling of northwestern Ohio informants

the other five tend to choose Midland variants (*bucket, slop*, and so on). The mid-line dividing the graph horizontally thus splits the informants into those who tend to choose Northern variants (above the line) and those who tend to choose Midland variants (below it). They are, in the terms we have used in discussing transitions in Chapter 8, 'more Northern' speakers as opposed to 'more Midland' speakers.

When we turn our attention to the remaining three informants (D2, O1, D1) who are found in the other quadrants, on the left, we can discover what it is that sets them apart. Their patterns of choices of the variants are unlike either of the other groups – sometimes they choose Northern variants, sometimes Midland, sometimes neither. They are all located near the mid-line, so their placement indicates their mixed usage, with two of them slightly more Northern and the other one very slightly more Midland.

Of course, none of these ten informants is a pure Northern or Midland speaker. To find informants who are, we would presumably have to look at informants further north and further south of the ten informants in the transition zone. But the multi-variate analysis shows that two of those informants are decidedly Northern speakers and five others are decidedly Midland speakers. The middle group is truly transitional, and although one of those, D1, is more like the Midland group than the other two are, all three are speakers of mixed lects.

The terms we have used to interpret the correspondence analysis of these dialects of northwestern Ohio are very similar to the terms we used earlier in describing the transition zone for (u) and (a) in the east midlands of England in Chapter 8. This is not at all surprising. It is natural to find the same range of lects in the two places, although one is in England and the other in the United States, because both are transition zones.

9.4.5 *Linguistic distance and geographic distance*

One possible objection to multidimensional scaling is that it eliminates geographic distance in favour of statistical distance, so to speak. However, it is the difference between the two types of distance that proves to be one of the most telling aspects of the analysis. Compare the positions of the informants in Fig. 9-1 with their physical locations in Map 9-2. The similarities are remarkable, especially when you consider that the correspondence analysis encoded no information whatever about geography. Just as P1 and P2 are well removed from the others at the top of the scaling in Fig. 9-1, so their home town, Perrysburg, is removed from the others in the north on Map 9-2; V1, V2, US1 and US2 are at the bottom in the scaling and their home towns, Van Wert and Upper Sandusky, are the furthest south on the map; O2 is surrounded by the Vs and USs on the scaling and O2's home town, Ottawa, is between Van Wert and Upper Sandusky; D1 and D2 are in between the others just as Defiance, their home town, is between the other towns. The individual most out of line is O1, who is a considerable distance from his real-life neighbour O2 in the scaling, but a closer look at the map shows that the proximity of Ottawa to Defiance is about the same as its proximity to Van Wert. Evidently, some people in Ottawa speak more like their southerly neighbours in Van Wert and others speak more like their northerly neighbours in Defiance. The field records of Davis and McDavid fortuitously included one of each, and the multivariate analysis identified them as such.

The relationships among these ten informants are thus revealed with considerable precision by the quantitative analysis. It is hard to imagine a dialectologist, no matter how experienced, identifying those relationships as precise simply by making observations about the distribution of variants in the database. It is even harder to imagine drawing conclusions with perfect confidence based on observation alone. The database for this case study is small, just ten subjects using 59 variables with two or three variants each. Problems of reliable observation multiply when there are hundreds of subjects using hundreds of variables. Multivariate analysis and other statistical methods can be used to sort out the relationships in an impossibly complex database.

Quantitative methods in dialect geography make it possible for dialectologists to handle data in greater quantities than ever before. They also make it possible to deal with data of greater complexity. It is no longer necessary to place artificial restrictions on data-gathering in order to make dialect data manageable. It is no longer necessary, in other words, to abstract away from the natural variability of language – by, say, restricting the data to one question, or by recording only one answer, or by surveying only one speaker or one social group. When these strictures are removed, all areas look like transition areas.

The most elusive questions about language variation can only be answered by confronting linguistic variability in all its profusion – as ordinary human beings confront it daily as they go about their mundane tasks. Quantitative methods open the way to discovering patterns and relationships in even the most complex situations.

Further information

General discussions about the theoretical implications of variability in linguistic data may be found in Labov 1972b; Chambers 1995: chapters 1 and 5; and in Guy 1996.

Several articles and monographs have been written about the variable (C$\underline{C}$) in the various dialects in which it has been studied. For a general discussion of (C$\underline{C}$) in the black vernacular of New York City, see Labov 1972b: chapter 8; on the Detroit survey, see Wolfram and Fasold 1974: chapter 5. The study of (C$\underline{C}$) in rural northern England comes from Chambers 1982, based on the records from the SED as compiled in Orton and Halliday (eds.) 1962–3.

The striking example of implicational relationships in colour terms comes from Berlin and Kay 1969. The syntactic implication comes from Feagin 1979.

Dialectometry originates in Séguy 1973. One of Séguy's students, Dennis Philps, extended his methods influentially in *Atlas dialectométrique des Pyrénées* (1985). Influential applications of multivariate statistical programs to dialect data may be found in articles listed in the bibliography by Cichocki, Goebl, Kirk, Kretzschmar, Ogura, Thomas and Viereck.

For general discussion of multivariate statistics in linguistics, see Woods, Fletcher and Hughes 1986: chapters 14 and 15. See the classic article by Davis and McDavid 1950 and the response by Reed and Spicer 1952. The multidimensional scaling of the Ohio data is from Chambers 1997, an article that discusses many of the issues considered in 8.7 as well as in this chapter.

10

Diffusion: sociolinguistic and lexical

In this chapter and the next, we examine a number of hypotheses relating to diffusion, the study of the progress of linguistic innovations. The hypotheses attempt to answer different questions. First, we ask who the innovators are. The answer differs with the social circumstances surrounding the innovation, as we shall see, and we shall look at several studies from urban dialectology for the light they shed on the social factors behind the pattern of diffusion. Then we look at the topic more narrowly, seeking to discover what linguistic elements are the vehicles of innovation. A promising hypothesis, known as LEXICAL DIFFUSION, posits that the lexical formative is the primary vehicle for phonetic change at least. Finally, in the next chapter, we ask how innovations spread geographically and develop a geolinguistic model to account for it.

10.1 Real time and apparent time

Clearly, any study of the spread of a linguistic innovation will necessarily be comparative. The data must include evidence for the same population or at least for a comparable population from at least two different points in time. Ideally, one would like to have the results of a survey designed to elicit a particular variable at a particular time and then a replication of the same survey given to the same population after a lapse of several years. While it is inevitable that some members of the sample group would have altered their circumstances in the intervening years, moving upward socially, say, from the middle working class to the upper working class or changing neighbourhoods, there would nevertheless be large similarities between the populations that would permit nearly perfect confidence in the results of the comparison.

Unfortunately, such a replication, allowing a comparison of a population in two points of REAL TIME, is seldom possible. Too many other factors affect the sample group, such as unwillingness to participate a second time, emigration not only from the survey area but possibly even from the country so that some members cannot be located, death, and so on. A perfect replication is usually ruled out in practice.

However, it is possible to make a comparison of the data for a population in real time by lowering the standards somewhat from the ideal situation outlined above. If the same population cannot be located, it is still possible to locate a population in the survey area which is comparable to it. Thus one can control the independent variables by selecting a sample with the same numbers of males and females as the original survey, the same ethnic and social background, and even the same occupation, all in exactly the same survey area. The results obtained from the group can then be compared to the results obtained from the original group with a high level of confidence that any significant discrepancy between them is the result of a linguistic change in progress.

By correlating the data with the greatest discrepancies and the independent variables, one can determine which subgroups are the more innovative, which linguistic elements are carrying the innovation, and which districts within the survey area form the beach head of the innovation. In other words, one can study the mechanism of diffusion.

In fact, studies of populations in real time which involve comparable sample populations rather than identical populations have an obvious advantage in at least one respect. A comparable population can be surveyed at any interval following the original survey, be it a year, a decade, a century or (in theory, at least) a millennium. Needless to say, a survey of an identical population is constrained by the life span of its members. The unlimited interval is often necessary, because some innovations are notoriously slow – recall (u) and (a) in Chapter 8, which have progressed northward only a few miles in about three centuries – and some populations, such as the NORMs, are linguistically very conservative. Moreover, innovations tend to increase significantly from one generation to the next, more so than within the life span of the same generation, so that a survey which was constrained to the same generation might show an increase in some variable as time passed, but miss the much greater increase in the next generation which it might well have stimulated.

In theory, comparative studies based on real time spanning several generations provide the basis for describing linguistic diffusion. In fact, such studies are rare, and most of the attempts that have been made in this field are so hedged in by uncertainties and problems that they have not produced the strong hypotheses and principles that would stimulate research on diffusion.

The main cause is the inherent incomparability of much of the data that exists. Early surveys often were intended to 'cover' an area in a general way rather than concentrating on a particular variable. They are macro-surveys designed to elicit responses pertinent to several variables rather than micro-surveys intended to elicit a great deal of data about one or two variables. Researchers seeking to determine the progress of a variable must then dig out whatever data they can find from the earlier survey and attempt to design their own survey to elicit the same or similar data in the same stylistic context. Factors like these have seriously limited research based on real time.

Less ambitious real-time studies have, however, been undertaken, and their cumulative results are illuminating. Sociolinguists have revisited the sites of their earlier, more comprehensive urban dialect surveys and, in effect, double-checked the projections they made previously. The time lapse is necessarily brief – typically about fifteen years, although one project in Tsuruoka, Japan, has now completed three surveys at twenty-year intervals (1950, 1971, 1991). Real-time studies like these can provide crucial data for studies of innovation diffusion, social transmission, mechanisms of change, and many other fundamental concerns.

Research into diffusion has not depended upon studies in real time so much as on studies in APPARENT TIME (see 6.2). Studying the diffusion of innovations in apparent time involves surveying the differences between the speech of people of different ages in the same community, while controlling the other independent variables such as sex, social class and ethnicity.

Studies in apparent time as opposed to real time have the obvious disadvantage of limiting the time interval between the comparison groups, since the comparison groups must necessarily be made up of contemporaries. As was noted for real-time studies involving the same population, one life span may be too short an interval for studying diffusion.

Nevertheless, studies in apparent time have several advantages. Since the investigator of both comparison groups is the same person, factors like methodology, transcription and analysis can easily be made comparable. The data is not limited in artificial and unnatural ways either, since the researcher can simply go back for more as it is required. For these reasons, studies of diffusion have focused on apparent time rather than real time differences in recent research.

The validity of apparent-time studies hinges crucially upon the hypothesis that the speech of, say, 40-year-olds today directly reflects the speech of 20-year-olds twenty years ago and can thus be compared and contrasted meaningfully to the speech of 20-year-olds today. Differences in the speech of 40-year-olds and 20-year-olds with respect to some linguistic variable are attributed to the progress of a linguistic innovation in the twenty years that separate the two groups.

The relationship between real and apparent time may be more subtle than a simple equation of the two suggests. Social structures are dynamic, and any one of numerous social variables might alter in ways that impinge upon the progress of linguistic change and diffusion.

10.1.1 *Age-graded changes*

Sociolinguists are well aware of at least one kind of change that does not conform to the apparent-time hypothesis. These are age-graded changes, in which young people in a community alter their speech in predictable ways as they reach maturity. To take a simple example, many Canadian children learn the name of the last letter of the alphabet as *zee*, the name used by Americans. By the time they reach adulthood, however, most of them have changed their usage to *zed*, the name generally used in

Table 10-1. *Pre-adult groups in New York City approximate the speech of their parents more closely as they approach adulthood (from Labov 1964)*

Age	% conformity with adult norms
8–11	52
12–13	50
14–15	57
16–17	62

Canada (and, of course, everywhere but the United States). This change happens in successive generations. It is a recurring, continuous change.

If someone analysed an age-graded change like *zee*-to-*zed* in terms of the apparent-time hypothesis, they would be deceived. The results have the appearance of a change in progress: many children say *zee*, but fewer adolescents do, and almost no adults do. Making a prediction from this pattern that *zed* is being replaced by *zee* in Canada is clearly wrong. Instead, the pattern of diminishing use of *zee* as people mature recurs in successive generations.

Age-graded changes like these are among the ways that children accommodate to adult society as they grow older. They are part of growing up, like exchanging short pants for long trousers or a knapsack for a briefcase.

Minor adjustments in speech as children and adolescents attain adulthood may be more common than we have recognised. One indication of the complexity of the relationship is suggested by Labov's study of the children of some of his New York informants, which showed that the speech of the children underwent a continuous process of acculturation so that older children more closely approximated the speech of their parents.

The process of acculturation is shown in Table 10-1, where the older groups progressively show a higher percentage of conformity to their parents. In other words, the process of acculturation goes on long after language acquisition is completed, and discrepancies between two age groups may be resolved by the acculturation process rather than representing the diffusion of an innovation in the community (cf. 6.2.1).

However, data like these do not vitiate the hypothesis of apparent time because it is predicated largely on the speech of children and adolescents, whose flexibility as language users is well known. A comparison of the speech of two adult groups would show much less acculturation, perhaps even none.

Normally, differences in the speech of younger and older people in the same community represent changes in progress. The younger people retain the features as they grow older, as the apparent-time hypothesis predicts they will, and the next generation comes along and increases the difference between them and their elders. The historical pattern is one of waves of innovation moving through society in the course of time. Viewed from a great distance, the pattern results in cataclysmic long-term differences, as Shakespeare's contemporaries differ from our own. Viewed from up close, as sociolinguistics does, the pattern appears as relatively small, incremental variations between successive generations. In the next section, we look more closely at the carriers of those innovations.

10.2 Innovators of change

In the progress of any linguistic (or other) change, it is natural that some element of society should take the lead. Since the rise of urban dialectology, linguists have been able to ascertain the social groups that are in the vanguard of a particular innovation by correlating the linguistic variables with independent variables like age, sex, social class, ethnic group and geographical region. Very often, several of the independent variables combine to identify the innovating group but occasionally, usually under interesting social circumstances, one of the variables clearly takes precedence over all others and it is possible to identify the innovators as, say, women (regardless of age, social class, etc.) or young people (regardless of sex, social class, etc.) or some other social group. Some instances where one of the variables takes precedence are discussed in this section, because they are sociologically interesting and because they provide clear cases from which the more complex cases may be seen to follow. In the following sections, three such variables are discussed under the rubric class-based, sex-based and age-based.

10.2.1 *A class-based innovation in Norwich*

In studies of urban dialects to date, social class has proved to be the most likely independent variable to correlate with linguistic innovation. This fact would seem to be no more than the expected consequence of what most people know about society. That is, if we think of our society as being stratified into a working class and a middle class, it is common knowledge that it is the individuals in the groups closest to the middle who generally appear to be the most mobile, whereas those at either end tend to be the most stable or conservative.

If we make the stratification even finer, dividing the working class into lower, middle and upper strata and the middle class into lower and middle strata, we can identify the most mobile groups by the labels upper working class (UWC) and lower middle class (LMC). Since these groups tend to be most actively involved in changing (or 'improving') their place on the social scale, they also tend to be the groups whose speech diverges most markedly from the norms of the social groups below them on the scale. Hence a familiar pattern in a graphic representation of a linguistic variable is the one shown in Fig. 10-1, where the values along the abscissa range from more formal (word-list and reading-passage) styles at 0 to less formal (interview and

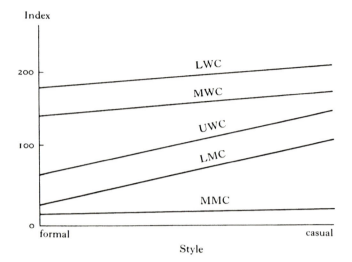

Fig. 10-1. Representation of a typical variable, with greater linguistic variation among the more mobile lower-middle and upper-working classes

casual speech) styles as one goes to the right. On the ordinate, the index values are scored in such a way that the lowest score, 0, represents the standard speech reflex (say RP, or urban Canadian English) for the variable under consideration and higher scores indicate a relatively greater frequency of nonstandard variants. The hypothetical situation shown in Fig. 10-1 is quite typical, if somewhat stylised. The upward slope of the lines show that the variable increases for all social classes in casual speech although the highest class, MMC, does not deviate from the standard much in any case. The two lowest groups, MWC and LWC, use nonstandard reflexes in all styles. However, the middle groups, UWC and LMC, while they hold their places relative to the MMC and the MWC, reveal a much greater variety, approaching the MMC norms in careful speech and the WC norms in casual speech. That is, their linguistic behaviour, at least with respect to the hypothetical variable considered here, directly reflects their greater mobility in the society.

Fig. 10-1 represents a situation that is common enough to be taken as the norm. Situations which diverge from it in striking ways are generally the result of a particular stratum of society asserting itself by taking the lead in an innovation. In a classic case, Labov discovered that fishermen on the island of Martha's Vineyard were at the leading edge of an innovation involving centralisation of diphthongs, and that the rest of the permanent population of the island had increasingly adopted this linguistic feature as a marker to distinguish themselves from the large tourist population that invades their island each summer.

Another striking divergence is shown in Fig. 10-2, based on the variable (e) studied in the city of Norwich (see 6.2.1). Variable (e) involves the pronunciation of /ɛ/ before

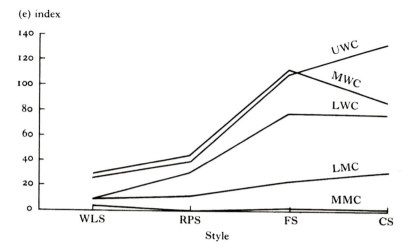

(e) index

Fig. 10-2. Class differences for the variable (e) in Norwich (after Trudgill 1974a). In contrast
to Fig. 10-1, the MWC and UWC speakers are unexpectedly further from the
standard than are the LWC speakers

[l] in words like *well, tell* and *bell*. The index score along the ordinate represents the
standard (RP) reflex [ɛ] as 0, a slightly centralised variant [æ̈ ~ ɜ] as 100, and a more
centralised variant [ɒ ~ Ẍ] as 200. As Fig. 10-2 shows, the UWC and MWC groups
are clearly out of line with other groups in Norwich. Comparing Fig. 10-2 with
Fig. 10-1, it seems clear that the MMC assumes its expected position, approximating
the standard norm in all styles, and the LMC, immediately above the MMC, is also
in a typical position. However, in the working-class groups, the class hierarchy has
been overturned, with both the MWC and UWC showing more centralisation than
the LWC. The configuration is explained by regarding the middle-class groups and
the LWC as the old order.

A generation or so ago, the UWC and MWC no doubt assumed typical positions
in the gap between LMC and LWC, but now they are initiating a change in terms of
centralisation. The relatively steep gradient for the LWC in Fig. 10-2 suggests that
this group is now starting to participate in the change, with significant centralising in
the more casual styles and much less in more formal styles. In other words, the unusual
representation of Fig. 10-2 results from the fact that Norwich is in the early stages of
a change with respect to centralisation of /ɛ/, and the UWC and MWC are the innovators of the change. (For another example of a class-based innovation, see 6.3.1.)

10.2.2 *A sex-based innovation in Belfast*

Research on two variables in Ballymacarrett, the working-class enclave
of Protestant east Belfast in Northern Ireland, reveals paradoxical results with respect

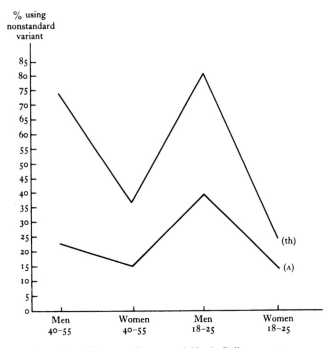

Fig. 10-3. Sex and age differences for two variables in Ballymacarrett,
Belfast (after Milroy 1976)

to the behaviour of males and females. Variable (th) measures the percentage of deletion of [ð] medially in words like *mother* [mɔːər], *brother*, *other* and *bother*; variable
(ʌ) measures the percentage of nonrounded [ʌ] in a set of lexical items that includes
pull, push, took, shook, would, stood (but never in *cook, book, wood, soot* and *wool*).

As Fig. 10-3 shows, younger men and older men all score significantly higher on
both variables than do women (and *all* speakers belong to the working class). Even
more striking, the variables are apparently on the rise in the male population since
younger men have higher scores than older men by about 6 per cent for (th) and
17 per cent for (ʌ) – while at the same time (ʌ) is about the same for younger and
older women and (th) is actually declining. Both variables are well-known markers
of working-class speech in Belfast, and (ʌ) is openly stigmatised there and a source of
embarrassment when it is discussed. Fig. 10-3 suggests that the men in Ballymacarrett
are remaining entrenched in the working class while the women are making linguistic
innovations in the direction of standard speech, and the social circumstances in
Belfast reinforce this interpretation.

To make sense of Fig. 10-3, it is essential to understand that Ballymacarrett is a
self-contained area in the sense that it has its own industrial district where most of
the men work, within a two-minute walk from their homes. They work in similar

occupations and interact socially within the district. When young men leave school, they generally enter the plants in the district and frequent the same pubs and clubs as their fathers. On the other hand, the women live much less restricted lives. Many older women work as office cleaners outside the district, and the younger women often have clerical jobs across the river. The younger women especially tend to have social as well as occupational ties beyond the boundaries of Ballymacarrett. Consequently, the women are the innovators of linguistic change in the district.

10.2.3 An age-based innovation in the Golden Horseshoe

For an innovation to be purely age-based, it must involve the replacement of a linguistic feature by all the younger speakers in a community regardless of their social class, sex and other social characteristics. Changes that are adopted by young people across the social spectrum are likely to be innovations that eliminate features that have become stigmatised or come to be regarded as old-fashioned.

In Canada, the recent fate of the lexical item *chesterfield* follows this pattern. In the first half of this century, *chesterfield* was the generic term for the upholstered piece of furniture that two or three people sit on in the living room. The term originated in England as the name for a particularly grand, horsehair-stuffed, leather-covered sofa that could be found in manor houses in the nineteenth century. Exactly how it got transplanted to the New World as the general term for any kind of long, upholstered seat, no matter how humble or grand, is unclear. It occurs as the generic term in a few American regions such as northern California but only in Canada was it the standard term used in all regions and by all social classes.

This situation started changing around mid-century, when young people began using other words in its place. Table 10-2 shows the proportions of people who use either *couch* or *chesterfield* or *sofa*, the three most common terms in Canada nowadays. (Note that the percentages do not add up to 100 in all rows because a few people gave minor responses or idiosyncratic words – *davenport, settee, love seat, love couch, lounge, divan, bank* and *chair*.) These figures come from a survey of almost a thousand people in the part of Canada known as the Golden Horseshoe, the U-shaped region at the western end of Lake Ontario where about 5 million people, almost one-fifth of Canada's population, live.

Table 10-2 subdivides the sample population into age groups, with teenagers (14–19) at the top, people over 80 at the bottom, and the middle groups by decades. It is important for our purposes here to emphasise that age is the only statistically significant social factor that correlates with the use of *chesterfield*; other factors such as sex, social class and ethnic background do not play a role in determining how the change is moving through society.

Reading down the columns in Table 10-2, the main directions of the change are readily apparent. *Couch* is easily the commonest term among the youngest groups, used

Table 10-2. *Occurrences of the words* couch, chesterfield *and* sofa *in the Golden Horseshoe (Chambers 1995a)*

Age	couch	chesterfield	sofa
14–19	85.0%	6.0%	6.0%
20–29	78.9	6.2	13.5
30–39	65.5	16.3	18.0
40–49	48.7	30.7	19.9
50–59	23.5	54.6	21.8
60–69	20.5	69.2	2.5
70–79	9.5	66.7	19.0
over 80	5.9	72.6	13.0

by 85 per cent of the teenagers. In fact, it is the majority term for everyone under 40. The distribution of *chesterfield* is almost the mirror-image: it is the majority term for everyone over 50.

Thus *chesterfield* shows a steady decrease and *couch* shows a steady increase. By contrast, *sofa* is sporadically represented. It is not the majority term for any age group, though it occurs as a variant in every age group. It appears to be a neutral alternative for people of all ages, because it is associated neither with the very old nor with the very young.

Chesterfield did become associated with the very old, and therein lies the key to its decline. Its use suddenly came to be considered quaint and old-fashioned. At first, *sofa* seems to have gained some currency as a possible alternative, but *couch* took hold in the speech of people now in their 40s, and from that point the use of *couch* accelerated. The rapidity of the change is illustrated in Fig. 10-4, which shows the age correlations for *couch* and *chesterfield* (ignoring other responses).

The chronology of the decline of *chesterfield* and the rise of *couch* can be inferred readily from the apparent-time display in Fig. 10-4. The lines on the graph intersect between the 40-year-olds and the 50-year-olds. In the 1930s, when the 50-year-olds were born, *chesterfield* was used by almost everyone in the community. In the 1950s, when the people in their 30s were born, it was declining as *couch* supplanted it, and by the 1970s, when the youngest group represented here was born, it was a word heard almost exclusively in the speech of older people.

Of course, there is nothing intrinsic in the word *chesterfield* that makes people think of it as an old-fashioned word. It is, in an objective sense, no older or younger than any other common word, including *couch* and *sofa*. The forces that underlie language change are sometimes impelled by attitudes, and sometimes those attitudes are formed by transitory fads and fancies. The rapid rise and decline of slang terms is an obvious example, and one that people are often very self-conscious about. But other

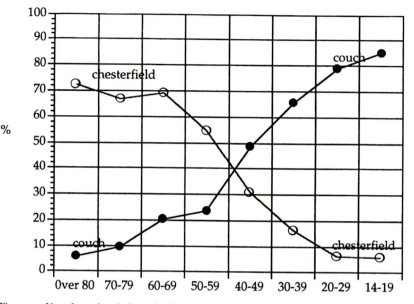

Fig. 10-4. Use of *couch* and *chesterfield* by different age groups (Chambers 1995a)

features of language can also be affected by fashion, and when they are, the fashionable trends often cut through social barriers and appeal to young people throughout the community.

10.3 **Lexical diffusion**

By correlating linguistic innovation with sociological variables, we are able to ascertain vital information about the social dimensions of linguistic diffusion. We would also like to understand the linguistic aspect of diffusion, that is, the means by which linguistic innovations get realised in the grammars of the speakers of a language. The history of linguistic science is not, of course, devoid of attempts to answer this fairly obvious question. However, the proposed answers have actually left in their wake a number of imponderables, and many linguists have begun to question the validity of the answers.

In recent linguistic history, there have been two slightly different ways of conceptualising the mechanism of change. We will call them structuralist and generativist, after the general frameworks in which the concepts originated. To illustrate the difference as simply as possible, consider a prototypical situation in which a particular language at time 1 has a phoneme /n/ that is realised phonetically as [ŋ] before velar consonants and as [n] elsewhere. Then in a later development at time 2, velar consonants are lost in some positions, but the velar nasals are retained. For the structuralists, language change is characterised by the maxim, 'Phonemes change'. Thus the change in the language at time 2 can fairly be described as a phonemic change with two phonemes, /n/ and /ŋ/, where at time 1 there was only /n/. For the generativists, this change might be seen as rule addition. At time 1, the language has a rule assimilating /n/ to [ŋ] before velar consonants. At time 2, when velar nasals occur in positions in which velar consonants do not follow them, the difference is the result of a rule of velar consonant deletion which applies after nasal assimilation. Thus the language has one more rule at time 2 than it had at time 1.

Either of these conceptions describes the situation adequately if we look no further than the static descriptions at time 1 and time 2. A more interesting question that arises with respect to both theories is the means by which the change was carried out. What happens if we look at the language in the interval *between* time 1 and time 2? Is there a moment in that interval when suddenly /ŋ/ emerges as a phoneme, or velar consonant deletion suddenly emerges as a rule? Such a development seems simply implausible.

In fact, neither school offers an answer to the question. The reason for their silence may be simply that neither school concerned itself seriously with the interval between time 1 and time 2. In order to look at the interval it is necessary to deal with variability. The dynamics of language change inescapably reveal contending variants in apparently unstable or unresolved distributions. Instead of completed changes, in the interval we are confronted with changes in progress.

At least one branch of structuralism maintained that one could not *in principle* observe a sound change in progress, thus ruling out studies of the interval. However, many of the most interesting developments of contemporary linguistics (and much of this book) result from observations of sound changes in progress, and there seems to be no real reason not to study the interval. By doing so, one must come to grips with the developmental stages between the initiation and the completion of phonemic change, or of rule addition.

Certainly one very important part of the answer appears to be what is known as LEXICAL DIFFUSION, the theory that a linguistic change spreads gradually across the lexicon, from word to word. In the hypothetical example we have been using, the emergence of velar nasals without following velar consonants, the words which at time 1 are heard with sequences of [ŋk] undergo change one at a time, so that at time 1[a] perhaps one or two members of the set are heard with [ŋ] alone or, more likely, occur variably with [ŋk] or [ŋ]; at time 1[b], other members of the set vary and some are exclusively heard with [ŋ]; at time 1[c], more members are involved in variability and change; and the change spreads throughout the lexicon in this fashion until at time 2, all – or, more realistically, most – of the words in the set have undergone the change. Thus the hypothesis of lexical diffusion maintains that *phonological change is lexically gradual.*

For dialectologists, the theory of lexical diffusion has instant credibility because it gives theoretical status to the kind of variety that is a commonplace of dialect surveys.

Table 10-3. *Lexical variants among speakers in the transition zone for the variable (u):* x = [ʌ]; o = *either* [ʊ] *or* [ɤ]; / = *variation;* – = *no data*

Lexical items	Speaker												
	1	2	3	4	5	6	7	8	9	10	11	12	13
must	x	x	x	x	x	–	x	/	x	x	o	o	o
dozen	x	x	x	x	x	/	x	o	o	o	o	/	o
other	x	x	x	x	x	x	x	/	/	o	o	o	o
come	x	x	x	x	x	x	x	o	o	o	x	x	o
stubble	x	x	x	x	x	x	o	x	x	o	o	o	o
does	x	x	x	x	x	o	–	o	o	o	o	o	o
cousin	x	x	x	x	x	o	o	o	o	o	x	o	o
done	x	/	x	x	x	/	o	o	o	o	/	o	o
duck	x	x	/	x	/	/	/	o	o	/	/	o	/
thumb	x	x	x	x	o	o	x	o	o	o	/	x	o
shut	x	x	x	x	x	o	o	o	x	x	o	o	o
sun	x	x	x	x	x	o	x	o	o	x	o	o	o
hungry	x	x	x	x	x	o	o	o	o	o	o	o	o
up	x	x	x	x	x	o	o	o	o	o	o	o	–
hundred	x	x	x	x	o	o	o	o	o	o	o	o	o
pups	x	x	x	x	o	x	o	o	o	o	o	o	o
cud	x	x	x	o	x	x	o	o	o	o	o	o	o
butter	o	x	x	x	o	x	x	o	x	o	o	/	o
gull	x	x	o	x	o	o	x	o	o	o	–	o	–
uncle	x	x	x	x	o	o	o	o	o	x	o	o	o

Consider, for example, variable (u), the slow-moving innovation centred in East Anglia and the east midlands of England discussed in Chapter 8 (especially 8.2 and 8.3). To the north, words like *must* and *dozen* occur invariably with the vowel [ʊ] in the stressed syllable, whereas to the south they have [ʌ]. In the transition zone between the two regions, either vowel can occur in any word.

Table 10-3 gives an indication of the variety by plotting the variation in twenty words. There are thirteen speakers, and some of them pronounce words like *must* and *dozen* with [ʌ], others with [ʊ] or [ɤ], and still others use both vowels. The items at the top of the list in Table 10-3 are ahead of the ones at the bottom (where 'x' marks the innovation and 'o' the old order), and many of them are heard with competing pronunciations (marked as '/') from the same speaker.

Faced with data like this and a hypothesis that 'phonemes change', what conclusion can a dialectologist draw? Determining any phonemic analysis on the basis of data like this is a problem, to say the least. The hypothesis that 'new rules are added' is no more helpful. The variety in Table 10-3 does not seem to be rule-governed, at least not in any sense that that term is used currently. However, the hypothesis that

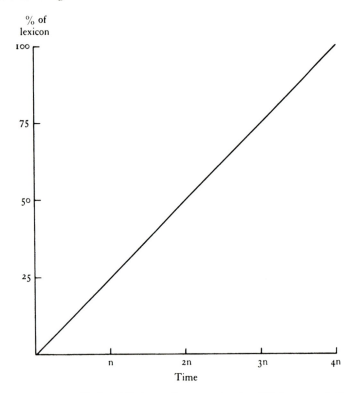

Fig. 10-5. Progress of lexical diffusion on the assumption that diffusion proceeds through the lexicon at a uniform rate

change is 'lexically gradual' fits the data, since it predicts that in any ongoing change some words will undergo the innovation before others. In other words, lexical diffusion accommodates the kind of heterogeneity that exists in transition zones.

If lexical diffusion can be studied at various stages of its progress, we should be able to determine how it proceeds through the lexicon. Here, the simplest hypothesis would be that diffusion occurs at a uniform rate. This situation is represented graphically in Fig. 10-5, which shows the percentage of lexical items that have undergone the change along the ordinate and the time interval on the abscissa. The progress of diffusion is uniform, taking in 25 per cent of the lexicon in each interval n.

It follows from this hypothesis that any case study of a change in progress should in principle have an equal probability of 'catching' it at any point in its progress. However, it happens that changes almost never are found in the middle of their time span – around 50 per cent – and are most often found at one of the two extremes – above 80 per cent or below 20 per cent. This remarkable fact is already such a common observation in variation studies that it effectively refutes an assumption of uniform rate of change.

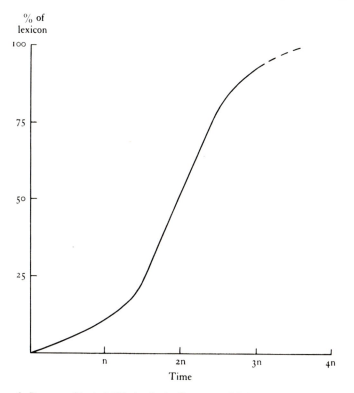

Fig. 10-6. Progress of lexical diffusion in the S-curve model, based on the assumption that diffusion is more rapid in the middle stages than at initiation and completion

In its place, we assume a rate of change that is quite rapid in the middle stages and slower at its beginning and end. This assumption is called the S-CURVE model of diffusion, after the figure that represents it, shown in Fig. 10-6. Here, the first 20 per cent of the diffusion is represented as taking about $1.5n$ and the final 20 per cent takes the same. In between, the rate of diffusion rises rapidly, so that the middle 60 per cent takes only $1n$. This representation predicts that studies of diffusion will much more commonly discover diffusions at the beginning stages and at the end stages than in the middle. This is strongly supported by the available evidence.

Looking again at the speakers with variable (u) in Table 10-3, it is possible to arrange them along a continuum according to the percentage of the lexical data for each that has undergone change from [ʊ] to [ʌ]. (The percentages are calculated from the data in Map 8-2 above.) Of the thirteen speakers, six fall into percentages above 79, and another five have percentages below 20. That leaves only two of them in the large middle area.

Fig. 10-7 is a graphic representation of these facts. As can be seen, the line in the graph forms a rough S-curve, of the type we have been discussing. However, one

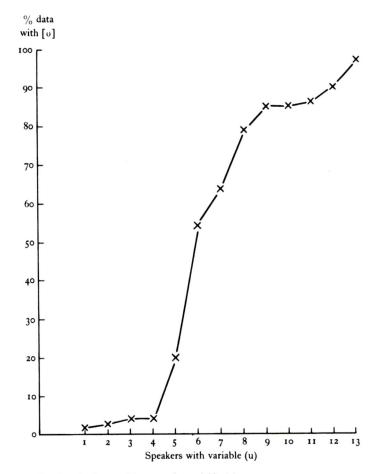

Fig. 10-7. Speakers in the transition zone for variable (u)

significant difference is seen by contrasting it with Fig. 10-6. While the ordinates in both figures represent the same value, the percentage of the lexicon that has undergone change, the abscissae represent different values, the former being time and the latter different speakers in the transition zone.

This distinction allows us to return to the discussion of real time and apparent time that opened this chapter, because Fig. 10-7 is really just an apparent-time representation of Fig. 10-6, which is based on real time. In other words, Fig. 10-6 could describe a single speaker in a transition zone who is recorded on several different occasions in real time (at time n, $2n$, etc.); in that case the S-curve would describe that speaker's personal progress through a linguistic change. However, in the research on variable (u), real-time data for any speaker is not available. Instead, the progress of the change is represented inferentially by describing contemporaries in the transition zone. Some people in the transition zone are further ahead in the change than others. Assuming that those people with low percentages will eventually move into the middle areas and then into the high percentages in the course of time, then the progress of this change can be viewed in apparent time by looking at the cross-section of speakers at different stages.

Further information

For a general discussion of real and apparent time, see Labov 1994: chapter 1. REAL-TIME studies in which sociolinguists revisit sites of earlier urban dialect surveys include Cedergren in Panama (1988), Trudgill in Norwich (1988), Thibault and Daveluy in Montreal (1989), and Bailey, Wikle Tillery and Sand in Texas (1991). The real-time study in Tsuruoka, Japan, and the age-graded change in Canada cited in this chapter come from Chambers 1995: chapter 4. APPARENT-TIME studies are more common, beginning with Labov's influential discussion (1966: chapter 9). Studies have been made by Gal in Oberwart, Austria (1979), Cheshire in Reading, England (1982), Horvath in Sydney (1985), Eckert in Detroit (1989), Chambers in the Golden Horseshoe (1998), and many others. The case of the fishermen on Martha's Vineyard is in Labov 1972b: chapter 1. The innovation by the working class in Norwich is in Trudgill 1974a, especially chapter 7. The sex-based innovation is adapted from Milroy 1976. The age-based innovation is in Chambers 1995a.

Of several very good papers on lexical diffusion, perhaps the most thorough discussions are by Chen and Hsieh 1971, Chen and Wang 1975 and Phillips 1984. The references in these articles provide a good indication of the research on lexical diffusion up to their publication dates.

11
Diffusion: geographical

For many years, people studying geographic diffusion assumed that innovations spread continuously along immigration routes or transportation lines. This conception was often expressed by analogy to a wave. The 'wave model' visualised innovation diffusion as a pebble-in-a-pond effect, with a centre of influence (the point of impact of the pebble) sending ripples outwards in all directions (the movement of the wave).

A more accurate analogy in the light of studies made in the last fifty years would be skipping a stone across a pond. Innovations diffuse discontinuously from one centre of influence to other centres (the successive points where the stone hits) and from each of those into the intervening regions (in waves that sometimes overlap). In other words, innovations leap from one place, usually a city, to another place, another city or large town, and then move into the places between, such as towns and villages.

This view is largely due to the Swedish geographer Torsten Hägerstrand, who tracked the spread of several innovations across the landscape. Although Hägerstrand's evidence came from non-linguistic innovations such as the spread of the automobile and of controls against bovine tuberculosis, there was no reason to think that the regional diffusion of linguistic innovations would work differently.

Indeed, dialectologists who know Hägerstrand's work and that of his followers are very likely to think of analogous cases having to do with linguistic innovations. Some well-known dialect features with hitherto puzzling distributions now become comprehensible. As we show in Map 11-6 below, the distribution of uvular /r/ in European vernaculars takes in not only a large continuous region encompassing Paris, Marseille, Stuttgart and Cologne, but also discontinuous areas on the periphery. The discontinuous regions are all dominated by large cultural centres: the Hague, Berlin, Copenhagen and Bergen. The distribution, of course, makes perfect sense when we know that innovations skip from one centre to others.

In this chapter, we look first at several examples of areal diffusion (11.1-4), and illustrate the dynamics of innovations that diffuse at different rates for different social groups (11.5-6). Finally, we develop a gravity model (in 11.7-8) that directly encodes the essential insight that geolinguistic diffusion is a function of population and distance.

11.1 Spatial diffusion of language

Linguistic changes may spread from social group to social group (sociolinguistic diffusion); from word to word (lexical diffusion); and from one linguistic environment to another (linguistic diffusion). They may also, as we have noted earlier in this book, spread from place to place. This spatial diffusion of linguistic innovations often constitutes a kind of reflection of the other types of diffusion.

To take a specific example: we know that there has been a linguistic change in English (see 6.1.3) such that /j/ has been lost before /uː/ in words like *rule* /rjuːl/ > /ruːl/ and *lute* /ljuːt/ > /luːt/. In the eastern counties of England it seems that this change was more general than in other areas, and that it has spread socially, so that working-class varieties have it to a greater extent than middle-class varieties; lexically, so that /j/-loss is less common in some words (such as *educate*) than in others (such as *due*); and linguistically, so that /j/-loss is more common after some consonants, such as /s/ *suit*, /t/ *tune*, /d/ *due*, than after others, such as /k/ *cue*, /v/ *view*. These three types of diffusion have also spread geographically, with the result that there is a higher level of /j/-loss ((a) for more speakers, (b) in more words, (c) after more consonants, (d) with a higher frequency) in the east of the region in question than on the periphery. In parts of Lincolnshire, for instance, it is perhaps only working-class speakers who demonstrate /j/-loss, and infrequently, in a relatively small number of words after relatively few consonants, while in eastern Norfolk most people have /j/-loss frequently, in most words, and after all consonants.

As we have shown in 8.7 and elsewhere, it is difficult to illustrate this kind of situation accurately on maps. Nevertheless, in order to achieve an understanding of geographical diffusion of linguistic forms, we must look at it in greater social and linguistic detail. It is therefore necessary to develop cartographical techniques and a methodology to enable us to do so. This will be especially valuable if we wish to learn how exactly it is that linguistic innovations are spread from one place to another.

11.2 Spatial linguistics

We have already discussed, in Chapter 7, the spread of changes along rivers and the presence of relic areas, which are all topics that presuppose an interest in geographical diffusion. Given the historical orientation of early dialectology, it was also of interest to dialect geographers to discover that dialect maps could be used as a research tool in investigating the probable route of a linguistic change and in shedding light on problems such as the relative age of two current linguistic forms.

Observations such as these in fact led to the development of a whole new school of linguistics. 'Neolinguistics', later 'spatial linguistics', was developed in Italy in the 1920s, and was based partly on five principles or areal norms which were to be used in the study of historical linguistics. The three of the norms that were genuinely geographical were:

1. If, of two linguistic forms, one is found in isolated areas and the other in areas more accessible, then the former is the older.

2. If, of two linguistic forms, one is found in peripheral areas and the other in central areas, then the former is the older.

3. If, of two forms, one is used over a larger area than the other, then that is the older.

'Spatial linguistics' eventually became discredited as a method of historical linguistics because the principles were sometimes contradictory, and many exceptions to them could be found. For example, full /j/-loss in England is geographically peripheral but is actually an innovation. That is, it conforms to principle (3) but contradicts principle (2).

The chief problem with 'neolinguistics' was that the school attempted to work with these principles as if they were laws, whereas they are really simply tendencies. As guidelines, rather than laws, they do however have considerable validity. Map 7-5 (p. 95), for example, shows the geographical distribution of postvocalic /r/ (see 3.2.1) in conservative dialects in Britain. The map shows that there are three main separate *r*-ful areas, but only one continuous *r*-less area. This suggests very strongly, as already discussed in 7.2, that it is the loss of postvocalic /r/ which is the innovation. It would be most unlikely for an identical innovation to have started in three widely separated areas at once. (We of course already know that /r/-loss is the innovation from the spelling and many other sources.) It can therefore be assumed that the loss of /r/ began somewhere in the east of the country. The innovation has subsequently spread northwards and westwards, forming wedgelike patterns which divided an originally unified, conservative *r*-ful area into three. (Note that there are also relic areas on the east coast. The *r*-ful area in southwest Wales is the result of early immigration from England.)

11.3 Linguistic areas

The diffusion of linguistic innovations can also have geographically more far-reaching consequences. It has often been observed that languages which are spoken in the same general geographical region tend to have features in common even if they are not closely related historically. Isoglosses can be drawn for many linguistic features which bear no relation to language frontiers. In continental Europe, for example, the front rounded vowels [ø] and [y] occur in a geographical area (see Map 11-1) which includes Finnish, Swedish, Norwegian, Danish, German, Dutch and French. Note that, while standard German has these vowels, many southern dialects do not, and that, while standard Italian does not have them, northwestern Italian dialects do. The affricate /ʧ/, on the other hand, occurs only in geographically peripheral languages in Europe. It is found in the standard varieties of English, Spanish, Italian, Hungarian and the Slavic languages, but not in German, Dutch, French or Scandinavian.

Map 11-1. Front rounded vowels in northwestern Europe (to the north and west of the line)

In many cases, we can assume that areal features of this type are the result of linguistic innovations originating in one dialect and then spreading to neighbouring varieties – the NEIGHBOURHOOD EFFECT – regardless of language boundaries, presumably through the medium of bilingual individuals. Where this type of diffusion has taken place on a large scale it is usual to talk of LINGUISTIC AREAS. (The German term *Sprachbund* is also used.)

The best-known linguistic area in Europe is undoubtedly the Balkans. The languages spoken in this area, particularly Romanian, Bulgarian, Macedonian, Albanian and Greek, are not for the most part closely related, but nevertheless show striking resemblances to one another in many respects. The most striking example of this similarity, and the best known, is the fact that four of these languages, Albanian, Bulgarian, Macedonian and Romanian, all have a postposed definite article:

> Romanian: *lup – lupul*
> Albanian: *ujk – ujku*
> 'wolf' – 'the wolf'

This feature does not occur in languages which are historically related to the Balkan languages but which happen not to be spoken in the Balkans, such as Italian (in the case of Romanian) or Russian (in the case of Bulgarian).

11.4 Uvular /r/ in Europe

One linguistic feature that has undergone a remarkable degree of geographical diffusion across language frontiers is the European uvular /r/. Originally, all the languages of Europe had a consonant /r/ pronounced as an apical trill [r] or flap [ɾ]. However, at some stage, the /r/ in Parisian French began to be pronounced with the back rather than the front of the tongue, as a dorsal uvular or velar trill, fricative or continuant [ʀ] or [ʁ]. Since that time this pronunciation has spread not only within French but also across language boundaries, with the result that today it is standard in French, German and Danish, and is quite normal in many varieties of Dutch, Swedish and Norwegian.

It is possible to plot its progress to a certain extent. Beginning in Paris probably in the 1600s, uvular /r/ had reached Copenhagen by 1780, and by 1890 had spread to southern Sweden, where it has remained stationary since the 1930s (see Map 11-2).

Map 11-2 shows the current distribution of uvular /r/ in Europe. Like most traditional linguistic maps, however, this map is inadequate in a number of ways. First, it is not able to take account of linguistic diffusion of the type discussed above (11.1). In a large area of Sweden, for example, [ʀ] has replaced [r] in some phonological environments but not in others: [r] occurs, for example, word-finally, and [ʀ] word-initially. The frontier area in southern Sweden where this occurs is shown in Map 11-3.

Secondly, Map 11-2 gives the impression that the situation is a static one rather than a dynamic one. There is, however, at least one area, a thousand miles from Paris, where the change is still spreading, three hundred years later. Map 11-4 shows those areas of southern and western Norway where speakers born about 1900 have uvular /r/, while Map 11-5 shows the – much larger – area where speakers born in about 1960 have this pronunciation.

Thirdly, Map 11-2 does not show the frequency with which [ʀ] is used, nor in how many words. In some parts of Norway and Sweden, for instance, many speakers use both types of /r/ inconsistently and in different proportions.

Finally, Map 11-2 gives no social detail, which is unfortunate, given our knowledge of the importance of social mechanisms in the diffusion of linguistic innovations. Map 11-6 is an improvement in this respect. It will be observed that, by giving more social information, Map 11-6 also gives us more useful information on the subject of *how* the uvular /r/ innovation was diffused. We can see that the change has taken place through gradual spread as far as large parts of France and neighbouring

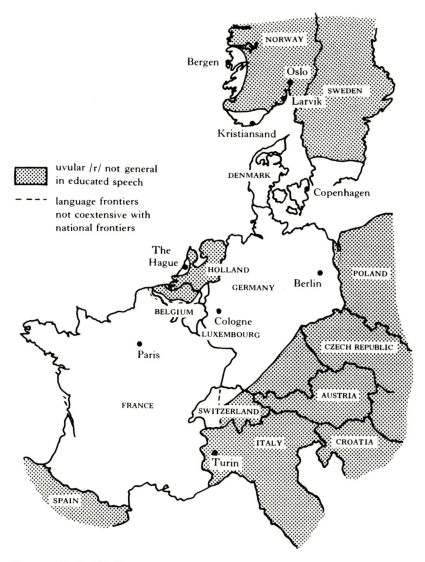

Map 11-2. Uvular /r/ in Europe (after Trudgill 1974c)

areas of Belgium, Switzerland and southwestern Germany are concerned. But it is also clear that elsewhere the diffusion has taken the form of 'jumping' from one urban centre to another, especially The Hague, Cologne, Berlin, Copenhagen, Kristiansand and Bergen. (This can also be seen in Maps 11-4 and 11-5.) Essentially Map 11-2 obscures the role of the urban centre in the diffusion of linguistic innovations.

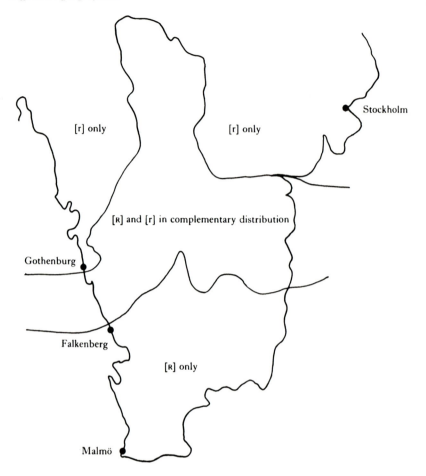

Stockholm

[r] only   [r] only

[ʀ] and [r] in complementary distribution

Gothenburg

Falkenberg

[ʀ] only

Malmö

Map 11-3. Uvular /r/ in southern Sweden

11.5 Diffusion down the urban hierarchy

It is, of course, no surprise that urban centres are important in the spreading of innovations, but our knowledge of how this works has recently become more detailed. For example, as in many other areas of the northern USA, the vowel /æ/ in Chicago English is gradually being raised and diphthongised from [æ] through [ɛ] to [eə], as in *bad* [beəd]. In other parts of the Chicago area of northern Illinois the same development is also taking place. In a recent study, younger speakers (female students at Northern Illinois University) were recorded, and ascribed index scores for the raising of /æ/, in the manner outlined in Chapter 4, using (æ) as a linguistic variable with the variants:

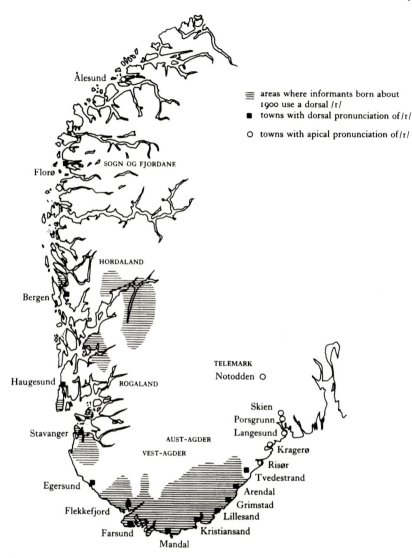

≡ areas where informants born about
  1900 use a dorsal /r/
■ towns with dorsal pronunciation of /r/

○ towns with apical pronunciation of /r/

Map 11-4. Uvular /r/ in Norway, older speakers (after Foldvik n.d.)

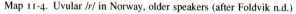

(æ)-1 = [εə]
(æ)-2 = [ε]
(æ)-3 = [ε˕]
(æ)-4 = [æ˔]
(æ)-5 = [æ]

These index scores were then averaged, not for social-class groups, as in the original quantitative urban dialect studies, but for geographical area – in this case counties.

173

areas where informants born about 1960 use a dorsal /r/

■ towns with dorsal pronunciation of /r/

○ towns with apical pronunciation of /r/

Map 11-5. Uvular /r/ in Norway, younger speakers (after Foldvik n.d.)

Map 11-7 gives the average score per county. It will be observed that there seems to be no pattern to the geographical distribution of vowel height, and that distance from Chicago appears to be relatively unimportant in spite of the fact that it is an obvious assumption that this very large urban centre will play a key role in the diffusion of the raising of /æ/.

This apparently chaotic pattern is actually the result of the fact that the neighbourhood effect (the gradual spreading of features from one place to the next, as with

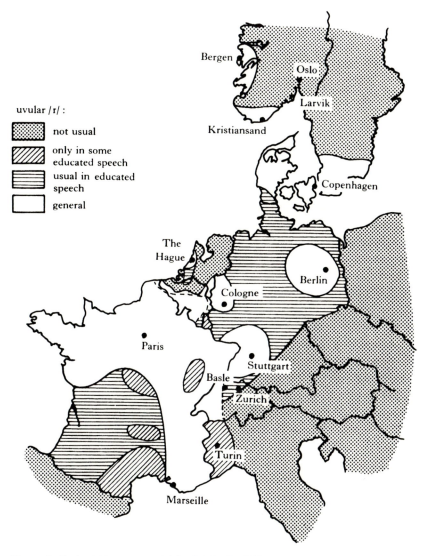

uvular /r/ :

▓ not usual

▨ only in some
  educated speech

▤ usual in educated
  speech

☐ general

Map 11-6. Uvular /r/ in greater social detail (after Trudgill 1974c)

uvular /r/ from France into southwest Germany) is complemented here, as again in the case of uvular /r/, by the jumping of the innovation from one large town to another, and from these to smaller towns, and so on. This is illustrated in Fig. 11-1 which shows that the height of /æ/ corresponds very closely with the *size* of the town in which the speaker lives and *not* (or not only) with its distance from Chicago. We shall return for further discussion of why this is so below (11.7).

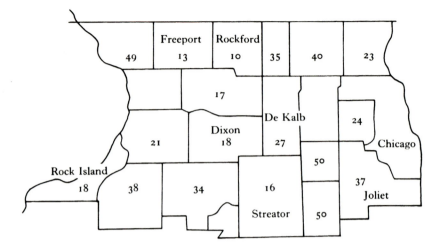

Map 11-7. /æ/-raising in northern Illinois

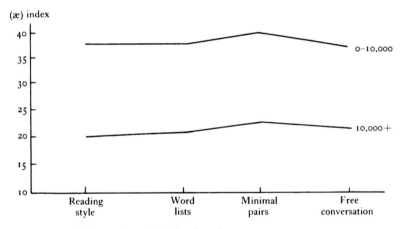

Fig. 11-1. /æ/-raising in northern Illinois by size of town

11.6 Cartographical representation of spatial diffusion

We have seen that urban centres are important in the diffusion of linguistic innovations, and that this role may well be obscured if our dialect maps are not sufficiently detailed – if they do not, for example, give adequate social information. One way in which improvements of this type can be made is for dialect geographers to attempt to develop quantitative techniques of the sort used by geographers and sociolinguists. If these can be devised to handle variability and gradient phenomena in language, then we shall be in a position, too, to portray with more accuracy the

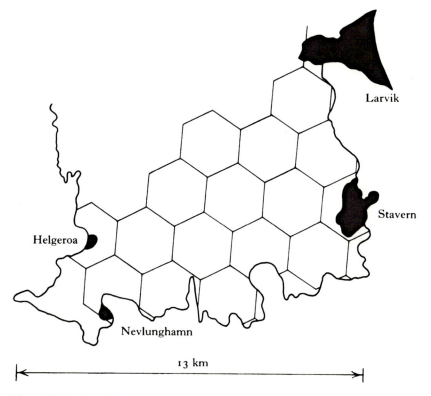

Map 11-8. Brunlanes, Norway

sort of gradual transition situation found, for example, in the case of /j/-loss (11.1; discussed also in Chapter 8).

11.6.1 *The Norwegian study*

The peninsula of Brunlanes in Vestfold, southern Norway, is an ideal location for the study of linguistic diffusion. An area with 6,500 inhabitants, it is surrounded by the sea on three sides, and bordered in the north by a wooded area with no roads of any consequence. It is dominated by Larvik, a town of 10,000 inhabitants at its northeastern corner through which all communications lie.

Human geographers have developed methods for studying and displaying the diffusion of technological innovations such as cars and agricultural techniques. These methods were adapted to the study of language forms in Brunlanes. The peninsula was covered with a hexagonal grid (see Map 11-8), and linguistic fieldwork with informants was carried out in each cell. (Note that this is similar to the methodology employed in the Illinois study, with the refinement here that each area is of uniform size and shape.)

One of the linguistic features studied was the pronunciation of (sj), corresponding to orthographic *sj* and *skj* in words such as *sjø* 'sea' and *skjære* 'cut'. The variable (sj) has variants as follows:

$$(sj)\text{-}1 = [sj]$$
$$(sj)\text{-}2 = [\int j]$$
$$(sj)\text{-}3 = [\int]$$
$$(sj)\text{-}4 = [\underset{.}{s}]$$

(Variant 4 is a retroflex fricative.) In Brunlanes (sj)-1 is the oldest pronunciation and (sj)-4 the most recent. Using the methods described in Chapter 4, average index scores were calculated for each geographical cell, consistent use of (sj)-1 giving an index of 0 and (sj)-4 an index of 300.

Maps were then drawn, using this information, after the manner of geographers producing maps with height contours. The maps were drawn showing not isoglosses in the traditional sense but rather isoglosses relating to these average index scores. The method is, briefly, as follows. If two hexagonal cells with centre points *a* and *b* have, respectively, (sj) index scores of 150 and 75, and if, on our map, *a* and *b* are 15 millimetres apart, then we can draw a 'contour line' representing an index score of 100 that passes between *a* and *b* at a point 10 mm from *a* and 5 mm from *b*. (Usually, of course, the arithmetic is more complicated than this.) Maps 11-9, 11-10 and 11-11 were produced in this way. They also involve the study of linguistic change in *apparent time* (see 6.2, 8.7, especially 8.7.2, and 10.1).

The maps show clearly that the linguistic change from [sj] through [∫] to [ş] is spreading outwards from Larvik but is also jumping, in the manner already discussed, to the much smaller towns of Stavern and Nevlunghamn, which in turn can be seen influencing their immediate neighbourhoods. It is also clear that, while the oldest informants use a high proportion of [sj] pronunciations, younger speakers have on average adopted a pronunciation varying between [∫] and [ş].

11.7 Explanations in sociolinguistic dialect geography

Given fuller descriptions of the details of the geographical distribution of linguistic forms of this type, the next step is to attempt to achieve a better appreciation of why this distribution comes to be what it is in the first place. One approach to a better understanding of what factors are involved has been to attempt to construct geographical diffusion models for the explanation and prediction of the spread of linguistic innovations, and hence the location of isoglosses, just as geographers have done for population movements and similar phenomena.

In a study carried out in East Anglia, a simple 'gravity' model of a type often used by geographers and others was developed. It is designed to account for the linguistic influence of one urban centre on another, based on the assumption that the interaction

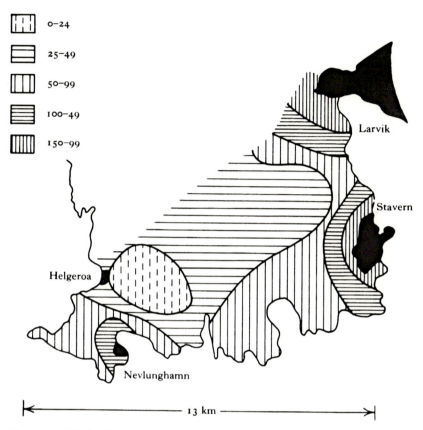

(sj) index

 0–24

25–49

50–99

100–49

150–99

Larvik

Stavern

Helgeroa

Nevlunghamn

|← ——————— 13 km ——————— →|

Map 11-9. (sj) in Brunlanes, speakers aged over 70

of two centres will be a function of their populations and the distance between them, and that the influence of the one on the other will be proportional to their relative population sizes. The formula reads:

$$Iij = S \cdot \frac{PiPj}{(dij)^2} \cdot \frac{Pi}{Pi + Pj}$$

Iij = influence of centre i on centre j
P = population
d = distance
S = index of prior-existing linguistic similarity (the higher the index the greater the similarity)

The factor *S* has been included to account for the fact that it appears to be psychologically and linguistically simpler to adopt features from a dialect that closely

179

(sj) index

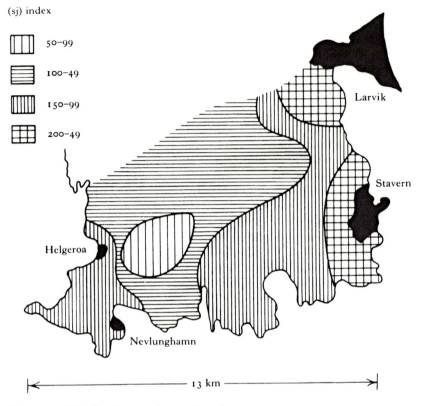

Map 11-10. (sj) in Brunlanes, speakers aged 25-69

resembles one's own than from one that is rather different. Where *j* is Norwich, *S* has been set at 4 for other centres in the same county (Norfolk), 3 for other centres in East Anglia, 2 for southeastern centres, 1 for other centres in England, and 0 for all others. With population calculated in thousands and distances in miles, the formula yields the following indices of influence:

	Index of linguistic influence
Centre	*of centre on Norwich*
London	156
Ipswich	11
Birmingham	5
Glasgow	0

This tallies well with the observation that almost all linguistic innovations occurring in Norwich English are derived from London speech, and not from anywhere else.

(sj) index

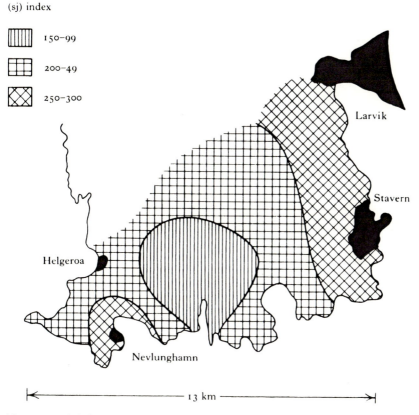

Map 11-11. (sj) in Brunlanes, speakers aged under 24

Note that, as it stands, the model is inadequate in a number of ways. For example, it predicts that smaller towns in the vicinity of Norwich will be more affected by London than they are by Norwich, because of their relative population size. This is obviously not the case. What we have to do is to recognise that these smaller towns are influenced by Norwich more than they are influenced by London, because of the relative distances, and will therefore only adopt London features after Norwich has done so. We have to note that centres compete in influence with one another, and handle this by subtracting scores for the different centres from each other (see below).

The influence of index scores, according to the formula, for the main northern East Anglian urban centres are given in Table 11-1. (For the location of the towns, see Map 11-12.) Clearly the first centre to be influenced by London will be Ipswich, and the second Norwich. But what happens after that? If we allow for competing influences, we get the following:

Table 11-1. *Influence index scores of London and East Anglian centres*

Influence on \ Influence of	London	Ipswich	Norwich	Lowestoft	K. Lynn	G. Yarmouth
Ipswich	351	—	10	1	0	0
Norwich	156	11	—	4	2	7
Lowestoft	60	5	25	—	1	50
K. Lynn	48	1	11	1	—	50
G. Yarmouth	36	3	45	50	50	—

Map 11-12. East Anglian centres

Sum of influence of London, Ipswich and Norwich on:		Subtract influence of other centres	Total
Lowestoft	90	51	39
G. Yarmouth	84	100	0
K. Lynn	60	51	9

Therefore the third centre to be influenced is Lowestoft. Finally we get:

Sum of influence of London, Ipswich, Norwich and Lowestoft on:		Subtract influence of other centres	Total
G. Yarmouth	134	50	84
K. Lynn	61	50	11

The fourth centre is thus Great Yarmouth, and the fifth centre King's Lynn. Note that this is *not* the order expected if we look only at the London influence scores (see Table 11-1) because here King's Lynn scores higher than Great Yarmouth.

How successful is this prediction on the part of the model? One feature that is currently being diffused from London into East Anglia is the loss of /h/ in words like *hum* /ʌm/ and *hat* /æt/. A survey produced average index scores for (h) as a linguistic variable in the different towns, for working-class speakers, as follows:

Order predicted by model	Centre	(h) index
1	Ipswich	56
2	Norwich	44
3	Lowestoft	40
4	G. Yarmouth	33
5	K. Lynn	21

The correlation is impressive.

The same type of operation can be carried out for the Illinois urban centres shown in Map 11-7. This will be rather more by way of an illustration of what can be done than an exercise in genuine prediction, as with the East Anglia data, because (a) we do not have such full information in this instance, (b) the urban centres shown in Map 11-7 are by no means the only important centres in northern Illinois, and (c) the scores given in Map 11-7 are not actually for the urban centres themselves but for the counties in which they stand. Table 11-2 gives the influence index scores for these northern Illinois centres, with the factor S set at 1.

Table 11-2 shows, as was obvious, that it is Chicago which has by far the greatest influence. It is also clear that Joliet is the town which is most influenced. The next

Table 11-2. *Influence index scores of northern Illinois centres*

Influence on \ Influence of	Chicago	Rockford	Joliet	R. Island	De Kalb	Freeport	Streator	Dixon
Rockford	6,381	—	77	20	109	97	3	14
Joliet	20,473	142	—	28	69	7	17	4
Rock Island	607	61	46	—	8	7	2	11
De Kalb	2,888	438	149	10	—	5	5	21
Freeport	720	508	19	13	7	—	2	28
Streator	730	31	80	7	10	3	—	4
Dixon	552	120	19	23	45	44	3	—

stage, then, is to note the combined influence of Chicago and Joliet on each of the remaining centres, taking account of the competing influences of other centres:

Sum of influence of Chicago and Joliet on:		Subtract influence of other centres	Total
Rockford	6,458	243	6,215
Rock Island	653	89	564
De Kalb	3,037	479	2,558
Freeport	739	558	181
Streator	810	55	755
Dixon	571	235	336

This shows that the next centre to be influenced will be Rockford. Note also that Freeport and Streator, which have very similar Chicago influence scores in Table 11-2, here have radically different indices.

Carrying through this process to its conclusion, the order of towns to be influenced by the innovation (together with the actual order of (æ) indices on Map 11-7) turns out to be:

Order on map	Order predicted by model	Centre	(æ) index score on map
1	1	Chicago	—
2	3	Rockford	10
3	5	Freeport	13
4	6	Streator	16
5	7	Rock Island	18
6	8	Dixon	18
7	4	De Kalb	27
8	2	Joliet	37

In spite of our lack of full information, only De Kalb and Joliet are out of place, although, it must be conceded, badly so. Note that the benefit of calculating competing influences from all centres is demonstrated by the fact that, while Streator has a higher Chicago influence score than Freeport in Table 11-2, it actually finishes lower overall, both in the model's prediction and, satisfyingly, on the map itself.

The model is also successful for Brunlanes. It produces the following order of influence, which can be checked against Maps 11-9–11-11:

> Larvik
> Stavern
> Nevlunghamn
> Helgeroa

11.8 Further refinements to the model

This model obviously has many inadequacies. Indeed, its main value perhaps lies in its ability to point to a lack of fit between its predictions and the actual linguistic facts and thus to lead the investigator to consider what *other* factors may be involved in the diffusion of innovations, and to what extent.

A good example of this is provided by a recent study of the diffusion of a linguistic innovation in modern Dutch. The Amsterdam urban dialect variant of standard Dutch /ɛi/, as in *rijs* /rɛɪs/ 'rice', ranges from [æ] to [ɑ], while the corresponding form in rural dialects in the areas around Amsterdam ranges from [æi] to [ɔi]. The monophthongal Amsterdam variant is currently spreading into these rural areas.

The study that was made of this process used the diffusion model of 11.7 to predict which places outside Amsterdam would be most affected by the innovation, and then investigated how accurate the predictions were. The predictions produced by the model were in fact almost entirely accurate: places with high Amsterdam influence indices were also the places with high numbers of monophthongs.

There were, however, a number of exceptions, of two different types. First, there were places where the change to a monophthongal form had taken place even though the model did not predict this. The explanation for this appears to be a linguistic one. It seems that the change in these cases has taken place independently. The evidence for this is that the vowel systems of the dialects in question are of a type that would lead phonologists to predict a high probability of this kind of monophthongisation occurring anyway.

Secondly, and more importantly for our purposes, the study found places with high Amsterdam influence scores but without the expected sound change. The explanation in these cases is again a linguistic one. The prior-existing phonological systems of these dialects, it seems, are unfavourable to the acceptance of this change in that they already have a vowel /ɑ/ (from a different historical source). The change from [ɑi] to [ɑ] thus spreads until it reaches an area which already has [ɑ] and where the acceptance of this innovation would lead to a vowel merger and the loss of contrasts. There is likely to be particularly strong resistance, it seems, if the two vowels involved in the potential merger are of high frequency.

This sort of work illustrates the advantages of attempting to develop an explanatory model. In those cases where it does not work we are led to ask why it does not work, and to look for further factors which may promote or inhibit the geographical diffusion of linguistic innovations. In addition to the linguistic similarity factor S, we now know that we need to add some other variable which will take account of those specifically linguistic factors, such as the nature of the original phonological system and the possibility of phonological mergers, that may slow down or accelerate linguistic diffusion processes. It is not enough to look at these processes in a kind of vacuum. We have also to think of the system into which the innovations are to be accepted or incorporated.

Once we have appreciated this point, it is easy to note further examples of the same factor at work. Map 11-6 shows that Dutch has been much less ready to accept the uvular /r/ innovation than its neighbours French and German. One explanation for this may be that there already exists in Dutch a back velar or uvular fricative, corresponding to orthographic *g*, with which some varieties of uvular /r/ might have merged had it been accepted.

Further information

The Italian school of neolinguistics is discussed in Bonfante 1947. For those who can read Italian, there is also Bartoli 1945. Map 11-1 is based on one in Trudgill 1975, which also gives references on the subject of linguistic areas. The seminal writings on the subject of linguistic areas were Jakobson 1949 and Trubetzkoy 1949. Current models are developed in Nichols 1992 and Thomason and Kaufman 1988. The diffusion of uvular /r/ and the development of a geographical diffusion model for language are discussed at greater length in Trudgill 1974b. The data on uvular /r/ in Norway are taken from Foldvik n.d. The data on southern Sweden come from Sjøstedt 1936 and Elert 1976. Some impression of early work by geographers in innovation diffusion can be gained from Hägerstrand 1967. The work on northern Illinois is from Callary 1975. The study of Brunlanes is reported in Trudgill 1974b and in Foldvik 1979. The East Anglian data referred to in 11.7 are taken from Trudgill n.d. The Amsterdam study is Gerritsen and Jansen 1980. The cartographical techniques discussed here are dealt with in greater detail in Robinson and Sale 1969; for linguistic applications, see Chambers 1997 and Kretzschmar 1996a.

12

Cohesion in dialectology

For much of its history, practitioners of dialectology viewed it as an autonomous discipline, with its own goals and unique methods. In this guise, it became established as an academic discipline and contributed a fascinating chapter to intellectual history. Its heritage is the classic dialect atlases of the first half of this century, and they continue to nurture and inspire research on dialects to this day – even, arguably, with greater impact now than a few decades ago.

One of our purposes in this book has been to make accessible the methodology and some results of autonomous dialectology or dialect geography to general readers and students. To that end, we devoted much of the book (Chapters 2, 3, 7 and 8 as well as parts of many other chapters) to traditional dialectology.

It forms one of the main streams of the modern discipline of dialectology. A second stream, and an enormously influential one, is the study of urban dialects, which is usually referred to under the general heading of 'sociolinguistics'. The methodology and results of urban dialectology and the crucial perspective it offers on linguistic innovation (as discussed especially in Chapters 4, 5 and 6; 10.1 and 10.2) belong to the foundations of modern dialectology as we see it.

Another of our purposes has been to demonstrate that the confluence of these two streams forms a coherent modern discipline. This may not be obvious to some readers who bring to the book a traditional perspective. We are well aware, of course, that the provenance of the two streams is so diverse that they might seem incompatible. Dialectology began in the nineteenth century, a product of intellectual currents (as outlined in Chapter 2) that now seem remote and perhaps exotic. Sociolinguistics had its effective beginning almost a century later, in the 1960s. The intellectual sources of dialect geography were evolutionary theory and Linnaean taxonomy in which the main linguistic current was comparative philology. Sociolinguistics was the run-off of the social sciences movement when it belatedly met with structural linguistics.

For all their differences, dialectology and sociolinguistics converge at the deepest point. Both are dialectologies, so to speak. They share their essential subject matter. Both fix the attention on language in communities. Prototypically, one has been centrally

concerned with rural communities and the other with urban centres, but these are accidental differences, not essential ones and certainly not axiomatic.

Along with anthropological linguistics and otherwise alone among the linguistic sciences, dialectology and sociolinguistics depend upon fieldwork. For most of their long histories, dialectologists and anthropologists struggled against the practical impossibility of apprehending the stream of speech in social situations. They survived by imposing controls on data-gathering. One common field format isolated speakers from their social milieu by putting them across the table from a recording secretary, the fieldworker, who bent over a clipboard making fine transcriptions of the speaker's responses. The method basically consisted of, as William Labov once said, 'a long question from the interviewer and a short answer from the subject'.

Sociolinguistics, coming along some seven decades later with the advantages of unprecedented technological developments, could devise freer data-gathering methods. Recording quality, playback devices, instrumental analysis, and other advances make the stream of speech accessible as never before. The empirical differences that arose out of the methodologies were significant. Where dialectology succeeded in documenting linguistic variety, sociolinguistics discovered variability. Though these differences were rooted in methodology, they occasionally became elevated to ideologies. Upstart claims of reactionary resistance to technical advances were met with piety for old-time practices as time-tested necessities.

A decade or two ago, it might have been possible to think that the common subject matter of dialectology and sociolinguistics counted for next to nothing. Now we know it counts for everything. Dialectology without sociolinguistics at its core is a relic. No serious perspective on dialectology can grant urban research and variation theory less than a central role.

There is also a third stream forming the confluence of the discipline as we see it, from the discipline of geography. Its inclusion here may seem less essential to linguists of any age or orientation, and less familiar. Nevertheless, at least the beginning of what we see as a fruitful interchange of hypotheses with geography should be evident in the discussion of cartographic methods (8.7, 9.4), geographic models of diffusion (11.7), and several other points. There is potentially a great deal more to come.

We put no stock whatever in statements such as this one, by a linguist: 'Geographical dispersions can be so chaotic as to challenge the plausibility of any hypotheses about the orderliness of language variation' (Bailey 1973: 86). Like the dialect geographers who discovered that dialectal variants were not distributed according to the simplest predictions of neogrammarian theory and ended up abandoning the theory, this conclusion also seems to set aside the crucial questions.

Instead of giving up on the relationship between linguistic orderliness and geographical dispersions, what is required is a richer set of hypotheses about language variation and a more profound understanding of spatial networks and the diffusion of innovations.

In recent decades, geographers have made important advances towards developing dynamic models of diffusion which go beyond static characterisations of the distribution of elements, involving social attitude and community networks as independent variables. Such studies are often brought together under the rubric 'human geography', and linguists who become aware of developments within that field can hardly fail to see parallels there to the development of variation models in their own field. Both groups have a great deal to learn from one another, and the interchange has barely begun.

We conceive the confluence of these three streams – dialect geography, urban dialectology, and human geography – as a unified discipline. Its goal, like any other subdiscipline of modern linguistics, is to elucidate the most accessible system of human knowledge, the capacity for language. Its unity is provided by the theoretical underpinning of variation theory, the set of premises and hypotheses which arises as a consequence of accepting the variable as a structural unit in the grammatical model (especially Chapter 9 and 10.3).

Urban dialectology has been for some years now a burgeoning field of inquiry, stimulated originally by the bizarre neglect of the social aspect of linguistic behaviour in linguistic theory. In the last decade or two, rural dialectology has been revitalised both by adapting techniques developed in urban studies and by developing powerful new tools of its own. We have presented them together in this book, as co-equals. Their integration into a coherent single discipline grows stronger as it gains practitioners trained in both traditions and, we hope, advocates of both without distinction.

Further information

The growing inclusiveness of contemporary dialectology is a minor theme in many recent publications cited throughout this book, and the major theme in a few. Johnston 1985 demonstrates the shared ground of regional surveys and urban studies. Kretzschmar 1996b points up the common concerns. Chambers 1993 does too. Labov 1994: chapter 17 revaluates the uses of dialect geography from a comparativist's perspective. Preston 1993a applies the human geographical concept of mental maps to dialect regions.

REFERENCES

Allen, H. B. 1973–6. *The Linguistic Atlas of the Upper Midwest*. 3 vols. University of Minnesota Press.

Anderson, J. A. 1973. *Structural Aspects of Language Change*. London: Longman.

Atwood, E. B. 1953. *A Survey of Verb Forms in the Eastern United States*. University of Michigan Press.

Bailey, C.-J. 1973. *Variation and Linguistic Theory*. Washington, DC: Center for Applied Linguistics.

Bailey, G. et al. 1991. *The Emergence of Black English*. Amsterdam and Philadelphia: Benjamins.

Bailey, G., T. Wikle, J. Tillery and L. Sand. 1991. 'The apparent time construct'. *Language Variation and Change* 3: 241–64.

Bartoli, M. 1945. *Saggi di linguistica spaziale*. Turin: Bona.

Baugh, J. 1983. *Black Street Speech: its history, structure and survival*. Austin: University of Texas Press.

Berlin, B. and P. Kay. 1969. *Basic Color Terms: their universality and evolution*. Berkeley and Los Angeles: University of California Press.

Bickerton, D. 1975. *Dynamics of a Creole System*. Cambridge University Press.

Bloomfield, L. 1933. *Language*. New York: Holt, Rinehart & Winston.

Bonfante, G. 1947. 'The neolinguistic position'. *Language* 23: 344–75.

Brun, A. 1936. 'Linguistique et peuplement'. *Revue de linguistique romane* 12: 165–251.

Butters, R. 1989. *The Death of Black English: divergence and convergence in black and white vernaculars*. New York: Peter Lang.

Callary, R. 1975. 'Phonological change and the development of an urban dialect in Illinois'. *Language in Society* 4: 155–70.

Cedergren, H. 1988. 'The spread of language change: verifying inferences of linguistic diffusion'. In P. Lowenburg (ed.), *Language Spread and Language Policy*. Washington, DC: Georgetown University Press. 45–60.

Chambers, J. K. 1973. 'Canadian raising'. *Canadian Journal of Linguistics* 18: 113–35.

Chambers, J. K. 1982. 'Geolinguistics of a variable rule'. *Discussion Papers in Geolinguistics* 5. North Staffordshire Polytechnic.

Chambers, J. K. 1993. 'Sociolinguistic dialectology'. In Preston 1993b. 133–64.

Chambers, J. K. 1994. 'An introduction to dialect topography'. *English World-Wide* 15: 35–53.

Chambers, J. K. 1995a. 'The Canada–US border as a vanishing isogloss: the evidence of *chesterfield*'. *Journal of English Linguistics* 23: 155–66.

Chambers, J. K. 1995. *Sociolinguistic Theory: language variation and its social significance.* Oxford: Blackwell.

Chambers, J. K. 1997. 'Mapping variability'. In A. R. Thomas (ed.), *Issues and Methods in Dialectology.* Bangor: University of Wales. 284–93.

Chambers, J. K. 1998. 'Social embedding of changes in progress'. *Journal of English Linguistics* 26: 5–36.

Chambers, J. K. and P. Trudgill. 1991. 'Dialect grammar: data and theory'. In P. Trudgill and J. K. Chambers (eds.), *Dialects of English: Studies in Grammatical Variation.* London and New York: Longman.

Chen, M. and H.-I. Hsieh. 1971. 'The time variable in phonological change'. *Journal of Linguistics* 7: 1–14.

Chen, M. and W. S.-Y. Wang. 1975. 'Sound change: actuation and implementation'. *Language* 51: 255–81.

Cheshire, J. 1978. 'Present tense verbs in Reading English'. In Trudgill 1978.

Cheshire, J. 1982. *Variation in an English Dialect: a sociolinguistic study.* Cambridge University Press.

Cichocki, W. 1989. 'An application of dual scaling in dialectometry'. In Kretzschmar, Schneider and Johnson. 91–6.

Coates, J. 1986. *Women, Men and Language.* London and New York: Longman.

Cochrane, G. R. 1959. 'The Australian English vowels as a diasystem'. *Word* 15: 69–88.

Combrink, J. 1978. 'Afrikaans: its origin and development'. In L. Lanham and K. Prinsloo (eds.), *Language and Communication Studies in South Africa.* Oxford University Press.

Davis, A. and R. I. McDavid. 1950. 'Northwestern Ohio: a transition area'. *Language* 26: 186–9.

De Camp, D. 1958. 'The pronunciation of English in San Francisco'. *Orbis* 7: 372–91.

De Camp, D. 1959. 'The pronunciation of English in San Francisco'. *Orbis* 8: 54–77.

Douglas-Cowie, E. 1978. 'Linguistic code-switching in a Northern Irish village: social interaction and social ambition'. In Trudgill 1978.

Eckert, P. 1989. *Jocks and Burnouts: social categories and identity in the high school.* New York and London: Teachers College Press.

Elert, C. 1976. 'Gränsen för det sydsvenska bakre *r*' [The boundary of the south Swedish dorsal *r*]. *Svenska Landsmål och Svenskt Folkliv*, 7–20.

Fasold, R. W. 1972. *Tense Marking in Black English.* Washington, DC: Center for Applied Linguistics.

Feagin, C. 1979. *Variation and Change in Alabama English: a sociolinguistic study of the white community.* Washington, DC: Georgetown University Press.

Fintoft, K. and P. E. Mjaavatn. 1980. *Språksosiologiske forhold i Trondheim bymål.* Trondheim: Tapir.

Fischer, J. L. 1958. 'Social influences on the choice of a linguistic variant'. *Word* 14: 47–56.

Foldvik, A. K. 1979. 'Endring av uttale og spredning av ny uttale: generasjonsskilnader i Brunlanes, Vestfold' [Change of pronunciation and spread of new pronunciation: generation differences in Brunlanes, Vestfold]. In J. Kleiven (ed.), *Språk og Samfunn: bidrag til en norsk sosiolinguistikk.* Oslo: Pax.

References

Foldvik, A. K. n.d. 'The pronunciation of *r* in Norwegian with special reference to the spread of dorsal *r*'. Unpublished paper.

Francis, W. N. 1978. Review of Orton and Wright 1974. *American Speech* 53: 221–31.

Gal, S. 1979. *Language Shift: Social Determinants of Linguistic Change in Bilingual Austria.* New York: Academic Press.

Gerritsen, M. and Jansen, F. 1980. 'The interplay of dialectology and historical linguistics: some refinements of Trudgill's formula'. In P. Maher (ed.), *Proceedings of the 3rd International Congress of Historical Linguistics.* Amsterdam: Benjamins.

Gilliéron, J. 1902–10. *Atlas linguistique de la France.* 13 vols. Paris: Champion.

Glauser, B. 1985. 'Linguistic atlases and generative phonology'. In Kirk, Sanderson and Widdowson. 113–29.

Goebl, H. 1982. *Dialektometrie.* Vienna: Österreichischen Akademie der Wissenschaften.

Goebl, H. 1993. 'Dialectometry: a short overview of the principles and practice of quantitative classification of linguistic atlas data'. In R. Köhler and B. Rieger (eds.), *Contributions to Quantitative Linguistics.* Dordrecht: Kluwer. 277–315.

Green, E. and R. Green. 1971. 'Place names and dialects in Massachusetts: some complementary patterns'. *Names* 19: 240–51.

Gulbrandsen, Per P. 1975. 'Nye drag in Tønsbergs bymal' [New features in the urban dialect of Tønsberg]. Dissertation, Oslo University.

Guy, G. R. 1996. 'Post-Saussurean linguistics: toward an integrated theory of language'. In M. Meyerhoff (ed.), *Papers from NWAVE 24. Working Papers in Linguistics* 3. University of Pennsylvania, Philadelphia. 1–24.

Hägerstrand, T. 1967. *Innovation Diffusion as a Spatial Process.* Trans. A. Pred. University of Chicago Press.

Haugen, E. 1966a. *Language Conflict and Language Planning: the case of modern Norwegian.* Harvard University Press.

Haugen, E. 1966b. 'Semicommunication: the language gap in Scandinavia'. In S. Lieberson (ed.), *Explorations in Sociolinguistics.* The Hague: Mouton.

Haugen, E. 1968. 'The Scandinavian languages as cultural artifacts'. In Fishman et al. (eds.), *Language Problems of Developing Nations.* New York: Wiley.

Hockett, C. 1958. *A Course in Modern Linguistics.* London: Macmillan.

Holm, J. 1988. *Pidgins and Creoles.* Cambridge University Press.

Holmes, J. 1992. *An Introduction to Sociolinguistics.* London and New York: Longman.

Horvath, B. 1985. *Variation in Australian English: the sociolects of Sydney.* Cambridge University Press.

Hudson, R. A. 1996. *Sociolinguistics.* 2nd edn. Cambridge University Press.

Hughes, A. and P. Trudgill. 1996. *English Accents and Dialects: an introduction to social and regional varieties of English in the British Isles.* 2nd edn. London: Edward Arnold.

Hymes, D. (ed.). 1971. *Pidginisation and Creolisation of Languages.* Cambridge University Press.

Jaberg, K. and J. Jud. 1928–40. *Sprach- und Sachatlas des Italiens und der Südschweiz.* Zofingen: Ringier.

Jakobson, R. 1949. 'Sur la théorie des affinités phonologiques entre les langues'. Appendix in N. Trubetzkoy, *Principes de phonologie.* Paris: Klincksieck.

Jochnowitz, G. 1973. *Dialect Boundaries and the Question of Franco-Provençal*. The Hague: Mouton.

Johnston, P. A. 1985. 'Linguistic atlases and sociolinguistics'. In Kirk, Sanderson and Widdowson. 81–93.

Keyser, S. J. 1963. Review of Kurath and McDavid 1961. *Language* 39: 303–16.

King, R. D. 1969. *Historical Linguistics and Generative Grammar*. New York: Prentice-Hall.

Kirk, J. M., S. Sanderson and J. D. A. Widdowson (eds.). 1985. *Studies in Linguistic Geography*. London: Croom Helm.

Kirk, J. M. and G. Munroe. 1989. 'A method for dialectometry'. In Kretzschmar, Schneider and Johnson. 97–110.

Knowles, G. O. 1978. 'The nature of phonological variables in Scouse'. In Trudgill 1978.

Kolb, E. 1964. *Phonological Atlas of the Northern Region*. Berne: Franke Verlag.

Kretzschmar, W. 1992. 'Isoglosses and predictive modeling'. *American Speech* 67: 227–49.

Kretzschmar, W. 1996a. 'Quantitative areal analysis of dialect features'. *Language Variation and Change* 8: 13–39.

Kretzschmar, W. 1996b. 'Dialectology and sociolinguistics: same coin, different currency'. *Language Sciences* 17: 271–82.

Kretzschmar, W., E. W. Schneider and E. Johnson (eds.). 1989. *Computer Methods in Dialectology*. *Journal of English Linguistics* 22 (special edition).

Kretzschmar, W., V. G. McDavid, T. K. Lerud and E. Johnson (eds.). 1994. *Handbook of the Linguistic Atlas of the Middle and South Atlantic States*. University of Chicago Press.

Kurath, H. 1949. *Word Geography of the Eastern United States*. University of Michigan Press.

Kurath, H. 1972. *Studies in Area Linguistics*. Indiana University Press.

Kurath, H. and B. Bloch. 1939. *Handbook of the Linguistic Geography of New England*. Brown University Press.

Kurath, H. and R. I. McDavid, Jr. 1961. *The Pronunciation of English in the Atlantic States*. University of Michigan Press.

Kurath, H., M. Hanley, B. Bloch and G. S. Lowman, Jr. 1939–43. *Linguistic Atlas of New England*. 3 vols. Brown University Press.

Labov, W. 1964. 'Stages in the acquisition of standard English'. In R. Shuy (ed.), *Social Dialects and Language Learning*. Champaign, IL.: National Council of Teachers of English.

Labov, W. 1966. *The Social Stratification of English in New York City*. Washington, DC: Center for Applied Linguistics.

Labov, W. 1972a. *Language in the Inner City*. University of Pennsylvania Press.

Labov, W. 1972b. *Sociolinguistic Patterns*. University of Pennsylvania Press.

Labov, W. 1973. 'Where do grammars stop?' In R. W. Shuy (ed.), *Monograph Series on Language and Linguistics* 25. Georgetown University Press.

Labov, W. 1994. *Principles of Linguistic Change*, vol. 1. Oxford: Blackwell.

Lavandera, B. 1978. 'Where does the sociolinguistic variable stop?' *Language in Society* 7: 171–82.

Lehmann, W. 1962. 'Broadening of language materials: dialect geography'. In *Historical Linguistics: an introduction*. New York: Holt, Rinehart & Winston.

Macaulay, R. K. S. 1977. *Language, Social Class and Education: a Glasgow study*. Edinburgh University Press.

References

Macaulay, R. K. S. 1985. 'Linguistic maps: visual aids or abstract art?' In Kirk, Sanderson and Widdowson (eds.). 172–86.

Mather, J. Y. and H. H. Speitel (eds.). 1975, 1977. *The Linguistic Atlas of Scotland*, 2 vols. London: Croom Helm.

McDavid, Jr, R. I. 1957. 'Tape recording in dialect geography: a cautionary note'. *Journal of the Canadian Linguistic Association* 3: 3–8.

McIntosh, A. 1952. *An Introduction to a Survey of Scottish Dialect*. London: Nelson.

McMahon, A. 1994. *Understanding Linguistic Change*. Cambridge University Press.

Milroy, J. 1992. *Linguistic Variation and Change*. Oxford: Blackwell.

Milroy, L. 1976. 'Phonological correlates to community structure in Belfast'. *Belfast Working Papers in Language and Linguistics* 1 (August).

Milroy, L. 1984. *Language and Social Networks*. 2nd edn. Oxford: Blackwell.

Milroy, L. 1987. *Observing and Analysing Natural Language*. Oxford: Blackwell.

Mitzka, W. 1952. *Handbuch zum Deutschen Sprachatlas*. Marburg.

Montgomery, M. and G. Bailey (eds.). 1986. *Language Variety in the South: perspectives in black and white*. Tuscaloosa: University of Alabama Press.

Moulton, W. G. 1960. 'The short vowel systems of northern Switzerland: a study in structural dialectology'. *Word* 16: 155–83.

Mühlhäusler, P. 1986. *Pidgin and Creole Linguistics*. Oxford: Blackwell.

Newton, B. 1972. *The Generative Interpretation of Dialect*. Cambridge University Press.

Nichols, J. 1992. *Linguistic Diversity in Space and Time*. University of Chicago Press.

Nordberg, B. 1972. 'Morfologiska variationsmönster i ett centralsvenskt stadsspråk'. In B. Loman (ed.), *Språk och sawhälle*. Lund: Gleerup.

Ogura, M. 1990. *Dynamic Dialectology*. Tokyo: Kenyusha.

O'Neill, W. A. 1963. 'The dialects of modern Faroese: a preliminary report'. *Orbis* 12: 393–7.

Orton, H. 1960. 'An English dialect survey: Linguistic Atlas of England'. *Orbis* 9: 331–48.

Orton, H. 1962. *Survey of English Dialects: introduction*. Leeds: E. J. Arnold.

Orton, H. and M. Barry (eds.). 1969–71. *Survey of English Dialects. The Basic Material*, vol. 2 (3 parts): *The West Midland Counties*. Leeds: E. J. Arnold.

Orton, H. and W. Halliday (eds.). 1962–3. *Survey of English Dialects. The Basic Material*, vol. 1 (3 parts): *The Six Northern Counties and the Isle of Man*. Leeds: E. J. Arnold.

Orton, H. and P. M. Tilling (eds.). 1969–71. *Survey of English Dialects. The Basic Material*, vol. 3 (3 parts): *The East Midland Counties and East Anglia*. Leeds: E. J. Arnold.

Orton, H. and M. F. Wakelin (eds.). 1967–8. *Survey of English Dialects. The Basic Material*, vol. 4 (3 parts): *The Southern Counties*. Leeds: E. J. Arnold.

Orton, H. and N. Wright. 1974. *A Word Geography of England*. London and New York: Seminar Press.

Orton, H., S. Sanderson and J. Widdowson (eds.). 1978. *The Linguistic Atlas of England*. London: Croom Helm.

Palmer, L. R. 1936. *An Introduction to Modern Linguistics*. London: Faber.

Pederson, L. 1993. 'An approach to linguistic geography: the Linguistic Atlas of the Gulf States'. In Preston 1993b. 31–92.

Pederson, L., S. L. McDaniel, G. H. Bailey and M. Bassett (eds.). 1986. *The Linguistic Atlas of the Gulf States*, vol. 1: *Handbook*. Athens, GA: University of Georgia Press.

Pederson, L., S. L. McDaniel and C. Adams (eds.). 1988. *The Linguistic Atlas of the Gulf States*, vol. 2: *General Index*. Athens, GA: University of Georgia Press.

Pederson, L., S. L. McDaniel and C. Adams (eds.). 1991. *The Linguistic Atlas of the Gulf States*, vol. 5: *Regional Pattern*. Athens, GA: University of Georgia Press.

Pederson, L. and S. L. McDaniel (eds.). 1992. *The Linguistic Atlas of the Gulf States*, vol. 7: *Social Pattern*. Athens, GA: University of Georgia Press.

Petyt, K. M. 1977. 'Dialect and accent in the industrial West Riding'. PhD thesis, University of Reading.

Petyt, K. M. 1985. *Dialect and Accent in Industrial West Yorkshire*. Amsterdam and Philadelphia: John Benjamins.

Phillips, B. S. 1984. 'Word frequency and the actuation of sound change'. *Language* 60: 320–42.

Philps, D. 1985. *Atlas dialectométrique des Pyrénées centrale*. Thèse d'État, Université de Toulouse.

Pickford, G. R. 1956. 'American linguistic geography: a sociological appraisal'. *Word* 12: 211–33.

Pop, S. 1950. *La dialectologie: aperçu historique et méthodes d'enquêtes linguistiques*, vol. 1: *Dialectologie romane*, vol. 2: *Dialectologie non romane*. Louvain: Centre internationale de dialectologie générale.

Preston, D. R. 1993a. 'Folk dialectology'. In Preston (ed.). 333–78.

Preston, D. R. (ed.) 1993b. *American Dialect Research*. Amsterdam and Philadelphia: John Benjamins.

Pulgram, E. 1964. 'Structural comparison, diasystems and dialectology'. *Linguistics* 4: 66–82.

Reed, D. and J. L. Spicer. 1952. 'Correlation methods of comparing dialects in a transition area'. *Language* 28: 348–59.

Robinson, A. and R. Sale. 1969. *Elements of Cartography*. London: Wiley.

Romaine, S. 1978. 'Postvocalic /r/ in Scottish English: sound change in progress?'. In Trudgill 1978.

Romaine, S. 1988. *Pidgin and Creole Languages*. London and New York: Longman.

Sankoff, G. and H. Cedergren. 1971. 'Les contraintes linguistiques et sociales de l'élision du l chez les Montréalais'. In M. Boudreault and F. Moehren (eds.), *Actes du XIIIe Congrès Internationale de Linguistique et de Phonologie Romanes*. Laval University Press.

Saporta, S. 1965. 'Ordered rules, dialect differences, and historical processes'. *Language* 41: 218–24.

Séguy, J. 1952. *Atlas linguistique et ethnographique de la Gascogne*, vol. 1. Paris: Centre national de la recherche scientifique.

Séguy, J. 1973. *Atlas linguistique de la Gascogne*, vol. 6. *Notice explicative*. Paris: Centre national de la recherche scientifique.

Shuy, R. W. et al. 1968. *Field Techniques in Urban Language Study*. Washington, DC: Center for Applied Linguistics.

Sivertsen, E. 1960. *Cockney Phonology*. Oslo University Press.

Sjøstedt, G. 1936. *Studier över r-Ljuden i sydskandinaviska mål* [Studies in the *r*-sound in south Scandinavian dialects]. Lund University.

Thibault, P. and M. Daveluy. 1989. 'Quelques traces du passage du temps dans le parler des Montréalais 1971–1984'. *Language Variation and Change* 1: 19–46.

Thomas, A. R. 1967. 'Generative phonology in dialectology'. *Transactions of the Philological Society*. 179–203.

References

Thomas, A. R. 1981. 'Networks, nuclei and boundaries in areal dialectology'. In H. Warkentyne (ed.), *Papers from the Fourth International Conference on Methods in Dialectology*. University of Victoria, Canada. 171–91.

Thomason, S. G. and T. Kaufman. 1988. *Language Contact, Creolization, and Genetic Linguistics*. Berkeley: University of California Press.

Thorne, B. and N. Henley. 1975. *Language and Sex: difference and dominance*. Newbury House.

Todd, L. 1974. *Pidgins and Creoles*. London: Routledge & Kegan Paul.

Trubetzkoy, N. 1949. 'Phonologie et géographie linguistique'. In *Principes de phonologie*. Paris: Klincksieck.

Trudgill, P. 1972. 'Sex, covert prestige and linguistic change in the urban British English of Norwich'. *Language in Society* 1: 179–95. Reprinted in Thorne and Henley 1975.

Trudgill, P. 1974a. *The Social Differentiation of English in Norwich*. Cambridge University Press.

Trudgill, P. 1974b. 'Linguistic change and diffusion: description and explanation in sociolinguistic dialect geography'. *Language in Society* 3: 215–46.

Trudgill, P. 1975. 'Linguistic geography and geographical linguistics'. In C. Board et al. (eds.), *Progress in Geography*, vol. 7. London: Edward Arnold.

Trudgill, P. (ed.). 1978. *Sociolinguistic Patterns in British English*. London: Edward Arnold.

Trudgill, P. 1983. *On Dialect: social and geographical perspectives*. Oxford: Blackwell.

Trudgill, P. 1988. 'Norwich revisited: recent linguistic changes in an English urban dialect'. *English World-Wide* 9: 33–49.

Trudgill, P. 1995. *Sociolinguistics: an introduction to language and society*. 2nd edn. Harmondsworth: Penguin.

Trudgill, P. n.d. 'A sociolinguistic study of linguistic change in urban East Anglia'. Report to the SSRC.

Ulseth, B. n.d. 'Stress and toneme as used by Trondheim speakers: a sociolinguistic study'. Department of Linguistics, University of Trondheim.

Underwood, G. N. 1976. 'American English dialectology: alternatives for the Southwest'. *International Journal of the Sociology of Language* 2: 19–39.

Upton, C., S. Sanderson and J. Widdowson. 1987. *Word Maps: a dialect atlas of England*. London: Croom Helm.

Upton, C., D. Parry and J. D. A. Widdowson. 1994. *Survey of English Dialects: the dictionary and grammar*. London: Routledge.

Upton, C. and J. D. A. Widdowson. 1996. *An Atlas of English Dialects*. Oxford University Press.

Vasiliu, E. 1966. 'Towards a generative phonology of Daco-Rumanian dialects'. *Journal of Linguistics* 2: 79–98.

Viereck, W. 1966. *Phonematische Analyse des Dialekts von Gateshead-upon-Tyne*. Berlin: De Gruyter.

Viereck, W. 1985. 'Linguistic atlases and dialectometry: the Survey of English Dialects'. In Kirk, Sanderson and Widdowson. 94–112.

Wakelin, M. F. 1972. *English Dialects: an introduction*. Edinburgh: Athlone Press.

Walshe, M. 1965. *Introduction to the Scandinavian Languages*. London: André Deutsch.

Weinreich, U. 1954. 'Is a structural dialectology possible?' *Word* 10: 388–400. Reprinted in J. Fishman (ed.), *Readings in the Sociology of Language*. The Hague: Mouton, 1968.

Wells, J. C. 1982. *Accents of English*. 3 vols. Cambridge University Press.

Wolff. H. 1959. 'Intelligibility and inter-ethnic attitudes'. *Anthropological Linguistics* 1: 34–41.

Wolfram, W. 1969. *A Sociolinguistic Description of Detroit Negro Speech*. Washington, DC: Center for Applied Linguistics.

Wolfram, W. 1971. 'Black–white speech differences revisited'. In W. Wolfram and N. Clarke (eds.), *Black–White Speech Relationships*. Washington, DC: Center for Applied Linguistics.

Wolfram, W. 1974. *Sociolinguistic Aspects of Assimilation: Puerto Rican English in New York City*. Washington, DC: Center for Applied Linguistics.

Wolfram, W. and D. Christian. 1976. *Appalachian Speech*. Washington, DC: Center for Applied Linguistics.

Wolfram, W. and R. Fasold. 1974. *The Study of Social Dialects in American English*. New York: Prentice-Hall.

Woods, A., P. Fletcher and A. Hughes. 1986. *Statistics in Language Studies*. Cambridge University Press.

INDEX

Lightning Source UK Ltd.
Milton Keynes UK
UKOW05f1812080813

215084UK00001B/71/P